D1555514

THE SWEETEST IMPRESSION OF LIFE

THE SWEETEST IMPRESSION OF LIFE

The James Family and Italy

Edited by James W. Tuttleton
and Agostino Lombardo

CT
274
.J35
S84
1990
west

New York University Press
New York

Istituto della Enciclopedia Italiana
Rome

1990

Copyright © 1990 by New York University
All rights reserved
Manufactured in the United States of America

Library of Congress Cataloging-in-Publication Data
The Sweetest impression of life: the James family and Italy / edited
by James W. Tuttleton and Agostino Lombardo.
p. cm.
Includes bibliographical references.
ISBN 0-8147-8183-7 (alk. paper)
1. James family. 2. James, Henry, 1843–1916—Knowledge—Italy.
3. James, William, 1842–1910—Influence. 4. Italy in literature.
I. Tuttleton, James W. II. Lombardo, Agostino.
CT274.J35S84 1990
813'.4—dc20   89-27387
CIP

New York University Press book are printed on acid-free paper,
and their binding materials are chosen for strength and durability

Book design by Ken Venezio

For Glauco Cambon

Writers have to have two countries, the one where they belong and the one in which they live really. The second one is romantic, it is separate from themselves, it is not real but it is really there.

—GERTRUDE STEIN

Italy remains firm while other things come and go—remains, on the whole, I mean, the sweetest impression of life.

—HENRY JAMES

Contents

Acknowledgments

*T*HIS VOLUME represents the labor and devotion of many hands. The editors wish especially to thank Dr. Vincenzo Cappelletti, Director General of the Istituto della Enciclopedia Italiana (Rome), for convening in New York the Italian scholars who contributed to *The James Family and Italy: A Symposium* in April of 1988, where most of the essays in this volume were presented as conference papers, and for co-sponsoring the publication of this book. Dr. John Brademas, President of New York University, Dr. Aileen Ward, Albert Schweitzer Professor of the Humanities, Dean C. Duncan Rice and Dean Ann M. Burton of the Faculty of Arts and Science at New York University were also gracious hosts who assembled in New York City the American critics and scholars who contributed to the conference and to this volume. We owe them our thanks for making this conference and the volume that has issued from it a genuine contribution to learning.

Thanks are likewise due to the Organizing Committee of the symposium, which included Dr. Luigi Ballerini, Professor and Chairman of the Department of Italian at New York University, Dr. John Maynard, Chairman of the Department of English at New York University, and Dr. Gianni Eugenio Viola, Director of Cultural Activities of the Istituto della Enciclopedia Italiana. To Dr. A. Richard Turner, Director of the New York Institute for the Humanities, to Ms. Leslie Berlowitz, Associate Vice-President for Academic Affairs at New York University, and Mr. Ennio Troili, Acting Director of the Italian Cultural Institute of New York City, we also express our thanks for various courtesies and generous forms of assistance. Dr. Kenneth Silverman and Dr. Josephine Gattuso Hendin of the Department of English, Dr. Aldo Scaglioni of the Department of Italian, and Dr. Paul Baker of the Department of History at New York University, as well as Mr. Louis Auchincloss, are also to be thanked for their contributions. Dott. Monica Ricci Sargentini was especially helpful with research and translations, and Mrs. Luisa Liberati and Ms. Silvia Casagrande of the Istituto della Enciclopedia Italiana were indispensable, in various important ways, in making this volume a reality.

Preface

*I*TALY, since the earliest day of the American Republic, has always occupied a special place in the imagination of American travelers, writers, and artists. The glorious land and seascapes, the manifest palimpsest of her history from pagan, medieval, and Renaissance times to the present, the richness of her artwork, the complexity of her social and cultural organization, even the weather itself—all of these have contributed to what, for Americans, Henry James called "the Spirit of the South." The meaning of this intangible spirit, to the American mind, arises in part out of the impressions of eighteenth- and nineteenth-century Anglo-American travelers in Italy, together with figures like Stendhal and Goethe, whose accounts of the country served to create a complex image of a congenial people whose history was marked by an ancient pagan and Catholic religious tradition, remarkable social and historical density, ambiguous moral complexity, and recurrent internecine political turbulence. Perhaps above all else, for American travelers, Italy came to be seen as a land of aesthetic glory.

On the other hand, America during the nineteenth century was a relatively new nation created out of the intermingling of peoples of diverse ethnic, racial, national, and religious origins. (The unparalleled growth and development of America was to include, of course, the immigration of hundreds of thousands of Italians.) The nationalist agenda, especially for writers like Emerson and Whitman, required the celebration of all things American and the virtual repudiation of Europe: her monarchical governments, her political aristocracies, her class structure, her state religion, and her blood-soaked history. As Emerson put it in "The American Scholar" (1837), "We have listened too long to the courtly muses of Europe."[1] Given the course of Italian political and cultural history since the Renaissance, it was perhaps inevitable that nineteenth-century American travelers should accept as natural the fact of Italian cultural decline—what Edgar Allan Poe had summed up in the phrase "the grandeur that was Rome." The present and the future seemed to point to the New World.

But the comparative infancy of American cultural institutions and the primitiveness of American social forms were evident to any witness not blinded by American nationalism, and American confidence in the cultural glories yet to come in the New World did not always compensate for the perceived "cultural thinness," as Henry James called it, of the American scene. Hence we have the phenomenon of a good many nineteenth-century American "backtrailers" —travelers who preferred to return to see Europe or even to settle there as expatriates rather than to sit still in the undeveloped East or to go West and grow up with the raw new country. To these backtrailers—Irving, Cooper, and Longfellow, for example—the idea of an absolute break with the European past and European culture was illusionary and detrimental to America's proper development. Europe still had much to boast of, much to teach the fledgling American nation.

The reappropriation of Europe for the purposes of indicating a standard for American cultural development required sympathetic American thinkers and writers to create a counterargument emphasizing the character of European greatness. Faced with evidence of Italy's manifest economic and political decline since the Renaissance, American writers created a countermyth of Italy in which that country came to be seen as the land of rich aesthetic traditions, spontaneous poetic passions, and insouciant carnal and spiritual freedoms. "To the imagination," Henry Wadsworth Longfellow told a Harvard audience in 1851, "Italy has always been, and always will be, the land of the sun, and the land of song; and neither tempest, rain nor snow will ever chill the glow of enthusiasm that the name of Italy excites in every poetic mind. Say what ill of it you may, it still remains to the poet, the land of his predilection, to the artist, the land of his necessity." An instance of how the mere name of Italy could excite the enthusiasm that Longfellow mentions is suggested by C. Waller Barrett in *Italian Influence on American Literature:* when the novelist James Fenimore Cooper rode over the Simplon Pass on his first visit to Italy in 1828 and the coachman cracked his whip and called out "Italy," Cooper wrote: "I pulled off my hat in reverence."[2]

The westward-looking nationalist enthusiasm for the American future and the backtrailing passionate attraction to Europe, and especially to Italy, are nowhere more evident than in the family of Henry James, Sr. To this wealthy, independent, and eccentric religious and social thinker—the author of *The Secret of Swedenborg* (1869) and *Society The Redeemed Form of Man* (1879)—the proper development of his five children (William, Henry Junior, Garth Wilkinson, Robertson, and Alice) required not only academic tutoring but, more importantly for our purposes, a "sensuous education" that only Europe could provide. Frequent travelers to Europe, the members of the James family illustrate and contribute to the complex image of Italy that is still reflected in American imaginative and artistic thought.

This image of Italy—when all is said and done—shares much with the "oddly persistent Anglo-Saxon" myth, dating from the Renaissance, which Carl Maves has described in *Sensuous Pessimism: Italy in the Work of Henry James*. On the one hand, this myth saw Italy as

a venerable relic of the Roman Empire, as purveyor and exemplar of culture and civilization, a land of carefree sensuous enjoyment and sunny skies inhabited by [as Howells put it in *Italian Journeys*] "simple and natural folks, pleased . . . with little things, and as easy and unconscious as children in their ways," while on the other hand viewing it, like Roger Ascham in *The Scholemaster* (1570), as the sink of elegant vice and luxurious corruption, of subtle treachery with dagger and poison, of cynical sensual indulgence and Machiavellian casuistry, a moral hothouse pullulating with Jesuits, assassins, and courtesans.[3]

The attitude toward Italy of Henry James, Sr., resembles somewhat the latter viewpoint and shares much with Hawthorne's ambivalent response to the country in *The Marble Faun*, where the crushing weight of the past is viewed as a giant corpse suffocating the life of contemporary Italy. As Father told Henry Junior, he sensed, under the acclaimed picturesqueness of Italy, "all the pent-up moaning and groaning soul of the race, struggling to be free or to come to consciousness." He remarked that "the historical consciousness rules to such a distorted excess in Europe that I have always been restless there, and ended by pining for the land of the future exclusively."[4]

William James, the great philosopher and psychologist, likewise insisted on the vitality of the present American moment and its glorious future. Appalled by decadence wherever he found it, he was disturbed by evidence of Italy's "moribund Latinity" and "sweet decay," and he celebrated the purer air and the "superior morality" of the Swiss. Yet in the course of his several visits to Italy, the charm of the country and its people also came to enchant him. "I surrender to Italy," he once wrote, "and I should think that a painter would almost go out of his skin to wander about from town to town."[5] Wandering about Lake Como, Milan, Turin, Venice, Torcello, and Verona in 1872, his sister Alice found the experience "crowded with sensations surprises and pleasures"—as her brother Henry reported to their parents.[6] For Henry himself—the great novelist who set nearly a score of his stories and a half dozen of his novels in Italy—the country was "quella terra santa," "that Paradise that makes every other place a purgatory at best."[7] No European pilgrimage was more passionate than his to Italy: in fact, he made fourteen visits to Italy over a period of thirty-eight years. As he told Grace Norton in 1892, "Italy remains firm while other things come and go—remains, on the whole, I mean, the sweetest impression of life."[8] Even so, James felt that Italy kept him at arm's length, however passionate he wished his embrace to become. There remains something of the "sentimental tourist," if not the "brooding tourist," in James's travel writings about the country. And however celebratory his travel writings, the image of Italy in James's fiction, as Maves has argued, emphasizes the Anglo-American gothic trope of treachery, betrayal, and death as much as that of beauty and art and the glories of an old aesthetic tradition.

The connection between Italy and American literature and philosophy, especially in relation to one or another member of the James family, has already elicited the interest of a number of distinguished Italian and American critics. Aside from Carl Maves's *Sensuous Pessimism: Italy in the Work of Henry James* and C. Waller Barrett's *Italian Influence on American Literature*, we must salute Van Wyck Brooks's *The Dream of Arcadia: American Writers and Artists in Italy, 1760–1915*, Nathalia Wright's *American Novelists in Italy, The Discoverers: Allston to James*, and several Italian studies—Cristina Giorcelli's *Henry James e l'Italia*, Barbara and

Giorgio Melchiori's *Il gusto de Henry James*, Marilla Battilana's *Venezia sfondo e simbolo nella narrativa di Henry James*, Sergio Perosa's *L'Euro-America di Henry James* and *Henry James e Venezia*, edited by Sergio Perosa. But granted the preeminence of Henry Junior in fiction and William in philosophy and psychology, none of the available comparative criticism undertakes to look at the mutual influences linking the James family as a whole to the Italy they knew and—however ambivalently—loved.

The purpose of the present volume is to pay tribute to Italy as a source of inspiration to American thought and imagination, and to present a series of critical and scholarly essays that trace that inspiration in the lives and works of one of the most creative and impressive families in American cultural history. For the James family gave to each other, and to all Italians and Americans, both vivid accounts of their travels in Italy and rich testimony of the impact of that country's philosophy, art, and literature on the works they themselves composed. The following chapters trace the travels of the family in Italy and elucidate their responses to the art, history, philosophy, and culture of the nation. In the opening chapter, Leon Edel, the preeminent figure in Henry James studies, tracks the changing meaning of Italy to the novelist as, during the course of nearly four decades, Henry appropriated the country to his fictional purposes. Then I present an overview of the whole family's travels to Europe and offer a précis of their conflicting responses to the Italian scene.

Several of the chapters incisively demonstrate the uses to which the novelist Henry put his travel experience in the Italian novels and stories he published. Josephine Gattuso Hendin demonstrates the point of convergence between the Italian and the American sensibilities in *Roderick Hudson* and *The Princess Casamassima* and, in doing so, discriminates amongst the several regions of an Italy then undergoing complex political and cultural change. Daniel Mark Fogel, the editor of the *Henry James Review*, explores the motif of American girlhood innocence, betrayed in Italy, as James develops it in *Daisy Miller* and *The Portrait of a Lady*. Sergio Perosa, the foremost Italian critic of Henry James, defines, on the other hand, the hidden ambiguities of an international theme that is ordinarily oversimplified in James criticism, and in doing so he discovers new dimensions in several of the short stories, *The Aspern Papers*, and *The Wings of the Dove*. And Agostino Lombardo, in elucidating Italy as the scene of romantic love and death in James's fiction, argues convincingly that James's Italian works also disclose the hidden theme of fictional creation itself.

But these chapters are not merely excursions through an Italian fictional terrain. They take into account elements of biography, art, travel writing, and philosophy as well. Adeline Tintner, past president of the Henry James Society, illustrates the impact of Venetian rococo art on James and the reflection of Pietro Longhi in a number of James's novels and stories. Bonney MacDonald focuses on Henry James's qualities of perception and the implied phenomenology of vision that underlies such travel works as *Italian Hours*. The chapter by Maria Antonietta Saracino characterizes Alice's response to the country, explores the meaning of Italy in Alice's letters and diary, and defines her present stature with Italian readers. Lyall H. Powers gives an account of Henry James's criticism of Italian literature. Denis Donoghue reflects on the nineteenth-century Anglo-American expatriates in Italy and James's biography *William Wetmore Story and His Friends*, while Claudio Gorlier and Gerald E. Myers demonstrate not merely the influence of Italy on William James but the impact of his philosophy on a circle of Italian pragmatists and political theorists that included Giovanni Papini and Giuseppe Prezzolini. In sum, these chapters touch on a wide range of issues at the point where the James family and Italy converge. In doing so, they not only throw light on the specific subjects that they address but they symbolize those deep and abiding cultural ties between Italy and the United States that are celebrated by this volume.

New York University   *James W. Tuttleton*

Notes

1. Ralph Waldo Emerson, "The American Scholar," in *Ralph Waldo Emerson: Essays and Lectures* (New York: Library of America, 1983), 70.
2. C. Waller Barrett, *Italian Influence on American Literature* (New York: The Grolier Club, 1962), 13, 15.
3. Carl Maves, *Sensuous Pessimism: Italy in the Work of Henry James* (Bloomington: Indiana University Press, 1973), 5.

4. F. O. Matthiessen, *The James Family: Including Selections from the Writings of Henry James, Senior, William, Henry, and Alice James* (New York: Alfred A. Knopf, 1947), 289.

5. Quoted in Ralph Barton Perry, *The Thought and Character of William James* (New York: Harper, 1964), pp. 202–3.

6. *Henry James Letters*, vol. 1, *1843–1875*, ed. Leon Edel (Cambridge: Harvard University Press, 1974) 1: 296.

7. Quoted in James W. Tuttleton, "Henry James and the Venice of Dreams," in *Henry James e Venezia*, ed. Sergio Perosa (Florence: Leo S. Olschki Editore, 1987), 52.

8. *Henry James Letters*, vol. 3, *1883–1895*, ed. Leon Edel (Cambridge: Harvard University Press, 1980) 394.

ONE *The Italian Journeys of Henry James*

LEON EDEL

*I*N 1869, during his first tour of western Europe, Henry James characterized England as "a good married matron" and Switzerland as "a magnificent man." He did not characterize France, but if we follow his earlier designations he might have described the French Republic as a stalwart *dame de comptoir* hoarding her civilization and keeping her accounts. Italy, which James saw for the first time during the autumn of 1869, had quite a different appeal. The words he found for the Italian peninsula were "a beautiful dishevelled nymph." In the end James would live with the matron; he would cross to Paris and sit in the cafés of the *dame de comptoir*; but as often as possible he would pursue the dishevelled nymph in a series of cities whose names we all know. It might be useful however to further translate James's geography: England was society, tradition, and his literary ancestry; France was mind, amenity, and relaxed morals. Italy was a passion. He laid siege and captured London. Paris was a pleasurable way station to Italy. In Italy he tasted, as he became a relaxed puritan, his selective *dolce vita* during the period of his life when he debated whether to cultivate an art or a passion. He ultimately—but too late—learned that one could, in reality, cultivate both.

The solution for him happens to have been, however, that he was most comfortable cultivating an art. He could feel, from time to time, the pulse of passion: but he felt it intellectually and as spectator and observer. During his four and almost five decades in

© 1988 by Leon Edel

Europe he often forsook maternal England for Italy. He made four-teen journeys in all—winters in Rome, springtimes in Venice, long quiet residences on Bellosguardo in Florence or slowly paced ram-bles in the little towns including those hilltops that lie between Rome and the spread of Umbria.

James took possession of Italy by degrees; he had to accommodate himself slowly to the different layers of its civilization. He per-ceived first the Italy of Stendhal, and of the romantics. He under-standably identified himself with the other voyagers who had pre-ceded him—Goethe and his Italian journey, the passionate pilgrimages of Bryon, and the encounters with death in Italy of Shelley and Keats. Then came another phase which we can read in his early tales: the discovery of the early centuries. A New Yorker, like a New England puritan, is not supposed to allow for disturbing depths of feeling. We can trace the lines of an early guilt at permit-ting himself to be captured by so intense and erotic and ancient a nymph: it would require a number of years to find a balance. Disin-terred statues need to be reburied. Roderick Hudson is killed by his passions in Italy. Daisy Miller dies of insouciance and a Roman fever. Hyacinth Robinson with his shallow socialism discovers in Venice that he wants to experience the bourgeois immediacies of life, not the treacheries of revolutions. He resolves his schizoid being, created here by a novelist's faltering hand, in his suicide. Isabel Archer discovers the treacheries of the expatriate Americans in Florence and Rome. Milly Theale goes to Venice, the city of beauty and ruins, to die. However, at the end, in *The Golden Bowl*, Henry James can bring off the marriage between America and Italy —that is Europe. Maggie keeps her Italian prince, and bears him a child, a signal of the race's survival. Maggie has to pay a high price for not upsetting the applecart: the price Eve paid when she tasted of the Tree of Knowledge.

Such is the creative spiritual geography and moral history of James's Europe and especially Italy. Physically for James, Italy was a land where he could shed the woolen wrappings of England and listen to his senses. Within the sensuality of Italy James heard the organ tones of history—Rome and grandeur, the collapse of Empire, the brightness and desolation of Venice, the gloom and chill of Florence but also its Renaissance endurance, its arts and crafts, together with the cosmopolitan salons and the dilettantism of the outsiders settled there from many lands. As we look at the volumes of the New York Edition, we recognize the deep reach of Italy into the heart of this lonely pen-driving American—and we remember that in the end, in his late maturity, he wrote two essays devoted to two Italian writers—D'Annunzio and Matilde Serao—to try to define their kind of passion then called illicit in the Anglo world, and what it did to the novel. James's *Sacred Fount*, that little *jeu d'espirit* created at the beginning of this century, which his readers found so bewildering, was a kind of D'Annunzio-inspired novel in which James however wanted to say how vulnerable passion renders humans. "I saw," he writes of his observer, studying the mysterious lady in the novel, "I saw as I had never seen before what consuming passion can make of the marked mortal on whom, with fixed beak and claws it has settled as on a prey. She reminded me of a sponge wrung dry and with fine pores agape. Voided and scraped of everything, her shell was merely crushable."

The Italy of Henry James was a very particular Italy—entirely of his own creation, a profound part of his being, a happy pastiche of self-comfort. It is difficult for someone like myself who has read every word he wrote about the Italian cities and the Italian people to arrive at its essences. He was not writing about Italy as a social or economic entity, or as an assemblage of city states unified into a single country. His was, shall we say, a Proustian Italy, the Italy of historical impressionism, of an ultimately relaxed and accepting American who had learned adequately to speak and read Italian, who was deep and wise in Europe's ways, and who took each town, each square, each hilltop as an aesthetic experience. He was a wanderer in the old tradition—he traveled first with his volume of Ruskin, or the *Italienische Reise*, and closely consulted the guide-books of the time. We may get a sense of how saturated a traveler he was, how "knowing" and studious and observant, if we look at a passage in one of his Italian essays in which he describes a visit to Spezia and inevitably to nearby Lerici. What does he look for and at? His quest is for that which nourishes the eyes and through the eyes the sensibility. His sentimental pilgrimage takes him from Genoa first to Spezia itself where he notes that the place has become prosperous and ugly, home of the Italian fleet, filled with young men in blue flannel. A new big hotel at the edge of the sea speaks for the developers of the time. Its guests are grave-looking English tourists who walk about looking respectable and bored. He notes they hold a Church of England service in a gaudily frescoed parlor. He is happier as he makes his way to little Porto Venere, which acquired its name from having been the site of an ancient temple of Venus and later a ruined church on the same site. "If Venus ever revisits her desecrated shrine," he writes, "she must sometimes pause a moment in that sunny stillness and listen to the murmur of the tideless sea at the base of the narrow promontory." He reads an inscription in Italian and English that here the great Byron "defied the waves of the Ligurian sea." To which James rejoins "Byron was always defying something." If such slabs were put up wherever this performance occurred, he remarks, the commemorative tablets would be thick as milestones in many parts of Europe.

The great merit of Spezia was that he could have himself rowed across the Gulf one October afternoon to the little bay of Lerici to pay tribute to an English-Italian past. Lerici he found charming. The hills closed it in and there was a wonderful, presiding old castle, without which Jamesian Europe would be incomplete. In the middle of the curving shore stands the desolate little villa in which Shelley spent the last months of his short life. Here we can read James's feelings within his prose strategies, his sense of the poetry of the thing "outlived and lost and gone."

The house [Shelley] occupied is strangely shabby and as sad as you may choose to find it. It stands directly upon the beach, with scarred and battered walls and a loggia of several arches opened to a little terrace with a rugged parapet, which, when the wind blows, must be drenched with the salt spray. The place is very lonely—all overwearied with sun and breeze and brine—very close to nature, as it was Shelley's passion to be. I can fancy a great lyric poet sitting on the terrace of a warm evening and feeling very far from England in the early years of the century. In that place, and with his genius, he would as a matter of course have heard in the voice of nature a sweetness which only the lyric movement could translate. It is a place where an English-speaking pilgrim himself may very honestly think thoughts and feel moved to lyric utterance. But I must content myself with saying in halting prose that I remember few episodes of Italian travel more sympathetic . . . than that perfect autumn afternoon; the half-hour's station on the little battered terrace of the villa; the climb to the singularly felicitous old castle that hangs above Lerici; the meditative lounge in the fading light, on the vine-decked platform that looked out toward the sunset and the darkening mountains and, far below, upon the quiet sea, beyond which the pale-faced tragic villa stared up at the brightening moon.

There you have a perfected Jamesian travelogue in which his voyaging is related to literature, to the English poetic past in Italy, and to the extrapolation of history—literary history—within his own sensuous observances of nature and the Italian seacoast. Later we will see James placing himself into the Roman, the medieval, the Italian city-states of the peninsula. He journeys with history in his mind's eye and his feelings, and books of history in his language, as his library later revealed.

He decidedly does not journey like Tocqueville in America, or so many other travelers imbued with a desire to understand the great and irresistible forces working in national societies. He is always aesthetic. One of the qualities residing in Balzacian novelists is to see the world as it exists, not as it should be or might be. James has no blindness to poverty and he confesses to its adding its realities to his art; or human struggle, or the vain posturings of successive generations. He confines himself to narrow yet deep passageways of a quest for beauty and harmony, and the powerful awareness that is possible to humans to remind themselves that a given soil has been trampled by many feet in the lapse of the centuries; that strange and curious things have come to be—cities built and desolated, works of architecture overlaid again and again by succeeding works of architecture. He is that particular voyager, a leisurely American endowed with a love for the visitable past. As a novelist he wants to know old manners, customs, usages; old ways of constructing human existence in a cruel world that preys constantly upon itself.

This was "the poetry of the thing outlived and lost and gone." Yet remembered, and re-infused with posthumous feeling. He was, as a traveler, a kind of archaeologist of feeling, and when we trace his Italian attachments we see that the process he used was to take possession of the old cities until he knew them and had made them a part of himself.

His first Italian journey of 1869 was mainly a journey of discovery —a journey feverish and excited, in which for the first time he experienced a climate less intense than he had ever known, a sense of history that had never gone as deep, and a feeling of cities and people that seemed to him vitally anarchic. He entered Italy reading Stendhal and saturated with Ruskin. I am fairly certain he carried Goethe with him, and in Rome we know he bought—and kept—the *Lettres familières écrites d'Italie* by a man best remembered for his quarrel with Voltaire. I refer to the Président de Brosses. We know also that he bought in 1869 Jules Zeller's *Entretiens sur l'histoire d'Italie.* He was ready for all kinds of emotions; and in his fantasy-story "At Isella" he described a young man rescuing a woman fleeing from her husband. She possesses "the rich capacity of the historic womanhood of Italy," of Lucrezia Borgia or Bianca Capello. His fancy ran to history. He wanted to learn about a civilization more rooted and relaxed than his own. "It is rather a melancholy mistake," he would write, "in this uncertain life of ours, to have founded oneself on so many rigidities and rules—so many siftings and sortings." Beyond his cerebral self lay the unexplored depths of his own senses. However, in his old age he would be able to write of "the loved Italy . . . so much more loved than one has ever been able, even after fifty efforts, to say!" And also "I nourish for Italy an unspeakably tender passion." His writings, his journalism, and his fiction reveal this in full.

The process of taking possession began in Florence where, like so many cultured travelers, he found the compact city by the Arno tugging at him by its artistic appeal and its Renaissance glories: "that vague aftertaste of evil things that lurks so often, for a suspicious sensibility, wherever the terrible game of the life of the Renaissance was played as the Italians played it." In Florence he began work on his first novel, living in rooms in the heart of the city. Bit by bit he found that Florence had become for him a city of withdrawal, of meditation, of dilettante cosmopolitanism, a secretive and yet sociable city. Enclosed by mountains, and confining gloomy narrow streets, in which stood the moldy elegance of a palatial past, Florence possessed not only the richness of its old paintings but the artefacts, the plate, the silver and gold, the mute testament of opulence and grandeur in the lower rooms of the Pitti and elsewhere. James came to like Florence and its intellectual qualities, its nourishment of craft and beauty. Later he saw it as engaged in social measurements not unlike those of London. After dining with various Russian expatriates and observing the expatriated Americans, and enjoying the friendships of cultured ladies like Vernon Lee and sundry duchesses and countesses, or making friends with the American physician William Wilberforce Baldwin —for whom Florence was the center of an international practice— James found Firenze charming enough but "queer, promiscuous, polyglot." And he enjoyed being lionized by it. Still it was a society from which he detached himself; a friend who observed him closely enough remarked, "I have never seen anyone to be so run after as Mr. James was while in Florence."

James took possession of Rome by stages. His first visit finds him writing home in ecstasy a letter to William filled with the sense of history, and of a civilization both ancient and modern. We must also think of his parents reading this in snowbound Cambridge, by lamplight, far removed from the Vatican and Catholicism, in a suburb puritanical and Unitarian, suspicious of southern laxities and the sins of history. The letter has been much quoted, and will be I am sure again and again:

At last—for the first time—I live! It beats everything: it leaves the Rome of your fancy—your education—nowhere. It makes Venice—Florence—Oxford—London—seem like little cities of pasteboard. I went reeling and moaning thro' the streets, in a fever of enjoyment. In the course of four or five hours I traversed almost the whole of Rome and got a glimpse of everything—the Forum, the Coliseum (stupendissimo!), the Pantheon, the Capitol, St. Peter's, the Column of Trajan, the Castle of St. Angelo— all the Piazzas and ruins and monuments. The effect is something indescribable. For the first time I know what the picturesque is. In St. Peter's I stayed some time. It's even beyond its reputation. It was filled with foreign ecclesiastics—great armies encamped in prayer on the marble plains of its pavement—an inexhaustible physiognomical study. To crown my day, on my way home, I met his Holiness in person—driving in prodigious purple state—sitting dim within the shadows of his coach with two uplifted benedictory fingers—like some dusky Hindoo idol in the depths of its shrine. Even if I should leave Rome tonight I should feel that I have caught the keynote of its operation on the senses. I have looked along the grassy vista of the Appian Way and seen the topmost stone-work of the Coliseum sitting shrouded in the light of heaven, like the edge of an Alpine chain. I've trod the Forum and I have scaled the Capitol. I've seen the Tiber hurrying along, as swift and dirty as history! From the high tribune of a great chapel of St. Peter's I have heard in the papal choir a strange old man sing in a shrill unpleasant soprano. I've seen troops of little tonsured neophytes clad in scarlet, marching and counter-marching and ducking and flopping, like poor little raw recruits for the heavenly host. In fine I've seen Rome, and I shall go to bed a wiser man than I last rose—yesterday morning.

James would temper these first enthusiasms. He would come to see Rome less ecstatically as a muddy provincial city in which papal power was shrinking even while he was visiting it. He caught it at the last moment of its old splendor—the romance of antiquity aside. "A leaf out of the Middle Ages," he wrote as he saw the pope arrive at a church opposite his hotel, surrounded by cardinals and ambassadors. He remembers the Vatican draped in scarlet, the scarlet coaches of the cardinals, the monsignori in their purple stockings followed by solemn servants, the sobriety of the papal newspapers, the traces that Lords Spiritual still presided by divine emanation over the rites of mere humans. The great meeting of the Ecumenical Council was taking place in 1869; it would proclaim the dogma of papal infallibility in its final attempt to solidify the papacy, even as the pope was moving into symbolic terrain. Instead of the City of Rome he would have only the City of the Vatican. But the first glimpse of Pius IX in his gilded coach remains. We can read it in *Roderick Hudson*.

Secular Rome, and above all antique Rome, touched Henry James more profoundly. The Pantheon loomed out of centuries with a "delicacy" in its grandeur; it seemed to him more worshipful than the most mysterious and aspiring Gothic. St. Peter's was a "first-class sensation"; he could feel "the heart-beats of the Church"; but the Protestant side of Henry James turned away to admire the statue of Marcus Aurelius at the Capitol. He found in it—in consonance with Hawthorne—"an audible personal voice."

This was the beginning of a profound involvement with Rome. He returned to live there for the better part of two years. He threw himself into the city and the surrounding countryside. He rode horseback in the Campagna, where he felt himself on the edge of a long past, charged "with the murmur of extinguished life." He visited many Roman neighborhoods, as if he were walking about in paintings by Claude Lorrain. The Colosseum had not yet been excavated. It was filled with the earth of the centuries and covered with wild flowers. James also sounded the depths, during this period, of the American art colony, those artists who sculptured Americans and dressed them in togas. He saw the ensconced life of William Wetmore Story, the amateur sculptor who was prized in England and lived in Rome for half a century in his princely forty-room apartment in Palazzo Barberini. James visited a more modest craftsman, Luther Terry, in his flat in the Odiscalchi. Rome would glow in his memory with all sorts "of poetic, romantic lights." Winters of sunshine without clouds, picnics in the Alban and Sabine hills with lively painters and sculptors and food "spread upon the warm stones of ruined temples and tombs; of splendid Catholic processions and ceremonies; of friendly, familiar evenings, prolonged very late, in the great painted and tapestried saloons of historic palaces. It was the slumbrous, pictorial Rome of the Popes, before the Italians had arrived or the local colour departed." I am quoting here from one of his later tales.

During the ensuing years there were accretions of discovery, and deepened feelings. The Roman excavations had begun under the secular government. James did his own emotional excavating. His tales, like "The Last of the Valerii" or "Adina," suggest to us that the old buried things both of history and the psyche troubled him. One tale describes the disinterring of a statue of Juno and its effect on a young Roman of ancient family who has married a modern American girl. The statue arouses pagan feelings and pagan worship and the Roman withdraws from his troubled transatlantic wife. Her New World realism however is prompt and sure. She has the Juno buried again and the atavism is held in check. In "Adina" a predatory American takes from a young shepherd a topaz found in the Campagna; the American's betrothed is wooed by the shepherd and he wins her: in some way the occult evil in the topaz, which had belonged to the cruel emperor Tiberius, acts upon her. The shepherd announces that the girl is much better than the topaz. Still the stone's evil must be exorcised. The chastened American, who has flirted with ancient evil, from the middle of a Tiber bridge casts the glittering jewel into the river. He lets it "return to the moldering underworld of the Roman past." James thus warns his readers that it is dangerous to exhume dormant uncanny life. Contemporary life is evil enough.

Gradually the novelist passes his maturity and reaches the retrospective years of meditation and reflection; he comes to regard Rome as a part of a golden past. Late in life he writes William Wetmore Story's biography—the life of a subject he had never particularly liked—and wonders whether Story's Rome and the Rome of the *forestieri* from America had not been simply "a rare state of the imagination."

Venice offered itself to that kind of imagination. In his early visits he saw it as a city of dream and at first he denied his sensuous feelings, aroused by the water city's changing lights and colors.

In only one letter of this period is he a bit defensive about Venice, apparently attempting to dissipate William James's view that he is too aesthetic, too shallow, not sufficiently intellectual. To his mother he confesses that Oxford is perhaps more important than Venice, that it gave him "deeper and richer things." Perhaps at the time it had done so—although his visit to Oxford had been a fleeting one. This is the only letter I have found in which he is holding back or overlooking his feelings about the water-city. As time went on, he was quite willing to confess in his public writings—and in what we today would call highly erotic language—the effect of Venice on him: "The place seemed to personify itself, to become human and sentient, and conscious of your affection. You desire to embrace it, to caress it, to possess it; and finally a soft sense of possession grows up and your visit becomes a perpetual love affair." In Venice James was able to put his ever-hesitant arms around his disheveled nymph. By that time however the nymph of his imagination and dreams had herself undergone sea changes.

She—and Venice—reflected James's ambivalence, his wavering between what he called his "inexorable yankeehood," his desire not to over-romanticize Italy, and his own controlled and hidden deeper sensuality which he constantly verbalized—the caress of his eyes in the act of observation, his tender feelings for the gondolieri and their physical grace and strength. "It is charming," wrote James, "to wander through the light and shade of intricate canals with perpetual architecture above you and perpetual fluidity beneath." Almost a Freudian remark. His stay in Venice of 1881, when the full recognition of his love affair with the city occurred, was prolonged into weeks and months. "I seemed myself to grow young again," wrote James. He was only too aware of the approach of his fortieth

year. He stood at his window in his rooms on the Riva degli Schia-
voni. The view was *una bellezza*—"the far-shining lagoon, the pink
walls of San Giorgio, the downward curve of the Riva, the distant
islands." Again and again he imaged the Piazza San Marco as resembling a drawing room—the drawing room of all Europe; and in
his growing intimacy all Venice seemed to him like a collective
apartment—one could hear the inhabitants, the cries near and far
of the gondoliers and the people . . .

Without streets and vehicles, the uproar of wheels, the brutality of horses,
and with its little winding ways where people crowd together, where voices
sound as if in the corridors of a house, where the human step circulates as
if it skirted the angles of furniture and shoes never wear out, the place has
the character of an immense collective apartment, in which Piazza San
Marco is the most ornamental corner and palaces and churches, for the
rest, play the part of great divans of repose, tables of entertainment, expanses of decoration. And somehow the splendid common domicile, familiar, domestic and resonant, also resembles a theatre with its actors clicking
over bridges and, in straggling processions, tripping along fondamentas.

For James, Venice was dramatic and operatic. Beyond propinquity
and dissonances it was something else: it was a "sifted Cosmopolis,"
a place that drew to itself seekers of poetry and dispensers of romance.

It is a fact that almost every one interesting, appealing, melancholy, memorable, odd, seems at one time or another, after many days and much life,
to have gravitated to Venice by a happy instinct, settling in it and treating
it, cherishing it, as a sort of repository of consolations; all of which today,
for the conscious mind, is mixed with its air and constitutes its unwritten
history. The deposed, the defeated, the disenchanted, the wounded, or even
only the bored, have seemed to find there something that no other place
could give.

James would write some of this unwritten history, in *The Aspern
Papers*, and in the Venetian chapters of *The Wings of the Dove*, as
he had done in earlier works—say "Travelling Companions," briefly
and vividly in "The Pupil," or in a long chapter in *The Princess
Casamassima*.

Six years before his death, Henry James, in the final expression
of his love for Italy, assembled most of his Italian essays in a
sumptuous folio, illustrated by Joseph Pennell. He called it *Italian*

Hours. The book starts with five essays on Venice, early and late; its center contains six essays on Rome and its neighborhoods. He had written much less about Florence. There are two papers on that city, and in addition papers on the Umbrian hill towns, various Tuscan cities, Siena, Ravenna, Naples, and Capri, together with miscellaneous papers on his revisitings of Italy. He revised his Italian writings and added postscripts that were elegiac and nostalgic. One paper, called "Very Modern Rome," remained unpublished and was printed posthumously. It was found among the papers of Thomas Bailey Aldrich, and was intended for the *Atlantic Monthly*, which he edited. It seems to be of 1878 and, while charming as usual, adds little to some of his earlier impressions.

To read *Italian Hours* today is to rediscover James's care in distinguishing between the impressions of the *forestieri* and their beglamored vision of the peninsula, and the life of the Italians themselves. James could not enter closely into Italian lives—he touched them only generally. He is always careful to remind his readers that he is an outsider, a "sentimental tourist." At times he changes this, especially in his later papers to "brooding tourist." He constantly balances the response of his senses against such realities as he can observe. I need only quote a few sentences from his more mature observations to suggest the stages by which the novelist moved from his early romanticism to deeper reflection. At one point he reminds us

Young Italy, preoccupied with its economical and political future, must be heartily tired of being admired for its eyelashes and its pose.

Or again, as he is conscious of the new generation living under its secular government:

After thinking of Italy as historical and artistic it will do him [the traveler] no great harm to think of her for a while as panting both for a future and for a balance at the bank; aspirations supposedly much at variance with the Byronic, the Ruskinian, the artistic, poetic, aesthetic manner of considering our eternally attaching peninsula . . . nothing is more easy to understand than an honest ire on the part of the young Italy of today at being looked at by all the world as a kind of soluble pigment. . . . In one of Thackeray's novels occurs a mention of a young artist who sent to the Royal Academy a picture representing "A Contadino dancing with a Trasteverina at the door of a Locanda, to the music of a Pifferaro." It is in this

attitude and with these conventional accessories that the world has hitherto seen fit to represent young Italy, and one doesn't wonder that if the
youth has any spirit he should at last begin to resent our insufferable
aesthetic patronage.

Referring to the line of tram cars just then established from the
Porta del Popolo to the Ponte Molle, James added that it was on one
of those "democratic vehicles that I seem to see him [Italian youth]
taking his triumphant course down the vista of the future." And
James added: "Like it or not, as we may, it is evidently destined to
be; I see a new Italy in the future which in many important respects
will equal, if not surpass, the most enterprising sections of our
native land. Perhaps by that time Chicago and San Francisco will
have acquired a pose, and their sons and daughters will dance at
the door of the *locande*." James wrote this in 1877. He went on to
distinguish between Italy as a museum-world and Italy as a modern
state.

By being a brooding and reflective tourist James remembered
ultimately that a nation which had become the subject of our
romantic conception had been an ardently mercantile country as
well as a creator of frescoes and altar pieces. What had gone on in
James's sensibility had been a fusion of the literary tradition of Italy
—reflected in English classics such as *Othello* or *Volpone* or *Venice
Preserv'd*. He had grasped the operatic and melodramatic as well.
Out of the Italy of his own observation and imagination came the
Italy and the Italians of Henry James's later work—not only the
observed Venice of *The Aspern Papers* of 1888 but *The Wings of the
Dove* of 1902 and *The Golden Bowl* of 1904. Howells attempted an
Italian novel, and F. Marian Crawford had written romantic fiction
James knew well—and deplored. It was James however who brought
modern Italy into American fiction, as Shakespeare and Jonson and
Otway had used the Italy of the Renaissance for the drama. James
had written long before that "the sum of Italian misery is, on the
whole, less than the sum of the Italian knowledge of life." It is a
prince named ironically Amerigo who brings this knowledge to the
permissive father and innocent daughter of the *Bowl* in a drama
which uses old treacheries and evil to probe a modern dilemma.
When we read James's Italianate fiction—the Italy of *The Portrait
of a Lady* and the reflection of Italy in *The Golden Bowl*—we see

that his Italian experience touched the polarities of his creation—the evil and terror that lies within the sensuous beauty of existence, the heritage of the treacheries and beauties of the past.

Italy offered James not only the aesthetic values of its cherished art or of its way of life. It yielded him a sense of its past, the poetry of its mosaic, the secrets of its archaeology and architecture and their relatedness to the Italian modernity in which James had traveled and lived. If we understand this we can see how James outgrew his early pursuit of a disheveled nymph and in his later years saw her changed into a sophisticated and coiffed woman. She had lost her complexion, like Venice, "her figure, her reputation, even her self-respect; and yet, with it all, has so puzzlingly not lost a shred of her distinction." She was a product of "the defiant miracle of life and beauty." These were the alterations in his wondrous journey of discovery, the journey to Italy so often repeated, and so triumphantly converted by James's art into supreme fiction.

TWO "Dipped in the Sacred Stream": The James Family in Italy

JAMES W. TUTTLETON

*L*EON EDEL, in "The Italian Journeys of Henry James," has movingly characterized Henry James's passionate pilgrimage to Italy, the changing meaning and value of the country to him, and his use of Italian landscapes, scenes, and characters in his fiction. The task of the present essay is to bring forward into the Italian light the other members of the James family and to characterize their own experience of Italy. Providing something of the context in which the family thought of Italy and listening to the voices of his siblings and parents as they responded to the Italian scene will make more intelligible Henry's fervid rhapsody about that country and her people.

I shall not discuss William James of Albany, the progenitor of the James family in America, or the other ancestors who first came to this county from Ireland and settled in Albany and New York. It is enough to note that by the time of Henry James, Jr. (1843–1916), there had evolved a large tribe of relatives that Henry described in *The Wings of the Dove* as an "immense extravagant unregulated cluster, with free-living ancestors, handsome dead cousins, lurid uncles, beautiful vanished aunts, persons all busts and curls. . . ."[1]

Instead, I shall concentrate only on Henry James, Sr., and his five children: William, the great Harvard psychologist and philosopher, born in 1842 in a room at the Astor House, one of New York's finest hotels; Henry Junior, the novelist, playwright, critic, and short story writer, born in 1843 in Washington Place; Garth Wilkinson, born in 1845, also in Washington Place; Robertson, born in 1846 at 50 Pearl Street in Albany; and Alice, the diarist, born in 1848 at

54 West 14th Street in New York City.[2] I cite their places of birth the better to emphasize that the James family was exceptionally peripatetic, frequently on the move.

The father, Henry Senior, was fortunately wealthy, through inheritance, and had no obligation to work or pursue a profession, and was thus permitted to follow his frequently eccentric inclinations. Although he fathered two much more important sons, this remarkable progenitor of genius was unquestionably "a magnificent personality in his own right."[3] But living with him produced its problems for the children. Since they were thrown in with others at school, as Henry Junior reported, the siblings found it "tasteless and even humiliating that the head of our little family was *not* in business, and that even among our relatives on each side we couldn't so much as name proudly anyone who was." Writing many years later, the novelist remarked:

I perfectly recover the effect of my own repeated appeal to our parent for some presentable account of him that would prove us respectable. . . . I remember my friend Simpson's telling me crushingly, at one of our New York schools, on our hanging back with the fatal truth about our credentials, that the author of *his* being . . . was in the business of a stevedore. That struck me as a great card to play—the word was fine and mysterious; so that "What shall we tell them that you *are*, don't you see" could but become on our lips at home a more constant appeal. It seemed wantonly to be prompted for our father, and indeed greatly to amuse him that he should put us off with strange unheard-of attributions, such as would have made us ridiculous in our special circles; his "Say I'm a philosopher, say I'm a seeker for truth, say I'm a lover of my kind, say I'm an author of books if you like; or, best of all, just say I'm a Student," saw us so very little further.[4]

Passionately anti-Calvinist, Henry Senior had embraced a religion of spiritual mysticism, based on Swedenborg and deepened by his association with Concord transcendentalists like Emerson and Alcott. Emerson called him "true comfort—wise, gentle, polished, with heroic manners, and a serenity like the sun."[5] However, this serenity was purchased by a sublime indifference to most of the practical problems in life. Henry Senior described himself as loving to give "ecstatic hours to worship or meditation but moments spent in original deed, such as putting a button upon my coat or cleansing my garden-walk of weeds, weigh very heavily upon my shoulders."[6]

The fruits of his otherworldly meditation were the several books Henry Senior published during his lifetime: *Christianity the Logic of Creation* (1857), *Substance and Shadow* (1863), *The Secret of Swedenborg* (1869), and *Society the Redeemed Form of Man* (1879). (After his death, William, his dutiful but scientifically minded son, edited his *Literary Remains* [1884]). To discuss the spiritual character of these remarkable books is beyond the scope of this essay. It is sufficient to remark that they were passionate with intellectual conviction, an attribute of the education he gave his sons and daughter in the James household. The great *Nation* editor, E. L. Godkin, once remarked that

> There could not be a more entertaining treat than a dinner at the James house, when all the young people were at home. They were full of stories of the oddest kind, and discussed questions of morals or taste or literature with a vociferous vigor so great as sometimes to lead the young men to leave their seats and gesticulate on the floor. I remember, in some of these heated discussions, it was not unusual for the sons to invoke humorous curses on their parent, one of which was, that "his mashed potatoes might always have lumps in them!"[7]

However much the children divagated from their father's cloudy mysticism, Godkin commended Henry Senior as "a writer of extraordinary vigor and picturesqueness, and I suppose there was not in his day a more formidable master of English style."[8] A sense of style, indeed, was the father's precious gift to all his children.

But style and passionate conviction aside, it is his effect on his children, especially in relation to the topic of Italy, that most concerns us here. Henry Senior had a morbid dread of formal education, which he feared might stultify and narrow his children, whom he deeply loved. The key to their education was to be "spontaneity," its object virtue. "I desire my child," he said, "to become an upright man, a man in whom goodness shall be induced not by mercenary motives as brute goodness is induced, but by love for it or a sympathetic delight in it. And inasmuch as I know that this character or disposition cannot be forcibly imposed upon him, but must be freely assumed, I surround him as far as possible with an atmosphere of freedom."[9]

However, as his son Henry Junior remarked, this excess of freedom had peculiar effects on the children. Father, while "delighting ever in the truth," was "generously contemptuous of the facts," so that, "the literal played in our education as small a part as it perhaps ever played in any, and we wholesomely breathed inconsistency and ate and drank contradictions."[10] A restless man in search of a spontaneous education for his children, Henry Senior moved the children from one dame school to another in New York and Albany, gave them private tutors, and—once they got to Europe— moved them about from city to city, searching for what he thought could most prepare them for a free and virtuous life. Of course they came to see churches and castles, museums and galleries, the life of the street, the square, and the plaza. And, in Europe, they picked up French and German, and immersed themselves in books.

But of these disruptions of schooling Henry Junior later remarked: "We couldn't have changed oftener, it strikes me as I look back. . . ." He found it odd "that my main association with my 'studies,' whether of the infant or the adolescent order, should be with almost anything but the fact of learning—of learning, I mean, what I was supposed to learn."[11] Alice likewise remarked that their parents purged the children's minds of superstitions, "leaving them *tabulae rasae* to receive whatever stamp our individual experience was to give them, so that we had not the bore of wasting our energy in raking over and sweeping out the rubbish."[12] However free of rubbish their minds might be, Father's transcendental educational theories left the children ill-equipped for success in any profession, vocation, or trade. Henry Junior later described his father's educational experiments as "no plotted thing at all, but only an accident of accidents," and he defined their early education as "small vague spasms of school."[13] And Alice was later to wonder

whether if I had had an education I should have been more or less of a fool than I am? . . . It would have deprived me surely of those exquisite moments of mental flatulence which every now and then inflate the cerebral vacuum with a delicious sense of latent possibilities, of stretching one's self to cosmic limits; and who would ever give up the reality of dreams for relative knowledge?[14]

Properly to account for the influence of Italy on the James children requires postponing a discussion of their journeys to Italy in favor of a consideration of what the Jameses knew about Italy, by way of a preparation for it, before they ever left New York. And to understand this complex matter we must turn to Henry Junior's last writings, the autobiographical volumes *A Small Boy and Others* and *Notes of a Son and Brother*. While it is true that these are *ex post facto* accounts of his discovery of the country and her people, they are remarkably of a piece with his earliest responses to Italy. In these autobiographical works of his old age, James undertook nothing less than to account for the two most important features of his personal and artistic development: (1) the dawning of his aesthetic sensibility and (2) the development of "that 'sense of Europe' to which I feel that my very earliest consciousness waked."[15] In the growth of these elements of his mind and imagination, Italy had a surprisingly central role to play. As young children, of course, the James siblings could not distinguish precisely the individual nations of Europe. In fact, the distinctive national features of the European states tended, in the James family, to be rather blurred. One went to "Europe," not always specifically to Italy or France or Switzerland. This may have been the consequence of how Henry Senior spoke of these countries. For it was his belief that people in Europe were "all destined to be recast and remoulded into the form of a new and *de-nationalized humanity*, a universal form which, being animated by God's own infinite spirit, the spirit of human fellowship, will quickly shed all the soils it has contracted in the past."[16] (Henry Junior, it is fair to say, tried to become this denationalized European—embracing Italy, Switzerland, France, and England with grandiloquent encomiums for each.)

But Henry Junior's autobiography makes plain that, even before the family got there, the idea of Italy played a central role in their developing imaginations. Recounting the story of their growing up in Washington Square in the 1840s and 1850s, the elderly novelist Henry dredged the deep pool of memory for the most significant of his childhood experiences. Although there were perhaps only ten or twelve thousand Italians in New York at that time, a remarkably large number of Italians figure in James's autobiographical recollection of how his aesthetic sense arose and of what Europe stood for in his imagination. Let us then consider, as a preliminary to the Jameses' actual experience of travel to the country, how they "had Italy" even before they left New York.

In the James household, there were of course many art books and paintings. Henry Junior mentions his childhood fascination with "the female figures in those volumes of [S. G.] Gavarni then actual, then contemporaneous, which were kept in a piece of furniture that stood between the front-parlour windows in Fourteenth Street."[17] Henry Junior also recollected a "view of Tuscany" by the French painter Lefèvre, on the parlor wall in their Fourteenth Street house, which occasioned debates in the household as to whether the scene was really Tuscany. That painting gave young Henry "my very first chance, on such ground, for active participation" in art criticism: " 'Why of course,' I can hear myself [as a child] now blushingly but triumphantly intermingle [in the conversation]—'the softness and the haze of our Florence there: isn't Florence in Tuscany?' "[18] Such is the mystery of experience that James recollects this minor episode as having played a major role in his development as a critic of the arts.

Henry Junior also mentions "the ample canvas of Mr. [Thomas] Cole . . . which covered half a side of our front parlour. . . . It depicted Florence from one of the neighbouring hills—I have often since wondered which, the picture being long ago lost to our sight: Florence with her domes and towers and old walls, the old walls Mr. Cole had engaged for, but which I was ruefully to miss on coming to know and love the place in after years." James speculated in later life that the setting of the painting with "the contemplative monk seated on a terrace in the foreground, a constant friend of my childhood, must have been the convent of San Miniato, which gives me the site from which the painter wrought." Then he goes on to say that "We had Italy again"—a phrase that I emphasize for obvious reasons—"in the corresponding room behind—a great abundance of Italy I was free to think while I revolved between another large landscape over the sofa and the classic marble bust on a pedestal between the two back windows, the figure, a part of the figure, of a lady with her head crowned with vine-leaves." This bust, James recollected, "was known and admired among us as the Bacchante; she had come to us straight from an American studio in

Rome, and I see my horizon flush again with the first faint dawn of conscious appreciation, or in other words of the critical spirit."[19] As these recollections make plain, young James—and to a lesser extent the other children—was sensitized to the aesthetic character of Italy long before his family made its first trip there.

Then too there were Italian paintings in New York. The children were taken to art exhibitions at the Stuyvesant Institute and Bryant's Gallery of Christian Art, reached by an "omnibus after dinner," where, among other paintings, they saw the newly discovered and shockingly different Italian primitives then generally regarded as without merit. The experience, given what they had already seen of art, "cast a chill, this collection of worm-eaten diptychs and triptychs, of angular saints and seraphs, of black Madonnas and obscure Bambinos, of such marked and approved 'primitives' as had never yet been shipped to our shores."[20]

Italy also came to the James family in New York in the form of letters to the parents from Mary Temple and Edmund Tweedy, "an absent pair in whom our parents were closely interested and whose communications, whose Roman, Sorrentine, Florentine letters, letters in especial from the Baths of Lucca, kept on, in our air, more than any other sweet irritation, that 'question of Europe' which was to have after all, in the immediate years, so limited, so shortened a solution."[21]

But one must not neglect to mention perhaps the most delectable foretaste of Italy available to the James family on Fourteenth Street: those performances which the young James children, prowling the precincts of lower Fifth Avenue and Washington Square, saw announced on posters, attended, or heard their parents describe. It is not always possible to know whether the performers whom James mentions were in fact Italians and he concedes that some of the performances were probably amateurish by any distinguished standard, but they were enchanting to the children and conjured up a vision of Italy that stimulated their wanderlust. If the New York operagoer Walter Whitman was to effect his self-transformation in part through surrendering to "Italia's peerless compositions," if he was to celebrate "Composers! mighty maestros! / And you, sweet singers of old lands, / Soprani, tenori, bassi!" ("Proud Music of the

Storm"), young Henry James likewise expanded with enthusiasm at the memory of the old Park Theater,

to which it was just within my knowledge that my elders went for opera, to come back on us sounding those rich old Italian names, Bosio and Badiali, Ronconi and Steffanone, I am not sure I have them quite right; signs, of a rueful sound to us, that the line as to our infant participation *was* somewhere drawn. It had not been drawn, I all the more like to remember, when, under proper protection, at Castle Garden, I listened to that rarest of infant phenomena, Adelina Patti, poised in an armchair that had been pushed to the footlights and announcing her incomparable gift. She was about of our own age, she was one of us, even though at the same time the most prodigious of fairies, of glittering fables.[22]

Salvatore Patti, her father, was of course the co-director of the Astor Place Opera House at Cooper Union.

James also remembered with affection *A Midsummer Night's Dream* at the Broadway Theatre, with Madame Ponisi as Oberon, "Madame Ponisi whose range must have been wide, since I see her also as the white-veiled heroine of The Cataract of the Ganges, where, preferring death to dishonour, she dashes up the more or less perpendicular waterfall on a fiery black steed and with an effect only a little blighted by the chance flutter of a drapery out of which peeps the leg of a trouser and a big male foot." He also recollected her, "though presumably at a somewhat later time, or in strictness *after* childhood's fond hour, as this and that noble matron or tragedy queen. I descry her at any rate as representing all characters alike with a broad brown face framed in bands or crowns or other heavy headgear out of which cropped a row of very small tight black curls. The Cataract of the Ganges is all there as well, a tragedy of temples and idols and wicked rajahs and real water."[23]

At Niblo's Garden, Wallack's Theatre, and the Metropolitan Hall, the James children saw many different musical and variety entertainments, both high and low, featuring many Italian performers— still vividly memorable to Henry in old age. Of these we may mention "the wonderful exhibition of Signor Blitz, the peerless conjurer"; "the high and hard virtuosity of [the actress] Madame Ristori"; "Franconi's, which we more or less haunted and which, aiming at the grander style and the monumental effect, blazed with fresh paint and rang with Roman chariot-races up there among the deserts of Twenty-ninth Street"; and the "wondrous Martinetti Jocko" of melodrama fame. Then there was

Signor Léon Javelli, in whom the French and the Italian charm appear to have met, who was he, and what did he brilliantly do, and why of a sudden do I thus recall and admire him? I am afraid he but danced the tight-rope, the most domestic of our friends' resources, as it brought them out, by the far stretch of the rope, into the bosom of the house and against our very hearts, where they leapt and bounded and wavered and recovered closely face to face with us.

In his wonderment as to why he should remember the "brave Signor Léon," who bounded "to the greatest height of all," James was led to the conclusion that it must have been Javelli who first prepared him for the "revelation of the ballet."[24]

James's memory of Javelli and the ballet also spurred his recollection of the dancing academy of Mr. Edward Ferrero, which the children attended in New York—"where the orgy of the senses and even the riot of the mind, of which I have just spoken, must quite literally have led me more of a dance than anywhere. Let this sketch of a lost order note withal that under so scant a general provision for infant exercise, as distinguished from infant ease, our hopping and sliding in tune had to be deemed urgent. . . ." James remembered Edward Ferrero as particularly "good-looking, romantic and moustachio'd," a "charming man of the world":

Remarkably good-looking, as I say, by the measure of that period, and extraordinarily agile—he could so gracefully leap and bound that his bounding into the military saddle, such occasion offering [during the Civil War], had all the felicity, and only wanted the pink fleshings, of the circus —he was still more admired by the mothers, with whom he had to my eyes a most elegant relation, than by the pupils; among all of whom, at the frequent and delightful soirées, he caused trays laden with lucent syrups repeatedly to circulate.

The "free lemonade, and the freedom of remark, equally great, with the mothers, were the lavish note in him."[25]

Ferrero's brother-in-law, M. Dubreuil, was an extra at the Academy of Music operas, and James remarked how the children's

air thrilled, in the sense that our attentive parents re-echoed, with the visit of the great [Giulia] Grisi and the great Mario, and I seemed, though the art of advertisement was then comparatively so young and so chaste, to see our personal acquaintance, as [Dubreuil] could almost be called, thickly sandwiched between them. Such was one's strange sense for the connections of things that they drew out the halls of Ferrero till these too seemed fairly to resound with Norma and Lucrezia Borgia, as if opening straight upon the stage, and Europe, by the stroke, had come to us in such force that we had but to enjoy it on the spot.[26]

These allusions to Italian paintings, performances, and personalities, here culled from James's autobiography, may seem insignificant. James recognized the risk in adducing these ephemera. "One's record becomes, under memories of this order," he remarked, ". . . a tale of assimilations small and fine; out of which refuse, directly interesting to the subject-victim only, the most branching vegetations may be conceived as having sprung. Such are the absurdities of the poor dear inward life—when translated, that is, and perhaps ineffectually translated, into terms of the outward and trying at all to flourish on the lines of the outward; a reflection that might stay me here weren't it that I somehow feel morally affiliated, tied as by knotted fibres, to the elements involved."[27] The strength of these memories, knotted like fibres, morally and aesthetically affiliated the boy to Italy, predisposed him for the passionate pilgrimage to come, and prepared him for the glories he would find once he crossed the Alps and headed south. Let us turn now to the family's actual experience of Italy.

The turning point in the education of the children, the event that was to open up the *real* Europe to them, occurred in 1849, when a new keyword entered Father's vocabulary: a "sensuous" education. Writing to Emerson that summer, Henry Senior remarked:

My wife and I are obliged—so numerous has waxed our family—to enlarge our house in town, and get a country house for the summer. These things look expensive and temporary to us, besides being an additional care; and so, looking upon our four stout boys, who have no playroom within doors, and import shocking bad manners from the street, with much pity, we gravely ponder whether it would not be better to go abroad for a few years with them, allowing them to absorb French and German and get a better sensuous education than they are likely to get here.[28]

American schools and American tutors might educate the mind, develop the intellect, and inculcate the abstract. But a sensuous education meant immersion in the life of seeing and hearing, walking and looking, tasting and touching, and absorbing that which was most absent in America: the European historical tradition in music and art, literature and languages, the sublime and the picturesque in landscape—all that layered palimpsest of the past, all that could enrich the sensibilities and cultivate the soul beyond the merely cognitive, all, in short, that was not available in America.

The journey, however, was postponed until 1855, when the children were old enough to profit more fully from the plan. On their first trip to Europe in that year, William was thirteen and Henry was twelve, Wilkie was ten, Bob nine, and Alice seven. They went first to Switzerland, but Father decided within a month that the schools touted by their Anglo-American friends were much overrated and so he decided to have all the children privately tutored. Yet before the end of the year, the family had moved on to England, where they stayed until the spring of 1856. From there they went to Paris, where the children were taught French, music, and literature. Henry later recollected this peripatetic period—with brevities of schooling at the Pension Roediger, at Châtelaine near Geneva, at the Institut Maquelin, and the Institute Rochette—as "an incorrigible vagueness of current in our educational drift."[29]

In 1857 they drifted back to America. Where should they live, where could the children best be educated—New York, Albany, Boston? Before the question could fairly be answered, Father was dissatisfied again. In 1858, William wrote to a friend: "Father has come to the conclusion that America is not the place to bring up such 'ingenuous youth' as myself and my brothers."[30] Whereupon, the following year, Father packed them all up and returned them to Geneva, where they were enrolled in the schools that he had formerly thought overrated. Within a year, however, they were back in America. Father's explanation was that the boys needed "friends of their own sex, and sweethearts in the other," but Henry Junior recollected a different reason. William wanted to study painting, and the decision was made to try William Morris Hunt's studio in Newport: "We went home to learn how to paint."[31] Indeed, although William had the greatest sketching talent, Henry and Bob also threw themselves into painting, and Henry remembered thinking that even he "might get to copy casts rather well, and might in particular see myself congratulated on my sympathetic rendering of the sublime uplifted face of Michael Angelo's [sic] 'Captive' in the Louvre."[32]

That excursion of 1859 was their last trip, as a whole family, to Europe, and indeed, after this point, the family more or less split up and went, to a certain extent, their different ways. But the paradox is that, having toured England, having lived in Paris and other French cities, and having schooled the children in Switzerland, Henry Senior—in search of a sensuous education for them—never took his family all the way down into Italy, an omission of fateful consequence, I believe, for all of them, especially for Henry Junior.

Let me turn now to the youngest boys, Wilkie and Bob. As teenage youth, schooled abroad, they thought their language skills might fit them for business. (Wilkie spoke of entering "a Boston Tailor Store with the signs *"Ici on parle français,"* and *"Hier spricht man Deutsch."*[33] But on the family's return to America in 1860 they were enrolled in the Sanborn School in Concord, Massachusetts, where they absorbed the fiery abolitionism of Frank Sanborn, one of the "Secret Six" who conspired with John Brown to smuggle escaped slaves into Canada. And when the Civil War broke out, both boys volunteered for the Union Army, where they were commissioned as officers in black regiments. Both served with great distinction, were wounded or suffered disabilities, and were mustered out as heroes of the Republic. Given their business ambition, it is not surprising that neither boy had any intellectual interests. Henry said of the young Wilkie that "the act of reading was inhuman and repugnant to him." And William, whose sketching and painting were coming on apace, drew a caricature of Wilkie sleeping and entitled it "Garth Wilkinson James hard at work reading."[34]

Unlike the other siblings, Wilkie and Bob went through the fires of war, and, having seen something of the new country, wanted a life of active commercial affairs. Consequently, they proposed that their father set them up as managers of a plantation in Florida that would employ the new black freedmen. Although they worked very hard at this agricultural venture, it failed within a few years. Both then wound up in Milwaukee, Wisconsin, where they worked for the railroad. But neither was particularly successful at that. Both married and had children, but Wilkie died prematurely in 1883, aged thirty-eight, of Bright's disease. And Bob, never able to compete with his older—and by now famous—brothers, became dependent on alcohol, obsessed by a religious mania, and periodically unstable. Eventually separating from his wife, Bob spent periods of time in the Arlington Asylum, near Cambridge, where he dabbled in painting and writing. Permanently confused by his father over the question of what kind of life he should lead, Bob was later to say to Alice that "I wish our own father had steered his sons into the Soap or Baking Powder line."[35] He told her in 1898 that if his biography were ever written, "It would have to be the biography of broken fortunes."[36] Robertson James died on 3 July 1910 at the age of sixty-three.

One goes thus into Wilkie's early death and Bob's poignant life because, in after years, when Henry James undertook to write his autobiography, he made much of their early promise and broken fortunes, linking their unhappiness to a less than fulfilled experience of Europe. In the autobiography, Henry made a great deal of the impact on Bob of that short visit Bob was lucky enough to make to Italy, in 1859, in the company of his Swiss schoolmaster and his pupils. (The other James children were not enrolled in this school and thus did not make the trip.) Henry vividly remembered this "most desirable, delicious excursion," for he followed it (through Bob's letter) "in envious fancy, as it included a descent to the Italian Lakes and a push on as far as Genoa." Under "the weight of the vision of Italy," Bob's letter, reporting on the journey, provoked Henry's

shade of wonder at this odd chance that made the least developed of us the subject of what seemed to me even then a privilege of the highest intensity; and there again keeps it company my sense, through all the after years, that this early glimpse of blest old Italy, almost too early though it appears to have but just missed being, might have done something towards preparing or enriching Bob the one little plot of consciousness in which his deeply troubled life was to find rest.

That area so enriching to Bob was of course painting, which he tried to cultivate as William and Henry were doing. Reflecting on Bob's talent as a painter, Henry connected its origin with the visit—the first of any of the James children—to Italy:

I have known no other such capacity for absorbing or storing up the minutest truths and shades of landscape fact and giving them out afterward, in separation from the scene, with full assurance and felicity. He could do this still better even than he cared to do; I for my part cared much more that he should than he ever did himself, and then it was, I dare say, that I made the reflection: "He took in the picture of Italy, with his firm hard gift, having the chance while William and I were still, comparatively, small untouched and gaping barbarians; and it should always be in him to do at some odd fine moment a certain honour to that." I held to it that that sensibility had played in him more than by any outward measure at the time. . . . At all events I was absolutely never to cease to remember for Bob, through everything—and there was much and of the most agitated and agitating—that he had been dipped as a boy into the sacred stream; to some effect which, thanks to two or three of his most saving and often so amusing sensibilities, the turbid sea of his life might never quite wash away.[37]

Italy, then, was the sacred stream into which Bob had earliest and first, so fortunately and with lifelong consequences, been dipped. And it was therefore quite natural, after the Civil War, when Henry Junior made his first trip to Europe alone, that he should have headed straight for Italy—the country his father had so surprisingly omitted from their sensuous education. And it is no wonder, considering the way in which Henry had "had Italy" before he ever left New York, that, under the first impact of discovery that Professor Edel has cited from the letters (see above, p. 14), he should have gone reeling and moaning through the streets of Rome in a fever of aesthetic rapture. A passionate pilgrimage indeed!

Henry's father, however, took his namesake's Italian rhapsody more soberly, for Henry Senior could not dissociate from the Italian scene the suffocating weight of the past represented by the Italian monuments of antiquity. Writing to his son from America, Henry Senior remarked:

It is very good to get your first impressions of Rome, and I can sympathize with you very fully. I feel that I myself should be horribly affected there by the historical picturesque. I should be extremely sensitive to it objectively, and would therefore all the more revolt from it subjectively, as hearing underneath it all the pent-up moaning and groaning soul of the race, struggling to be free or to come to consciousness. I am glad on the whole that my lot is cast in a land where life doesn't wait on death, and where consequently no natural but only an artificial picturesque is possible. The historical consciousness rules to such a distorted excess in Europe that I have always been restless there, and ended by pining for the land of the future exclusively. Condemned to *remain* there I should stifle in a jiffy.[38]

The father's response initiates what F. O. Matthiessen has called one of "the most engaging manifestations of the family mind in action"—the recurrent theme, debated in the family circle, of "the differences between America and Europe":

They responded to it almost as though they had assumed roles in a debate. Father almost invariably gave voice to the promise of American life. HJ, after he had settled abroad, became the family Anglophile; whereas Alice was no less passionately pro-American than she was pro-Irish. WJ was enthusiastic about Europe when he was in America, and eager for America when he was in Europe. He in particular, in the excitement of the debate, was perfectly capable of shifting his position and coming up with unexpected arguments for the other side.[39]

Some final judgment about Europe, and thus about Italy, was of momentous importance to Henry Junior, for the sensuous education he had received seemed a perfect preparation for the vocation of the novelist. Vacillating throughout the sixties and seventies over the question of whether America or Europe offered a more stimulating field for the novelist, Henry at last came down on the side of Europe. As he recorded in his notebooks:

I have made my choice, and God knows that I have now no time to waste. My choice is the old world—my choice, my need, my life. . . . One can't do both—one must choose. No European writer is called upon to assume that terrible burden, and it seems hard that I should be. The burden is necessarily greater for an American for he *must* deal, more or less, even if only by implication, with Europe; whereas no European is obliged to deal in the least with America. No one dreams of calling him less complete for not doing so.[40]

But before discussing the evidence in the fiction that justified that choice, it is first necessary to discuss Alice James in Italy.

Alice James was not unlike her father and brothers in being highstrung and temperamental, but this trait reached a pathological extreme in 1867 or 1868, when she suffered her own version of the Jamesian "vastation," broke down completely, and suffered "violent turns of hysteria."[41] Throughout a lifetime of this illness, she remarked, "pain was the essence of the Universe to my consciousness."[42] Periods of remission did not prevent serious periodic recurrence of an incurable neurasthenia, which kept her for many years bedridden and under the care of many different doctors who tried all known remedies—ice and electric therapy, hydrotherapy, massage, institutionalization in the Adams Nervous Asylum near Boston—for her mysterious psychological affliction. None of them worked. Consequently, this most precocious and youngest of the James children was, in her sickroom, virtually limited to what she called "my centimeter of observation," every member of the family lamenting what she called "the poverty of my outside experience."[43] Matrimony, which was the intended complex fate of all women in her class, was thus not available to her. In any case, just to be, she was taught by the father, was enough.

Whether Alice was reduced to the condition of an hysteric for psychological reasons having to do with being the only girl in a family dominated by the male Jameses, as some feminists have suggested, we shall perhaps never know. Leon Edel has remarked that "at least some part of her condition was the common one of Victorian restrictions on women. Elizabeth Barrett offers a record of an analogous kind of bedridden life and of her escape from it." However, it is Edel's conclusion that is most pertinent here: "no Robert Browning came to carry off Alice to some Italy of her own."[44]

However, since "a trip to Europe" does seem to have been "the family panacea for all ills,"[45] Alice was induced to travel abroad in 1872 with her aunt Kate, her brother Henry serving as a guide. Dipped in the sacred stream for the first time, Alice visited Lake Como, Milan, Turin, Venice, Torcello, and Verona. Although the summer heat and mosquitoes were oppressive, the trip seems to have been moderately therapeutic. Of their stay in Venice Henry remarked, "We left nothing unseen that we wished to see, lived in our gondola, and found abundant coolness on the water and in the darksome churches." Alice, as Henry told their parents, "has gained a multitude of impressions which she will forever value,"[46] and he singled out their visit to Torcello and their "little boat-journey on the Lake of Como" as particularly exquisite. Of the excursion to Torcello, he wrote: "We had two mighty gondoliers, and we clove the wandering breezes of the lagoon, like a cargo of deities descending from Olympus. Such a bath of light and air—color and general luxury, physical and intellectual!" Less intellectual than physical was their lunch at the Lido, "where we dined most breezily on a platform where bathers and diners were strewn in true Italian promiscuity"; they also spent "much time in St. Mark's, and had ample leisure to see all the desirable pictures. The weather was perfect, we ate innumerable figs, ices every night at Florian's and bought a few very beautiful photographs . . . so that our four days [in Venice] were a great success and seemed more like a fortnight."[47]

The poignant Alice, who suffered so much and had so little of the rich travel experience of her brothers, died of cancer in 1892 and was buried in the Cambridge Cemetery near her parents. In old age, when Henry finally visited her grave in 1905, he was profoundly moved to "the recognition, stillness, the strangeness, the pity and the sanctity and the terror, the breath-catching passion and the divine relief of tears." There, at Alice's grave, he found her final connection with Italy: it was an "exquisite little Florentine urn of Alice's ashes" placed there by his brother; he called it "William's divine gift to us, and to *her*." Upon that urn he read "William's inspired transcript"—the Dantean lines from the *Paradiso* (10: 128–29): "ed essa da martiro e da essilio venne a questa pace" (and herself from martyrdom and exile came unto this peace). William's Dantean selection, Henry wrote in his notebook,

took me so at the throat by its penetrating *rightness*, that it was as if one sank down on one's knees in a kind of anguish of gratitude before something for which one had waited with a long, deep *ache*. But why do I write of the all unutterable and the all abysmal? Why does my pen not drop from my hand on approaching the infinite pity and tragedy of all the past? It does, poor helpless pen, with what it meets of the ineffable, what it meets of the cold Medusa-face of life, of all the life *lived*, on every side. *Basta, basta*.[48]

William's choice was indeed inspired, inspired by several journeys, as an adult, to Italy. But William's response to the country, its people and its past, was much more ambivalent than that of his younger brother; he reacted much more like their father, who as he grew older, "grew ever stauncher in his preference for America as the land of the future."[49] After the family trips to Europe in the late

1850s, their father had turned away from Europe and emphasized America as the country of the future, the proper focus of their attention. "America," Father had said in his eccentric way, "is the lost Paradise restored to boys and girls."[50]

Increasingly, as he experienced Europe, William, like his father, claimed America as the wave of the future. Italy was too much covered with grime, sunk in decay, and preoccupied with its own past; its ruins lay too heavily on the modern Italian spirit, preventing the actualization of the energy, talents, and accomplishments of living men and women. William's temperament inclined to moral earnestness; he detested anything suggestive of moral decadence or physical decay. But at the same time, the philosopher and psychologist who had wanted to be a painter kept being struck with Italian incarnations of the sublime, the beautiful, and the picturesque. Simultaneously appalled by the decay and seduced by the enchantments of Italy, his letters record the wonderful ambivalence of his reactions. On a visit to Florence in 1873, intended to lift his melancholy spirit, he remarked that "For ten days after my arrival I was so disgusted with the swarming and reeking blackness of the streets and the age of everything, that enjoyment all took place under protest, as it were." A little later, in Rome, he deplored its "gaudy decay, its embalmed history, its traditional paganism,"[51] and expressed sympathy with Emerson's daughter Ellen, who feared she might come to think Rome a greater place than Concord, Massachusetts. To Alice he wrote: "The barbarian mind stretches little by little to take in Rome, but I doubt if I shall ever call it the 'city of my soul' or 'my country.' " The "hoary eld" of Rome, he remarked, "has done more to reconcile me to what belongs to the present hour, business factories, etc., etc., than anything I ever experienced."[52]

Gradually, however, he relearned to see and discovered the treasures hidden beneath the ubiquitous grime. He remarked that "It is easier in Italy than elsewhere because of the cheerfulness and contented manners of the common people. They don't take life anything like as hard as we do, and suffer privation without being made desperate by it as we are."[53] "Every day I sally out into the sunshine and plod my way o'er steps of broken thrones and temples until one o'clock," he told Alice, when I repair to a certain café in the Corso, begin to eat and read "Galignani" and the "Débats," until Harry [Henry Junior] comes in with the flush of successful literary effort fading off his cheek. (It may interest the sympathetic soul of Mother to know that my diet until that hour consists of a roll, which a waiter in wedding costume brings up to my room when I rise, and three sous' worth of big roasted chestnuts, which I buy, on going out, from an old crone a few doors from the hotel. In this respect I am economical. Likewise in my total abstinence from spirituous liquors, to which Harry, I regret to say, has become an utter slave, spending a large part of his earnings in Bass's Ale and wine, and trembling with anger if there is any delay in their being brought to him.) After feeding the Angel in his old and rather shabby striped overcoat, and I in my usual neat attire, proceed to walk together to the big Pincian terrace which overhangs the city, and where on certain days everyone resorts, or to different churches and spots of note.[54]

As the magic of Italy worked upon William's depression, Henry Junior reported back to their father that "Willy, who at first hung fire over Rome, has now quite ignited, and confesses to its sovereign influence. But he enjoys all the melancholy of antiquity under a constant protest, which pleases me as a symptom of growing optimism and elasticity in his own disposition."[55] Even so, the grumbling reappeared in a letter to Alice, where William remarked that

Italy is a very *delightful* place to dip into but no more. I can't imagine how, unless one is earnestly studying history in some way, it can't in the long run help injuring all one's active powers. The weight of the past world here is fatal,—one ends by becoming its mere parasite instead of its equivalent. This worship, this dependence on other men is abnormal. The ancients did things by doing the business of their own day, not by gaping at their grandfathers' tombs,—and the normal man of today will do likewise. Better fifty years of Cambridge, than a cycle of Cathay! Adieu. Your brutal and philistine brother.[56]

Even so, the philistine brother returned to Italy in 1882. To his father he wrote that, after twenty-three days in Venice, "I hate to leave the indescribable Italian charm, and to go back to the harsh North again. *The laissez aller* of everything in Italy is the most comfortable of all possible mediums to be plunged in,—just the antipodes of England." Particularly he hated to leave "the glorious pictures, which one has to see in such an infernally unsatisfactory way. They ought to be erected into a circulating library to which one might subscribe and have a masterpiece a month in his own house throughout the year. If anything can make one a fatalist it's the sight of the inevitable decay of each fine art after it reaches its maturity." The decline of Venice and its hordes of tourists greatly bothered him, and he observed that he could "imagine some old patrician starting into indignant life again, merely to drive us away with his maledictions. I'm sure we should all flee conscience-stricken at the sight of him; for the energy of old Venice, as I've been reading it, must have been something prodigious and incessant."[57]

A decade later, he was to take a sabbatical leave from Harvard and spend much of the year in Florence, visiting Padua and Venice. Representing Harvard at the Galileo Tercentenary at Padua, he received an honorary degree. Of Padua he wrote to his wife on 2 November that he had rarely in his life passed a day of "greater contentment":

I surrender to Italy, and I should think that a painter would almost go out of his skin to wander about from town to town. One wants to paint everything that one sees in a place like this—as a *town* Florence can't hold a candle to it. She has her galleries, her palaces and her bridges, but the rest is incumbrance, here it is the entire town that speaks to one in the most charming unpretending way. . . . I understand Giotto's eminence now. It started the tears in my eyes to see the way the little old fellow had gone to work with such joyousness and spirit . . . and it is an honor to human nature that so many people feel under his quaintness that he is a *moral* painter.

In Venice he toured the Academy and the Ducal Palace, exclaiming over Giovanni Bellini and other painters who "*possess* one's eyes." And he concluded: "I really enjoy this furiously."[58]

Furious enjoyment of Italy came to William again in 1905, when he returned to Italy for travel and recreation and attended a philosophical congress in Rome, where he was enthusiastically received by a group of Italian pragmatists who had been deeply influenced by his philosophical studies. But of this engaging instance of the intellectual interrelationship between a member of the James family and Italy, Gerald E. Myers and Claudio Gorlier have given a full account later in this book.

William James, as Ralph Barton Perry has said, "liked simplicity, purity, and wholesomeness, in life as well as in nature. That at the same time he was tolerant of difference, addicted to morbid psychology, and catholic in his love of art and literature is not to be denied, but rather recognized as proving how deeply rooted was the plant which could resist these opposing influences."[59] His ambivalence about Italian antiquity led him to idealize Switzerland as a contrasting focal point for Italy. On 25 April 1893, he remarked "I am glad to have said goodbye to the sweet rottenness of Italy, of which I shall always preserve the tenderest memories, but in which I shall always feel a foreigner. The ugly Swiss faces, costume and speech seem to me delicious, primeval, pure, and full of human soundness and moral good. And the air! there can be nothing like it in the world."[60] Again he writes: "Florence seems to me even more attractive than it was when I was here eighteen years ago. . . . But how sovereignly *good* is Switzerland! It meets all the major needs of body and soul as no other country does, in summer time. After the aesthetics, the morbidness, the corruptions of Italy, how I shall want again in *ihrem Thau gesund mich zu baden!*"[61]

We come back, then, finally, to Henry Junior, who had the deepest experience of Italy and who made the most extensive use, amongst the family members, of his travels and observations. The world has "nothing better to offer a man of sensibility"—a character remarks in the tale "Benvolio" (1875)—"than a first visit to Italy during those years of life when perception is at its keenest, when discretion has arrived, and yet youth has not departed."[62] James had such a first visit in 1869—as well as thirteen more visits over the following three decades. During his early visits he tended to see the country through the myths and images he had absorbed in Washington Square. Even though the country and its people manifestly changed during his long observation of it, he found it difficult to shake the fixed impressions he had acquired as a boy. Even as late as *Roderick Hudson* (1876), his character Rowland Mallet can say of the landscape around Lake Como:

It was all confoundingly picturesque; it was the Italy that we know from the steel-engravings in old keepsakes and annuals, from the vignettes on music-sheets and the drop-curtains at theatres; an Italy that we can never confess to ourselves—in spite of our own changes and of Italy's—we have ceased to believe.[63]

Since modern Italy came to be quite different from the sentimental image he had absorbed in youth, he tried resolutely to face the changes, and in "Italy Revisited" (1883) he was prepared to grant that "modern Italy is ugly, prosaic, provokingly out of relation to the diary and the album."[64] Even so, he kept hoping with every visit that Italy would remain unchanged in its aesthetic picturesqueness, that it would always be, for him, as it is for his protagonist in "Diary of a Man of Fifty" (1879), who remarks "everything is so perfectly the same that I seem to be living my youth over again; all the forgotten impressions of that enchanting time come back to me."[65]

While, at the beginning of his Italian experience, he sometimes felt an "absurd want of reciprocity between Italy itself and all my rhapsodies about it,"[66] and while at times the "cold and foreign mass" of an alien city like Venice made him feel "more and more my inexorable Yankeehood,"[67] he loved Italy for providing him aesthetic satisfactions, and freedom from the constraints of Boston and New York—in short, a Gypsy life of visual and social pleasures. But gradually he grew into the country and appropriated it to his fictive purposes. How could it be otherwise, given the fact of so many visits, which totaled approximately four years spent in Italy. It was this accumulating knowledge that led Mrs. Humphry Ward to say of James that

here in this Italian country, and in the Eternal City, the man whom I had so far mainly known as a Londoner was far more at home than I. . . . Roman history and antiquities, Italian Art, Renaissance sculpture, the personalities and events of the Risorgimento, all these solid *connaissances* and many more were to be recognized perpetually as rich elements in the general wealth of Mr. James's mind.[68]

Because of the wealth of James's knowledge of Italy, through reading, travel, and aesthetic "gaping," he thought long and hard about buying a *pied-à-terre* in Italy and living there much of the year. Although this plan came to nothing, he did imaginatively take possession of the country. He set some six of his twenty-two novels and at least eighteen of his 112 stories in Italy—as we will see below in the criticism of such masterworks as *Daisy Miller*, *The Portrait of a Lady*, and *The Aspern Papers*. And when it came time,

in *The Wings of the Dove* to identify the site where Milly Theale
should most intensely live, and die, where the "heiress of all the
ages" should experience the richest aesthetic satisfactions, the in-
tensest love, and her tragic betrayal and death, he chose the Venetian setting.

In the course of writing all of these stories and novels, as Carl
Maves has observed, James

moves steadily from uncontrolled and lavish romantic enthusiasm to a
more objective and ironic consideration of his subject, simultaneously providing us with the rubrics under which all his subsequent "Italian" fiction
may be grouped and understood: the voluptuous enchanting beauty of Italy
and its people, the power that the past there wields over the present, the
theatricalism of Italian life, the passivity and fatalism of the Italian character, its pragmatism, its talent for deception and its sexual vitality; and
also the danger of idealizing Italy, of confusing Sacred and Profane Love, of
attempting to emulate the Italians rather than merely observe them.[69]

"Dear blest old Italy" is the refrain that runs throughout James's
letters. Italy was for him a "terra santa," "a Paradise that makes
every other place seem a purgatory at best." He remarked to Grace
Norton in 1892, "Italy remains firm while other things come and go
—remains, on the whole, I mean, the sweetest impression of life."[70]
And he told Edith Wharton in 1907 that Italy was "the most beautiful country in the world—of a beauty (and an interest and complexity of beauty) so far beyond any other that none other is worth
talking about."[71]

If James longed to be a native of Italy, at Lamb House he even
affected an Italianate air. At least his amanuensis Theodora Bosan-
quet, who took his dictation in Rye, remarked in 1907 that with his
"grey eyes set in a face burned to a colourable sea-faring brown by
the Italian sun," James seemed neither English nor American, and
"only doubtfully Anglo-Saxon. He might perhaps have been some
species of disguised cardinal," she said, "or even a Roman nobleman
amusing himself by playing the part of a Sussex squire."[72] But the
pied-à-terre in Italy was a dream never to be fulfilled. Knowing in
old age that he would probably never return to that terra santa of
Italy, the elderly writer poignantly remarked to Edith Wharton: "I
have drunk and turned the glass upside down—or rather I have
placed it under my heel and smashed it—and the Gipsy life *with* it

—for ever."[73] In this respect, his brother William was perhaps right about Henry all along: "He's really . . . a native of the James family, and has no other country."[74]

Notes

1. Henry James, *The Wings of the Dove*, ed. J. Donald Crowley and Richard Hocks (New York: W. W. Norton, 1978), 79–80.
2. It may seem prejudicial to omit discussion of Mary Walsh James, the children's mother, and even Aunt Kate, who lived with them. But these estimable ladies play a negligible role in the children's response to Italy. All of the evidence tends to suggest that the mother was both passive and unintellectual, yet at the same time rather gubernatorial in managing the household of her impractical husband, who said of her that "She was not to me 'a liberal education,' intellectually speaking." Even so, as Henry Junior idealizingly remarked, hers "was a perfect mother's life—the life of a perfect wife. To bring her children into the world—to expend herself, for years, for their happiness and welfare—then, when they had reached full maturity and were absorbed in the world and in their own interests—to lay herself down in her ebbing strength and yield up her pure soul to the celestial power that had given her this divine commission." Quoted in F. O. Matthiessen, *The James Family* (New York: Alfred A. Knopf, 1947), 129.
3. Matthiessen, *James Family*, 7.
4. *Henry James: Autobiography*, ed. Frederick W. Dupee (Princeton: Princeton University Press, 1983), 278.
5. Matthiessen, *James Family*, 15.
6. Ibid., 5.
7. Ibid., 71.
8. Ibid., 14. Henry Senior's piquant style and its effect on his son the novelist are perhaps suggested by the father's comment on Carlyle: "He compassionates all his friends. . . . 'Poor John Sterling,' he used always to say, 'Poor little Browning' . . . as if the temple of his friendship were a hospital and all its inmates scrofulous or paralytic. . . . He enjoyed an inward power and beatitude so redundant as naturally to seek relief in these copious outward showers of compassionate benediction." Quoted in *Alice James: Her Brothers—Her Journal*, ed. Anna Robeson Burr (New York: Dodd, Mead, 1934), 9.
9. Matthiessen, *James Family*, 70.
10. Ibid., 69.
11. Ibid., 73.
12. Ibid., 71–72.
13. Jane Maher, *Biography of Broken Fortunes: Wilkie and Bob, Brothers of William, Henry, and Alice James* (Hamden, Conn.: Archon Books, 1986), 5.

14. Matthiessen, *James Family*, 84.
15. Henry James, *A Small Boy and Others* (New York: Scribners, 1913), 34.
16. Matthiessen, *James Family*, 287.
17. Henry James, *A Small Boy and Others*, 18.
18. Ibid., 271.
19. Ibid., 269–70.
20. Ibid., 268.
21. Ibid., 273.
22. Ibid., 114.
23. Ibid., 108.
24. Ibid., 115, 133, 169, 167–68.
25. Ibid., 237–38.
26. Ibid., 240–41.
27. Ibid., 182.
28. Matthiessen, 45.
29. Maher, *Biography of Broken Fortunes*, 5–6.
30. Ibid., 8.
31. Ibid., 7–8.
32. *Autobiography* (1983), 284.
33. Maher, *Biography of Broken Fortunes*, 22.
34. Ibid.
35. Ibid., 190–91.
36. Ibid., 195.
37. *Autobiography* (1983), 260–61.
38. Matthiessen, *James Family*, 289.
39. Ibid., 286.
40. *The Complete Notebooks of Henry James*, ed. Leon Edel and Lyall H. Powers (New York: Oxford University Press, 1987), 214.
41. *Alice James: Her Brothers—Her Journal*, 181.
42. Ibid., 130.
43. *The Diary of Alice James*, edited with an introduction by Leon Edel (New York: Dodd, Mead, 1964), 19–20.
44. Ibid., 8.
45. *Alice James: Her Brothers—Her Journal*, 51.
46. *Henry James Letters*, vol. 1, *1843–1875*, ed. Leon Edel (Cambridge: Harvard University Press, 1974), 296.
47. Ibid.
48. *The Complete Notebooks of Henry James*, 240. Agostino Lombardo has speculated below as to whether Henry James knew very much Italian. It is interesting to note that James slightly misquoted the Dantean inscription in his notebook, suggesting that he knew or could recollect the Italian passably well, if not perfectly.
49. Matthiessen, *James Family*, 11.
50. Gay Wilson Allen, *William James: A Biography* (New York: Viking Press, 1967), 32.

51. Ibid., 187.
52. Ibid.
53. Ibid., 186.
54. Ibid., 187–88.
55. Ralph Barton Perry, *The Thought and Character of William James* (New York: Harper, 1964), 138.
56. Matthiessen, *James Family*, 291.
57. Perry, *William James*, 151–52.
58. Ibid., 202–3.
59. Ibid., 217.
60. Ibid., 202–3.
61. Ibid., 217–18.
62. *The Complete Tales of Henry James*, ed. Leon Edel, 12 vols. (Philadelphia: Lippincott, 1961–64), 3: 391.
63. Henry James, *Roderick Hudson* (Boston: Osgood, 1876), 423–24.
64. Henry James, "Italy Revisited," *Portraits of Places* (Boston: Osgood, 1884), 44–45.
65. *Complete Tales*, 4: 389.
66. *The Letters of Henry James*, ed. Percy Lubbock (New York: Scribners, 1920), 1: 36–37.
67. *Letters*, 1: 137.
68. Mrs. Humphry Ward, *A Writer's Recollections*, 2 vols. (New York: Harper, 1918), 2: 195.
69. Carl Maves, *Sensuous Pessimism: Italy in the Work of Henry James* (Bloomington: Indiana University Press, 1973), 45.
70. *Henry James Letters*, vol. 3, *1883–1895*, ed. Leon Edel (Cambridge: Harvard University Press, 1980), 394.
71. *Henry James Letters*, vol. 4, *1895–1916*, ed. Leon Edel (Cambridge: Harvard University Press, 1984), 458.
72. Quoted in Matthiessen, *James Family*, xii.
73. *Letters*, 4: 458.
74. Quoted in Matthiessen, *James Family*, 69.

THREE *Italy in Henry James's International Theme*

SERGIO PEROSA

The ever hungry artist has only to *trust* old Italy for her to feed him at every single step from her hand.

The great private palaces that are the massive majestic syllables, sentences, periods, of the strange message the place addresses to us.

Italian Hours (1873)

*H*ENRY JAMES'S best-known motivation for his expatriation to Europe and for his choice of the international theme is in a notorious passage in his 1879 book on Hawthorne: "the flower of art blooms only where the soil is deep . . . it takes a great deal of history to produce a little literature . . . it needs a complex social machinery to set a writer in motion."[1] The absence of "all these things" in America had led Hawthorne into the airy regions of allegory and romance. But the post–Civil War American novelist, like his European confreres Balzac and Maupassant, Flaubert and Turgenev, had to face reality, to confront contemporary *moeurs*, to depict the customs of the age—*faire concurrence à l'état civil*, in Balzac's beautiful phrase. To write novels of manners, or indeed realistic novels, the American writer had therefore to go to Europe, where hierarchical, historical, and social aspects and signs were plentiful, and where, as James put it in a 1913 letter, "after a fashion part of the work of discrimination and selection and primary clearing of the ground is already done for one . . . whereas

48

over there in America I seemed to see myself . . . often beginning so 'low down' . . . that all one's time went to it and one was spent before arriving at any very charming altitude."[2]

One went to Europe, however, not to write about Europe as such, but to write about America *within the milieu and from the point of view of Europe.* This is made clear by a passage in James's *Autobiography:* "To be so disconnected for the time, and in the most insidious manner, was above all what I had come out for. . . . There were, it appeared, things of interest taking place in America, and I had had, in this absurd manner, to come to England to learn it."[3] Europe gave saliency by contrast to American features, characteristics, and idiosyncrasies. The "international theme"—the confrontation of American characters and *moeurs,* morals and manners (or lack of manners) with European characters and *moeurs,* manners and morals (or lack of morals)—was therefore not only a "burden" for the American writer ("for he *must* deal, more or less, even if only by implication, with Europe; whereas no European is obliged in the least to deal with America," as James had observed in the *Notebooks*),[4] but a necessary choice and a challenge.

Elsewhere, in a later Preface, with a surprising image, James was to write of the confrontation between America and Europe in terms of two ladies on a dusty stage, propping up each other's "infirmities."[5] Yet the choice of the international theme sustained most of James's fictional career and, as I have argued elsewhere,[6] allowed him to dramatize the complexities of human behavior on either side of the Atlantic, and as it were in between, through a functional and symbolic use of contrasting settings, characters and *moeurs.*

To put it briefly, for the sake of convenience and by way of introduction, the international theme had three main articulations in James.

First, the "passionate pilgrim" or, even better, the American artist, starved and deprived at home, going to Europe to find historical depth and artistic richness, passion and human warmth, to be inspired and elated—only to find that passion and warmth are there excessive, the colors too strong, the richness too rich, so that he is crushed by the very wealth of the inner and outer inspiration he has sought. (An easy formula could be: *if America does not create, Europe destroys.*)

Second, the businessman or the self-made man, the "new man," going to Europe to find leisure and the enjoyment of life, enlightenment and entertainment, a pleasurable use for his money, social refinement, possibly even a wife—and being of course defeated and betrayed by the complexities and the callousness of European society, the devious practices and the corruption, the lack of scruples and of morals, lurking under the luster of European manners. (Here the formula could be: *if Europe has manners, America has morals.*)

Third, the American girl, the flower of the New Continent, the so-called or self-proclaimed "heiress of all the ages," the free and open heroine of the expanding and unsubdued self, going to Europe to realize and express her freedom and her eagerness to live—only to find her innocence misunderstood, schemed upon, and betrayed, her aspirations "ground in the very mill of the conventional," her imperious self bruised, constrained, and imprisoned by "the hard carapace of circumstances." (The formula here: *if you act by conviction, you're crushed by conventions.*)

Readers of James will have immediately identified my obvious references—to *Roderick Hudson, The American, Daisy Miller,* and *The Portrait of a Lady* (in this order, and among others). In this complex game, the role of Europe is often ambivalent and paradoxical: she is glamorous and enticing, but treacherous and corrupting; rich in history and art, in social graces and social ease, but lacking in fundamental decencies and moral values, in honesty and human kindness, in seriousness of purpose. She pays with carelessness and corruption, moral insensitivity, physical as well as psychological violence, for her *savoir faire,* her historical depth, her artistic refinement. If you imagine a scissorlike movement,[7] Europe is up in manners but low in morals, whereas gauche and awkward America, so innocent of the world, is innocent in two ways—of social graces but also of corruption, of sophistication but also of deviousness: if she is down in manners, she is up in morals.

This is not, however, a clear-cut division: the good on one side, the bad on the other, good guy versus villain. The interest of James's contrast lies exactly in its problematic and ambivalent character, in what I have called its scissorlike movement: what you lose on one side, you gain on the other—the higher the level of morals, the lower the refinement of manners (in their all-encompassing sense, which includes art, history, tradition, a knowledge of the world) and vice versa.

In this complex articulation of the international theme, Italy plays a very specific, recognizable, functional, and symbolic role—especially involving the first and third narrative situations or strategies—and her ambivalent and paradoxical quality is beautifully exploited for the fictional purposes of contrast and definition. Italy is the land of beauty and of passion, of art and history, of longing and nostalgia, where the past is visible and visitable at almost every step, where it is indeed an inescapable presence; but Italy also proves again and again to be, in Conrad's terms, the destructive element; her beauty is terrible and devastating, her past a curse and a doom; her art and her social *moeurs* are unsettling, disturbing, often a trap for the unwary Americans.

In James's early stories on the international theme, Italy is very much the land of the picturesque, of artistic, historical, and sentimental exaltation. Some of these stories read like disguised Baedekers, barely fictionalized travelogues, and show the influence of both Ruskin and Hawthorne. Italy is predominantly and preeminently represented—mainly, however, as a background, a backcloth, a mere setting or a pretext for mildly inconsequential plots. She is the land where the passionate pilgrim can revel or be disquieted, but she is only incidentally connected with the development of narrative motifs.

In "Travelling Companions" (1870), for instance, most of Italy is "done"—from Milan to Venice, from Florence to Rome—with extensive descriptive passages that read like tourist guidebooks: the "enchanting romance of Italy," the beauty of her people as well as of her landscapes, overwhelm a group of American travelers who "must go in for the beautiful," are enthralled by the genius of the picturesque, are even tempted (as Hawthorne had already warned) by Catholicism. Love at first denied is, after the experience of Italy, accepted: but the story does seem a mere pretext for the description of cherished places.

In "At Isella" (1871), too, the romance of Italy is made to coincide with romantic love, and the figures of her stark and inspiring past, from Lucrezia Borgia and Bianca Cappello to the heroines of

Stendhal, are evoked. Nature is there "refined and transmuted to
Art"; one speaks of the "symptoms" of Italy as of a mild intoxication, and a lengthy passage spells out the magic and the lure of the
place, its "Platonic" idea,[8] for far too passionate pilgrims. It comes
as no surprise that the Italian heroine is freed from bondage by an
American hand which is ready to favor romance. In the opening
pages of Confidence (1880), which are set in Siena, we are made to
breathe in full "the charm of the Italian spring," to feel the spell of
the "high picturesque" (including a contadino with donkey), and
to see "what painters call a subject" in the view. Moving to Dresden
in chapter 2, after Siena and Venice, is a letdown for the novel
itself.[9]

Yet such idyllic and impassioned notes—which echo those lavishly provided by James in his travel essays—soon begin to betray
signs of undisguised tension. As the heroine of James's earliest novel,
Watch and Ward (1871), admits while traveling in Europe to as-
suage a sentimental crisis, "One grows more in this wonderful Rome
than in a year at home";[10] that growth and that knowledge are,
however, soon identified with a sense of danger, of dissipation, of
evil: "I had rather not meet you again in Italy. It perverts our dear
old American truth!" says a character in "Travelling Companions."
The experience of Italy, of its past as well as its present, is unsettling, to say the least, for the American devotee.

In "The Madonna of the Future" (1873), the speaking character
gives vent to a paradigmatic lament on Americans as the "disinherited of art," condemned to be superficial, excluded from the magic
circle, lacking the deeper sense; yet the American artist who has
gone to Florence—where the ghosts of the past are all over the
place—to paint a beautiful Madonna, finds himself in the evening
of time and sinks into oblivion. He is bogged down, as well as
sustained, by a bourgeois Egeria, must recognize that he has been
dawdling for twenty years and has become a failure. This is the
whimper of the failing artist in Italy, as against the bang we will
hear in Roderick Hudson.

And what happens if, dissatisfied with the present, one tries to
unearth and relive the past? In "The Last of the Valerii" (1874),
still very reminiscent of Hawthorne's The Marble Faun, the Ameri-

can heroine marries Count Valerio because "he's the natural man," "like a statue of the Decadence." But when a real statue of Juno is unearthed in the garden, what at first appeared as a Garden of Eden turns into a nightmare. The statue casts a spell, Rome betrays a chilling strain, and the past hovers over the present as a blight. The statue—and the past—must be buried again.[11] In a similar way, in another early tale, "Adina" (1874), the "blonde angel of New England origin" is made to go through a harrowing experience until the topaz belonging to the times of Tiberius, found in the Campagna, is buried again.[12]

These are rather conventional, even trifling stories, which only show James's appreciation of Italy as a setting. "Adina," in particular, reads very much like a disguised travel guide and an exercise in the picturesque. The germs of the dichotomy as to the double role, function, and nature of Italy in the international theme are, however, visibly there. They become more clearly apparent in the novels.

In *Roderick Hudson* (1875) we have a perfect rendering of place, and the paradigm of Rome's (and Italy's) destructive role. The young American artist is brought there in order to find the inspiration and the support he cannot have at home: he finds too much of it. Rome destroys him with its *excess* of beauty and of art, of activity and emotion (even "a passive life in Rome . . . takes on a very respectable likeness to activity", [4], and through its double nature: "if Roman life doesn't do something substantial to make you happier, it increases tenfold your liability to moral misery".[13] "Passion burns out, inspiration runs to seed" (6). If living in Rome "was an education to the senses and the imagination" (5), it nevertheless involves a deep sense of depression and mortality, a premonition of disaster and ruin, which are brought down on Roderick as much by Christina Light—"nominally an American. But it has taken twenty years of Europe to make her what she is!" (5)—as by the place itself.

Rome is "done" by James in this novel at length and at leisure, and often in a recognizably romantic way: Villa Ludovisi and the Colosseum, the Church of St. Cecilia, St. Peter's, of course, which (here and elsewhere) James insists on seeing as a great mundane

and vociferous social haunt. Yet another typical and revealing theme
is the long association of the Palace of the Caesars (28) with the
idea of vanity, decadence, dissipation, and death.[14]

An intoxication with Rome proves a subtle and destructive disease (it infects and unsettles even Roderick's fiancée Mary, from
Northampton, Mass.). It can suggest a Hawthornesque (or indeed a
Melvillian) idea of *felix culpa*, of a happy fall: "If I had not come
to Rome I shouldn't have risen, and if I had not risen I shouldn't
have fallen" (21).[15] But Roderick's agonized cry at the end sums up,
and gives out, the real nature of his experience and of its setting:
"take me at least out of this terrible Italy . . . where everything
mocks and reproaches and torments and eludes me! Take me out of
this land of terrible beauty, and put me in the midst of ugliness. Set
me down where nature is coarse and flat, and men and manners are
vulgar. There must be something awfully ugly in Germany. Pack
me off there!" (22). This is indeed a devastating conclusion for a
passionate pilgrim. Roderick is then brought to the placidity (not
the ugliness) of Lake Como, a kind of earthly paradise which is
presented as the epitome of the picturesque, where he could live
forever: but he is eventually lost in a precipice of the sublime Alps.[16]

Italy, then, the "dishevelled nymph," the "tousled *bonne fille*,"
rather then the *old coquine* or the *Hausfrau*, has wreaked a kind of
vengeance on the aspiring artist: too much is too much.[17] In *Daisy
Miller* the geographical path is reversed—we move from Switzerland down to Rome—but the result is pretty much the same. True,
"the child of nature and of freedom" is betrayed more by European-
ized Americans than by the Italians themselves; yet in Rome, so
lovely in the spring, one feels "the freshness of the year and the
ambiguity of the place reaffirm themselves in mysterious interfu-
sion" (4). The beauty is on the Pincio and in Villa Borghese, in airy
views of the city and its people that seem to remind us of Boldini's
paintings, on the Coelian Hill and the Arch of Constantine, even in
St. Peter's. The Colosseum, however, harbors its secret venom—the
malaria, the bad air, the Roman fever, the real as well as symbolic
poison of the place[18]—and in the final scene, which provides a
perfect example of *chiaroscuro* used for effect as much as for functional purposes, the unfortunate girl who has sought freedom and
affirmation in Europe, with innocence and naïveté, is also de-

stroyed by the ambivalent nature of Italy: "The historic atmosphere was there, certainly; but the historic atmosphere, scientifically considered, was no better than a villainous miasma" (4).[19]

In its expanded version, in *The Portrait of a Lady* (1881), Italy appears as a crucial setting after England (in chapter 21); it appears as the land of promise, comforted by endless knowledge, where the love of the beautiful prevails. Isabel pauses in San Remo on the edge of a larger adventure. We all know what beautiful Italy, and her Italianate American, Gilbert Osmond, have in store for her. The double nature of Italy and the type of experience she leads to is suggested mainly by and through her buildings. The Florentine villa, in 22, has a front which is a mask, not the face of the house; it has lids, but not eyes, its windows "seemed less to offer communication with the world than to defy the world to look in." It is again a prolepsis, or a premonition. One does acts of mental prostration to Italy (22); "Rome, as Ralph said, confessed to the psychological moment" (27); it is an exquisite medium for impressions (28). Isabel is struck by St. Peter's and pays "her silent tribute to the seated sublime." Yet she ends up in Palazzo Roccanera, "a kind of domestic fortress . . . which smelt of historical deeds, of crime and craft and violence," much in the tradition of the Gothic novel, where her aspiration to freedom and self-possession will be crushed by Gilbert's viciousness as much as by the spirit of the place.[20]

As we know, the land of beauty gives way to the place of oppression. Isabel's free and imperious self is crushed by the "hard carapace of circumstances" she has overlooked. Her "innocence" of the world and her wish to follow purely her inner convictions lead her to misery and ruin. Yet Italy becomes part of, or has a role in, that process of enslavement. Gilbert himself will warn her against the superstition of an excessive love for Rome (48),[21] and Isabel herself will eventually feel Rome's misery (40). Gardencourt, the English country house of the first chapters of the novel, stands as the opposite of her Italian edifice with its dark, cold dusk (54). Italy has turned into a land of oppression, a darkened world, in a physical as well as a psychological sense; and the Italian setting has much to do with Isabel's well-known sentiments during her vigil (42):

she had suddenly found the infinite vista of a multiplied life to be a dark, narrow alley with a dead wall at the end. Instead of leading to high places of happiness . . . it led rather downward and earthward, into realms of restriction and depression. . . . It was the house of darkness, the house of dumbness, the house of suffocation. . . . She seemed shut up with an odor of mould and decay.[22]

This sense of oppression and suffocation is what, tragically and paradoxically, the beauty and promise of Italy has left her with.

After *The Portrait of a Lady*, James took a deep breath and turned away from the international theme. Italy, however, appears in intriguing and crucial ways in some of his in-between studies. In *Washington Square* (1880), a purely American novel, in a lonely valley in the Italian Alps where the heroine has been sent—as usual—to get wise, Catherine Sloper confronts her father and tells him that she is not going to give up her dubious lover. She will be steady. In *The Princess Casamassima* (1886), a purely English novel, the crucial turning point of the young revolutionary, Hyacinth Robinson, is brought about by his experience of Paris and Venice in particular. In Venice, as he tells his mentor in his well-known "Letter from Venice" (30), he has had a "revelation of the exquisite," a vision of artistic beauty that totally unsettles his composure and leads him to renege on his pledge to destroy the existing order of society. Such a "splendid accumulation of the happier few," so "precious and beautiful," makes him feel "capable of fighting for them." "The monuments and the treasures of art, the great palaces and properties, the conquests of learning and taste," in spite of being based "upon the despotisms, the cruelties, the exclusions, the monopolies and the rapacities of the past," lead him to swerve from his vow. The beauties of Italy are a crucial experience for Hyacinth Robinson; nothing can or will be the same after such knowledge.

Venice is again overwhelmingly present in *The Aspern Papers* (1888), a tale that could be read, in fact, in the light of the international theme. Here, too, the city plays a fundamental, indeed, a double role, with new emphases and a possible twist. We have here the Venice of the tourist guide and the romantic imagination: St. Mark's as an "open-air salon," the ghostly church, the house within the garden in Rio Marin, an environment and atmosphere which form the perfect shrine for the custodians of the relics of the great American poet (even if the references, we read, "would have seemed

to carry one back to the rococo Venice of Casanova"). The Pi-
azzetta and Florian's are forcefully present as tourist places. Yet the
city acquires a strong symbolic connotation: the Grand Canal, on
the occasion of two gondola rides, the lagoon itself way out to the
Lido, become a perfect objective correlative of the windings of the
protagonist's mind, of his doubts and fears.[23] As he wanders about
in the city, we are told, he wonders: a strict connection is established in perfect Jamesian fashion between the physical and the
mental orders: "floating aimlessly about on the lagoon" is a way to
shed, or indeed to increase, bewilderment. Being lost in the labyrin-
thine city is, for the protagonist, the perfect way to be "lost in
wonder" (9). In the afternoon of that day of reckoning, moreover,
in which he has to make his choice, a prominent feature of the city,
the elevated statue of Colleoni, looking "far over his head," makes
him realize that his battles and stratagems are of a very different
kind; that he is no man of action, that he is imprisoned in the poor
logic of the intellectual and the amateur, that he is living his life
vicariously by preying on the ghosts of the past.

Venice, in *The Aspern Papers*, is a city of sociability, "without
streets and vehicles . . . the place has the character of an immense
collective apartment"; it is a theater of human life. Yet, in spite of
its Ruskinian touches, Venice—and by extension, Italy—acquires
here a direct bearing on the characters and their experience. It is
mildly unsettling, a crucial place for bringing their souls to a crisis.
"So right and left, in Italy—before the great historic complexity at
least—penetration fails. . . . But we exaggerate our gathered values
only if we are eminently witless," James was to write in the preface
to that tale. The "gathered values" of Italy (and of Venice in
particular, as Venice seems to become more and more one of James's
cherished settings)[24] will soon be in full force again.

In stories like "Georgina's Reasons" (1884) and "A Modern Warn-
ing" (1884), both loosely dealing with international themes, Italy
is purely incidental, a matter of simple local reference. In another
story, "The Solution" (1889), the pictorial Rome of the popes and
its Campagna, "before the Italians had arrived and the local color
departed," reappear in a purely romantic light: for impoverished
and unimaginative Americans, Rome is the capital where the least
money "would go furthest in the way of grandeur." Frascati is a

place for picnics and the Campagna is "like a haunted sea." The great church of St. Peter's reappears "as a public promenade, or rather a splendid international *salon*" which "protected conversation and even gossip."

Italy is here a perfect place for pleasant comedy, reverting back to Arcadian innocence, and evokes acts of pure chivalry: but it is mainly background. Two years later, in "The Pupil" (1891), Venice resurfaces as the topos for the young protagonist's crisis, which is cast in an almost sinister, autumnal light. Thus, romantic Italy becomes once more imbued with tragic potential.[25] The November rain lashing about in a livid lagoon is of course a central element— not merely a background—of the next, great "international" novel, where the Italian setting is featured in a prominent way: *The Wings of the Dove* (1902), James's swansong on the fictional use of Italy, and of Venice.

In *The Wings of the Dove*, the theme is the almost decadent one of "death in Venice," but the implications and the forces at work are tragic. Quite understandably, Milly Theale's premonition of her fate in Italy is Wagnerian: "It was the Wagner overture that practically prevailed, up through Italy, where Milly had already been" (3, 5). Her final tone is that of subdued surrender to silence and death.

The "potential heiress of all the ages," the American natural princess, "looking down on the kingdoms of the earth," "one of the finest, one of the rarest . . . cases of American intensity," hovering, rather than pouncing, on her destiny—"isolated, unmothered, unguarded, but with her other strong marks," rich and free as she is, with her big money that is a poor and treacherous compensation for her failing health, goes to Europe for its "remedial properties." And in Europe, desperately wanting to live as she is, she will naturally meet her death and transfiguration. First we have London, where the dangers are admittedly greater than in New York or Boston; Venice only witnesses the final steps of her extinction, but it is far more than an appropriate setting. It is the symphonic ambience and specular image of her fate. Milly is first "successfully deceived" in England and by English people, but the consummation of her deception, betrayal, and death finds in Venice the proper conditioning and the suitable echo.

Venice is "done" in the novel because of the city's relation to the heroine and because Milly is in full possession of the place (7,26): we have the Rialto and the Bridge of Sighs, with a central role assigned to St. Mark's as the "great social saloon," the "blue-roofed chamber af amenity" (8, 27).[26] But when the crisis comes, we all know, "It was a Venice of evil. . . . A Venice of cold, lashing rain from a low black sky, of wicked rain raging through narrow passes"; the "great drawing room, the great drawing room of Europe" is profaned by bad weather, and it is precisely there and in that climate, we remember, that Milly hears of her betrayal from Lord Mark—so that it comes as no surprise that "the vice in the air, otherwise, was too much like the breath of fate." I take it that this phrase is meant to emphasize the perfect coincidence of place and destiny, of locale and story: "The weather had changed, the rain was ugly, the wind wicked, the sea impossible, *because* of Lord Mark" (9, 30).

The rain *is* tears. The wind makes Milly face the wall, and when after three days "Venice glowed and plashed and called and dived again" (9, 32), the horrible feeling of an unprecedented, cold Venice in the rain is not dispelled. This death in Venice has a cutting edge, has nothing in common with Thomas Mann's. It is a bang, not a whimper, in spite of James's well-rehearsed silences and reticences. One might contend that Venice *after* the lashing rain ("the air was like a clap of hands, and the scattered pinks, yellows, blues, tea-greens, were like a hanging-out of vivid stuffs, a laying down of fine carpets," [9, 32]) prefigures Milly's eventual transfiguration into a dove hovering in the air with protective, outstretched wings: but this would be to forget that her wings are also threatening and doom Kate Croy and Merton Densher, the betrayers, to separation and defeat ("we shall never be again as we were!" as the last line reads). A streak of evil and destruction seems to pertain even here to the beauty of Italy—that beauty which is ominous and terrible. As such it is a double-edged gift of history, or of the gods. Doom is inherent in beauty, the wealth of art and money is chilled by a gust of rain.[27]

One might stress that the pressure of the place is here intense but less pervasive than in *The Portrait of a Lady*, a novel with which *The Wings of the Dove* is often compared, if only to show the path James traveled from his early to his late manner. One would have to ascribe this to James's increasing rarefaction of his backgrounds, and to his belief that in his "major phase" he was eschewing "international" notations and connotations.[28] Yet in *The Wings of the Dove* he reverted to a close correlation of theme with setting, and Italy plays there a crucial part in the long series of fictional exploitations I have been describing so far.

Just as, nearing the end of his career, James erected this complex setting for the betrayal and death of an American princess, so too did he contemplate the fall of Italian princes. In "Miss Gunton of Poughkeepsie" (1900), a little-known story revolving around a question of pique, a young and willful American girl breaks her engagement with a Roman prince ("one of the most ancient of princes"), and happily marries an American. Italy here is very much a shady background. And what about that great majestic structure of James's last years, *The Golden Bowl* (1903)? There is no description of places, no overwhelming presence of functional or symbolic locales in this most rarefied and abstract of his novels: only the frail Murano crystal as a central but elusive symbol. Yet Prince Amerigo is meant and made to embody, though mainly "by indirection," his Roman past and heritage, history and tradition, Renaissance as well as papal Rome. And this imposing figure, whom the American millionaire Adam Verver sees as a "great Palladian church" (1,7), and who in his daughter Maggie evokes the image of an outlandish pagoda (2, 1), is bought as "a rarity, an object of beauty, an object of price" (1,1) and exiled in London, in spite of his yearning and nostalgia for the sunny, and even the picturesque, side of Italy.[29]

The quintessence of historical and artistic Italy is here made to pay tribute to the acquisitiveness and tight control of a new American family. I do not wish to stretch the point—which would probably be unfair to both James's total absorption, at this stage, in the problems of consciousness, and to his late American pilgrims to Europe. I offer it only as an aftermath in the long, long story of James's "international theme," in which the beauty and the enticement of Italy prove a double-edged menace. Her sunny atmosphere harbors mischief; her magnificent past can be a blight; her exuberance proves destructive; her open vistas close like vices on unsuspecting pilgrims. There the weight of tradition lies heavy on the soul, and the pressure of social circumstances crushes the hopeful dream of the imperious American self. Knowing Italy, for most of James's characters, is equal to eating of the Tree of Knowledge, and this implies turning innocence into experience, an encounter with evil, often a premonition of death. "After such knowledge," one is tempted to say with T. S. Eliot, "what forgiveness?"—except that all this is done in James's beautifully paradoxical or chiastic way. Beauty is still there after disaster has come; the blast of evil is almost a fair price to pay for its existence.[30]

Notes

1. Henry James, *Hawthorne*, ed. Tony Tanner (London: Macmillan, 1967), 25.
2. *The Letters of Henry James*, ed. Percy Lubbock (New York: Scribners, 1920), 2: 297–98.
3. *Henry James: Autobiography*, ed. F. W. Dupee (New York: Criterion, 1956), 558–59.
4. *The Notebooks of Henry James*, ed. F. O. Matthiessen and K. B. Murdock (New York: Braziller, 1955), 24, 32–36.
5. *The Art of the Novel: Critical Prefaces by Henry James*, ed. R. P. Blackmur (New York: Scribners, 1934), 200–201:

   It does thus in truth come home to me that, combining and comparing in whatever proportions and by whatever lights, my "America" and its products would doubtless, as a theme, have betrayed gaps and infirmities enough without such a kicking-up of the dramatic dust (mainly in the foreground) as I could set my "Europe" in motion for; just as my Europe would probably have limped across our stage to no great effect of processional state without an ingenuous young America (constantly seen as ingenuous and young) to hold up its legendary train.

6. Sergio Perosa, *L'Euro-America di Henry James* (Vicenza: Neri Pozza, 1979).
7. It can be visualized as follows:

8. "I have come on a pilgrimage," I said. "To understand what I mean, you must have lived, as I have lived, in a land beyond the seas, barren

of romance and of grace. This Italy of yours, on whose threshold I stand, is the home of history, of beauty, of the arts—of all that makes life splendid and sweet. Italy, for us dull strangers, is a magic world. We cross ourselves when we pronounce it. We are brought up to think that when we have learned leisure and rest—at some bright hour, when fortunes smiles—we may go forth and cross oceans and mountains and see on Italian soil the primal substance—the Platonic 'idea'— of our consoling dreams and our richest fancies." *The Complete Tales of Henry James*, ed. Leon Edel (Philadelphia: Lippincott, 1961–64), 2: 327. In *Italian Hours* we read of "The way in which the Italian scene . . . seems to purify itself to the transcendent and perfect *idea* alone— idea of beauty, of dignity, of comprehensive grace, with all accidents merged, all defects disowned, all experience outlived, and to gather itself up into the mere mute eloquence of what has just incalculably *been*, remains forever the secret and the lesson of the subtlest daughter of History . . . when high Natural Elegance proceeds to take such exclusive charge and recklessly assume, as it were, *all* responsibilities" [1873]. *Italian Hours* (New York: Grove Press, 1959), 359. James also remarks on p. 165: "Man lives more with Nature in Italy than in New or than in Old England; she does more work for him and gives him more holidays" [1873].

9. At the very beginning of the novel we move from Siena, the "flawless gift of the Middle Ages to the modern imagination," to an Arcadian scene in the countryside, with a terrace, an empty church, a fresco and an old beggar woman, a wall with a stone bench, "what the painters call a subject" (pp. 1–3).

10. Cristina Giorcelli, in her *Henry James e l'Italia* (Rome: Edizioni di Storia e letteratura, 1968), 45, stresses the similarity of this concept with an idea by Nathaniel Hawthorne.

11. While visiting the Forum in Rome James had seen the past "bodily turned up with the spade and transformed from an immaterial, inaccessible fact of time into a matter of soil and surfaces" *(Italian Hours*, 143).

12. Before the gem is returned "to the moldering underworld of the Roman past," in the Capuchin convent James sets up a perfect scene in *chiaroscuro*, with candles burning in the dusk, where the American soul feels the strong attraction of Catholicism in a Hawthornelike way. *Complete Tales*, 3: 241ff.

13. Similar ideas are expressed in *Italian Hours*: "if in Rome you may suffer from ennui, at least your ennui has a throbbing soul in it" (p. 205); there "One has really vibrated too much" (p. 214), "the pulse of life beats fast" (p. 255). Text references, such as (7,27), are to book and chapter.

14. Though, in St. Peter's, Isabel Archer's "conception of greatness rose and dizzily rose . . . [and] she paid her silent tribute to the seated sublime,"

James adds immediately that there was "something almost profane in the vastness of the place," ministering to material as well as spiritual contemplation" (chapter 27); in "The Solution" (1889) we read that "If we treated the great church as a public promenade, or rather as a splendid international *salon*, the fault was not wholly ours" since St. Peter's protected conversation and even gossip harbored "a faith that has no small pruderies to enforce" (*Complete Tales*, 7: 365). In *Italian Hours*, that church is likened to Piccadilly, Broadway, and the Paris boulevards (p. 149). For the Palace of the Caesars, see *Daisy Miller*, chapter 4 ("that beautiful abode of the flowering desolation"). In the *Autiobiography* (1956) (pp. 153–54), James writes of the visual influence of Thomas Cole's ample canvasses—one of which was the celebrated view of the Palace of the Caesars as the seat of decadence.

15. This idea is echoed in "Four Meetings" (1877): "I should go crazy if I did not go to Europe, and I should certainly go crazy if I did." For Mary's puzzlement in Rome: "at home . . . things don't speak to us of enjoyment as they do here. Here it is such a mixture. . . . Beauty stands there . . . and penetrates to one's soul and lodges there and keeps saying that man was not made to suffer but to enjoy. This place has undermined my stoicism, but . . . I love it!" (chapter 22).

16. For Como as an earthly paradise: "it was the Italy that we know from the street engravings in old keepsakes and annals, from the vignettes on music-sheets and the drop-curtains at theaters; an Italy that we can never confess ourselves—in spite of our own changes and of Italy's—that we have ceased to believe" (chapter 23). One is reminded, in passing, that a crucial scene of confrontation between father and daughter in *Washington Square* (1880) is set in the Alps (chapter 24).

17. Cf. *Letters*, (Lubbock) 2: 80, and in *Italian Hours*, p. 330: "the sense of a supremely intimate revelation of Italy in undress, so to speak (the state, it seemed, in which one would most fondly, most ideally, enjoy her); Italy no longer in winter starch and sobriety . . . the brilliant performer, in short, *en famille* . . . thanks to which she is by so much more the easy genius and the good creature as she is by so much less the advertised *prima donna*"; and p. 331: "the tousled *bonne fille* of our vacational Tuscany." James reserves for Italy (and particularly for Venice) his only expressions of almost physical love.

18. Cf. "The waning moon is veiled in a thin cloud-curtain; the empty arches of the dusky circle of the Coliseum are cavernous shadows, but the arena is clear and silent; there is a fusion of deep shade and luminous dusk. Of course one has to read lines out of Byron's *Manfred* there" (chapter 4).

19. Similar ideas are expressed in *Italian Hours*: "The Roman air is charged with an elixir, the Roman cup seasoned with some insidious drop" (p. 205), or in this passage about the waste of the Casino of Villa Madama

[1909]: "Endless for the didactic observer the moral, abysmal for the story-teller the tale" (p. 208).

20. In *Italian Hours* James had identified Italy with the "extraordinary in the romantic" and referred to her Gothic potentialities. The Benedictine convent at Subiaco, "which clings to certain more or less vertiginous ledges and slopes of a vast precipitous gorge, constitutes, with the whole perfection of its setting, the very ideal of the tradition of that *extraordinary in the romantic* handed down to us, as the most attaching and inviting spell of Italy, by all the old academic literature of travel and art of the Salvator Rosas and Claudes" [1909] (p. 221).

21. We also read that "Italy, all the same, has spoiled a great many people. . . . It made one idle and dilettantish and second-rate." For Osmond, "there is nothing tonic in Italian life." See Giorcelli, *Henry James e l'Italia*, 145.

22. For an extended treatment of this aspect of the novel, see Charles R. Anderson, *Person, Place, and Thing in Henry James's Novels* (Durham, N.C.: Duke University Press, 1978). One may recall, in passing, that *The Portrait of a Lady* was finished in Venice, with James having shut the windows to keep the bustle of the city from interfering with his writing.

23. In *Italian Hours* we are warned that "Venice isn't in fair weather a place for concentration of mind" (p. 13); yet in *The Aspern Papers*, in early autumn, the freshness of the weather from the sea is conducive to meditation and thought. "I wanted to walk, to move, to shed some of my bewilderment"; we also read of a "long day of confusion, which I spent entirely in wandering about, without going home, until late at night; it only comes back to me that there were moments when I pacified my conscience and others when I lashed it into pain" (chapter 9).

24. See *The Art of the Novel*, 160. As for James's well-known description of Venice in this tale, it is worth quoting again:

Without streets and vehicles, the uproar of wheels, the brutality of horses, and with its little winding ways where people crowd together, where voices sound as in the corridors of a house, where the human step circulates as if it skirted the angles of furniture and shoes never wear out, the place has the character of an immense collective apartment, in which Piazza San Marco is the most ornamental corner and palaces and churches, for the rest, play the part of great divans of repose, tables of entertainment, expanses of decoration. And somehow the splendid common domicile, familiar, domestic and resonant, also resembles a theater in which actors clicking over bridges and, in straggling processions, tripping along fondamentas. As you sit in your gondola the footways that in certain parts edge the canals assume to the eye the importance of a stage, meeting it at the same angle, and the Venetian figures, moving to and fro against the battered scenery of their little houses of comedy, strike you as members of an endless dramatic troupe. (Chapter 9)

25. In *Italian Hours*, Venice is at length and variously described as "the most beautiful of tombs" (p. 32), providing a "terrible standard of enjoyment" (p. 20), and representing all Europe (p. 69). Under the weight of her treasures, she is "insupportably sad"; in contrast, Florence offers "the sense of saving sanity" (p. 274). The Arcadian side of Italy is stressed in the almost contemporary tale "The Solution" (1889).

26. Yet in the Palazzo Leporelli, Milly Theale also feels "as in a fortress," "a painted idol." We think for a moment of Isabel Archer. And Milly wanders (and wonders) in Venice much as the narrator of *The Aspern Papers* had done. See Giorcelli, *Henry James e l'Italia*, 93.

27. For an extended analysis of the implications of the Venetian setting, see Marilla Battilana, *Venezia sfondo e simbolo nella narrativa di Henry James* (Milan: Laboratorio delle Arti, 1971; reprint 1987).

28. *The Art of the Novel*, 198–99. In a letter, Edith Wharton had been one of the first to remark on the rarefaction of James's settings in his later novels.

29. On Prince Amerigo as an epitome of Italy, and related aspects of *The Golden Bowl*, see also Carl Maves, *Sensuous Pessimism: Italy in the Work of Henry James* (Bloomington: Indiana University Press, 1973).

30. Much as he preferred the pre-1870 "romantic" Italy, James was also aware of the "new" Italy after unification, and has revealing aperçus in *Italian Hours*: "Young Italy, preoccupied with its economical and political future, must be heartily tired of being admired for its eyelashes and its pose" (p. 111); "It is in this attitude and with these conventional accessories that the world has seen fit to represent young Italy, and one doesn't wonder that if the youth has any spirit he should at last begin to resent our insufferable aesthetic patronage" (p. 112). He had seen Rome "in its superbest scarlet in 1869" (p. 198) and has nostalgic pages on papal Rome, but he also draws a comparison between present and past Italy (p. 248) and wishes "to try at least to read something of the old soul into the new forms" (p. 271). As for my reading of the role of Italy in James's novels, I refer to my second epigraph: "the great private palaces that are the massive majestic *syllables, sentences, periods,* of the strange message the place addresses to us" (*Italian Hours*, 252; my emphasis) as providing a crucial key.

FOUR

The Uses of Italy in Roderick Hudson and The Princess Casamassima

JOSEPHINE GATTUSO HENDIN

T HAT JAMES loved Italy has never been in doubt. After he wrote his brother, William, from Rome, "I went reeling and moaning thro' the streets, in a fever of enjoyment," James went on to write the essays collected in *Italian Hours* that showed his life-time experience of Italy as an ecstasy of sight and sensation, of happy "hazards" that made aesthetic experience synonymous with sensuality, spontaneity and chance. Rome, Venice, and the South, regions of major interest to James, arrested him by their power to interfuse antiquity with the living moment. What drew James forward with the urgency of a lover was that alchemical process in which "the present appeared to become again really classic."[1] From that encounter of tradition and modernity, James evolved distinctive psychological and social statements about the relation of ancient culture and modern character.

The power of Italy to enliven the present with the force of its complex history is nowhere more evident than in *Roderick Hudson* and *The Princess Casamassima*. Animated by the Italian-American princess, Christina Light, whose birth and marriage symbolize the mixture of nations, these novels use Italy to disclose complexities that both express and transcend what is conventionally known as James's "international theme." The glimpse that James offers into the workings of culture and character is deeper than what is generally found in his early novels, which tend to focus exclusively on the impact of Europe on American—frequently puritan—sensibility. In the Christina Light novels, what distinguishes James's Italy is the distinctive use he made of it: his exploitation of specific Italian regions to focus on aspects of Italian character and his use of a heroine of mixed ancestry to explore possibilities of cultural fusion.

For James, Italy is not only a place for revealing the clash between European fatalism and American hopes, but the locus of an active effort at retrieving and reexperiencing the past. The very writing of *Roderick Hudson* reveals this process. In his preface to the New York Edition, written over thirty years after the novel's publication, James said:

> One fact about it indeed outlives all others; the fact that, as the loved Italy was scene of my fiction—so much more loved than one has ever been able, even after fifty efforts, to say!—and as having had to leave it persisted as an inward ache, so there was soreness in still contriving, after a fashion, to hang about it and in prolonging, from month to month the illusion of the golden air. Little enough of that medium may the novel, read over today seem to supply; yet half the actual interest lurks for me in the earnest, baffled intention of making it felt. A whole side of the old consciousness, under this mild pressure flushes up and prevails again; a reminder, ever so penetrating, of the quantity of "evocation" involved in my plan, and of the quantity I must even have supposed myself to achieve.[2]

The "quantity of evocation" achieved may not have been fully appreciated by James. He describes the novel in terms that have become conventional for discussing his "international" fictions. He identifies its structure as one of opposites: counterpointed are the poles of Northampton, Massachusetts, and Rome; Mary Garland's puritan severities and Christina Light's urbanity; and Roderick's labile genius and Singleton's disciplined competence. These antitheses were to be suspended in the mind of Rowland Mallet, whom he calls "the centre of interest," who could "feel certain things happening to others . . . so the beauty of the constructional game was to preserve in everything its especial value for *him*"[3] and to sustain the dialectic between Italy and America. Yet James doubted his success. He faults the novel for "pointing almost too stern a moral,"[4] for making Roderick's collapse too easy, too simply the product of weakness and the catastrophic effect of Christina, and he further cites his failure to make Mary Garland a sufficiently strong antithesis to her. All of these assessments have encouraged a view of the novel as a cautionary tale, interesting in parts, but, on the whole, morally simplistic.

Notable discussions of *Roderick Hudson* are marked by a sense of its stark oppositions. As Leon Edel argues: "Art versus passion, then, is at the heart of *Roderick Hudson;* and beside it there is the other conflict I have mentioned: America versus Europe."[5] For Philip Rahv, the novel expresses a prototypical conflict between the life of duty and the life of pleasure evident in Mary Garland's declaration, on a lovely Roman night:

> At home . . . things don't speak to us of enjoyment as they do here. Here it's such a mixture; one doesn't know what to believe. Beauty stands here —beauty such as this night and this place and all this sad strange summer have been so full of—and it penetrates one's soul and lodges here and keeps saying that man wasn't made, as we think at home, to struggle so much and to miss so much, but to ask of life as a matter of course some beauty and some charm. This place has destroyed any scrap of consistency that I ever possessed, but even if I must say something sinful I love it![6]

Yet Italy is present in *Roderick Hudson* as a far grander force than can be encompassed by Mary Garland or contained by absolute moral opposites. It is itself a living character, an active spirit disclosing and reviving the pagan world in its energies, guiding concepts, frenzies, and even in its decline. James uses specific parts of Italy to effect a journey back and forward in time, to implement a replication of the process of creation. Rome emerges in the novel as the Eternal City perpetually welcoming that process of literal and spiritual creation. From James's early descriptions in *Italian Hours* of the sculpture and gardens of the Villa Ludovisi whose walls edge the pagan city of Rome, to the many descriptions of St. Peter's, named for the saint who is gatekeeper to the spiritual world and center of papal Italy, Rome is the place where the spirit, history, and the present flow into each other, forming an aesthetic whole.

In his preface, James raises the question of the nature of the "state of civilization" which "provided for art." The question overflows simple comparison between Northampton and Rome and reaches to the relationship between artist and environment, culture and character. For James, Rome is the place where art, divinity, and history have, for centuries, been so cohesive as to enable the artist to formulate the social and political context of life in aesthetic terms. That James tended to evaluate life in Italy by aesthetic standards is evident if one compares the Rome of *Italian Hours* of 1873 with that of *Roderick Hudson*, written during 1874–1875. In *Italian Hours* James comments on political change as a change in style, the result of a decline in the power of the pope. Papal Rome had a unique value whose loss was registered in the "look" of the city. James writes:

> The spectacle on the Corso has seemed to me, on the whole, an illustration of that great breach with the past of which Catholic Christendom felt the somewhat muffled shock in September 1870. A traveller acquainted with the fully papal Rome, coming back any time during the past winter, must have immediately noticed that something momentous had happened —something hostile to the elements of picture and colour and "style." My first warning was that ten minutes after my arrival I found myself face to face with a newspaper stand. The impossibility in the other days of having anything in the journalistic line but *Osservatore Romano* and the *Voce della Verità* used to seem to me much connected with the extraordinary leisure of thought and stillness of mind to which the place admitted you. . . . Rome reading unexpurgated news is another Rome indeed. For every subscriber to the *Libertà* there may well be an antique masker and reveller less. As striking a sign of the new régime is the extraordinary increase [of] . . . gentlemen, . . . spotless flowers of fashion. . . . They proclaimed . . . that by force of numbers, Rome had been secularised.
>
> An Italian dandy is a figure visually to reckon with, but these goodly throngs of them scarce offered compensation for the absent monsignori, treading the streets in their purple stockings . . . for the mourning gear of the cardinals' coaches that formerly glittered with scarlet and swung with the weight of the footmen clinging behind, for the certainty that you'll not, by the best of the traveller's luck, meet the Pope sitting deep in the shadow of his great chariot with uplifted fingers like some inaccessible idol in his shrine.[7]

James's favorite Rome was a Rome of poetry and prayer, not news; ritual song and not "free" speech. The political inadequacies of his position are less important than his astonishing ability to conflate moral, political, and aesthetic judgments. James subordinates all other forms of discussion to aesthetic discourse. As a journalist in his travel writing, he makes it clear that he is aware of the claims of the populace against the "stillness of mind" supported by papal authority. As a novelist, he follows his heart all the way to

an infatuation with the notion of a living church, a religion embodied in a vigorous "idol" of a pope whose passage through the streets
and paternal guidance of Rome made of the entire city a shrine. It
is into the ethos of that Rome, which had in reality already been
eclipsed by the time he was writing the novel, that James plunges
Roderick Hudson.

Drawn to the Vatican above all other places, Roderick finds that
"the old imperial and papal city altogether delighted him; only
there he really found what he had been looking for from the first—
the sufficient negation of his native scene. And indeed Rome is the
natural home of those spirits with which we just now claimed
fellowship for Roderick—the spirits with a deep relish for the element of accumulation in the human picture and for the infinite
superpositions of history. It is the immemorial city of convention;
and in the still recent day the most impressive convention in all
history was visible to men's eyes in the reverberating streets, erect
in a gilded coach drawn by four black horses."[8] The pope embodied
for James the past as present, presiding over rituals that represented
the long historical process that lay behind them. Like the shining
toe of the statue of St. Peter, polished by the lips of pilgrims who
had kissed it, Rome itself had been burnished for James by the pope's
passage to the brightness of metaphor; the streets of the Eternal City
lead back to the beginning of time.

James populates his Rome with artists who flock to this Eden of
art to learn the secrets of creation. Rome for James is a palimpsest
in which pagan, Christian, and modern elements can be read only
by those chosen artists who can understand that the present may
accommodate all time. Yet the tree of aesthetic knowledge bears
fruits which may contain seeds of corruption. The artists James
assembles each reflect not merely different kinds of art, but different
uses and misuses of the aesthetic impulse. In its most benign lapse,
art can be perceived as and distorted to technical craft, subordinat-
ing instinct and talent to skill. Although Singleton, who represents
the artist as hardworking craftsman, is often held up by critics as an
example of the "good" artist in contrast to Roderick's unreliability,
he appeals less for his work than for his earnest modesty and decency. James refers to him affectionately as the "little artist man."
Art can also be reduced to the mild dilettantism of Miss Blanchard,

who paints mostly flowers and has a fortune, but is not above selling pictures which reflect the trivialization of art to decoration. Gloriani, the most complex of James's "Romans," suggests deeper debasements of art under the pressure of modern doubts about the purity of the creative act. Gloriani reveals the corruption of art by moral-aesthetic relativism. He believes that

there is no essential difference between beauty and ugliness; that they overlap and intermingle in a quite inextricable manner; . . . that it is a waste of wit to nurse metaphysical distinctions and a sadly meagre entertainment to caress imaginary lines; that the thing to aim at is the expressive and the way to reach it is by ingenuity; . . . that a consummate work is a sort of hotch-potch of the pure and the impure, the graceful and the grotesque.[9]

Gloriani has learned to make moral and aesthetic anomie work for him. Not simply the man who knows how to make "capital of his talent," as James says, Gloriani capitalizes on that moral and aesthetic neutrality in which the prime duty of art is "to report on an aesthetic adventure"; in other words, to be about itself. Denying differences between the beautiful and the ugly, and their Jamesian corollaries, good and evil, Gloriani advocates ingenious ambiguities.

Against this "corruption," James situates Roderick's ambition "to produce the sacred terror," to create forms so powerful that they render the observer "blue" or "faint." Teased by Gloriani that the pagan deities have already been done, Roderick insists that he will do all the "Forces and Elements and Mysteries of Nature. . . . Morning, . . . Night . . . the Ocean and the Mountains, the Moon and the West Wind. I mean to make a magnificent image of my Native Land."[10] He shifts quickly from classical deities to the religion of nature, and just as quickly turns toward Christianity, insisting that he will improve on Christ by making him "more idealistic"[11] by stressing a perfection of form. Pagan, Christian, and an American religion of nature are subsumed in Roderick's vision of art as equal to divine creation and of the artist as capable of transcending the limitations of time, place, and self.

Roderick is not simply the American corrupted by exposure to European complexity, but a person chronically displaced, an eternal artist looking for a vantage point outside himself. In Northampton he is an uprooted Southerner whose dress, manner, and sensuous apprehension of reality all place him at odds with an environment collaborating, as Cecelia puts it, "to keep him quiet," but clearly boring him to death. James treats him as having a predisposition to pagan art. His subjects for sculpture—the water bearer, the memorial statue to his brother as the the fallen soldier —are reminiscent of those fallen gladiators and cup bearers of antiquity who are deep drinkers themselves.

Roderick's operative impulse is a Dionysian recoil against the quotidian in which self-obliteration can be seen as self-transcendence. That his character is Dionysian in its sentiments is clear in Northampton when Roderick declares "I want to do something violent and indecent and impossible—to let off steam!"[12] Italy provides Roderick with the tools of self-transformation. Adopting European dress, wearing a Venetian watchchain and Roman intaglio, and expressing attitudes that Mary Garland would find "corrupt," he is drawn to the Vatican as to the obliteration of his former self, for only there does he find the "sufficient negation of his native scene."[13] In his "revolt" Roderick practices that art that aligns pagan and Christian in its emphasis on transport and self-transformation.

Past, present, and future are enfolded in James's amazing portrait of Christina Light, Roderick's most "fitting" subject. Christina enters the novel under the aegis of the pagan goddess and queen, Juno. As Roderick sketches the mask of Juno in the Villa Ludovisi, James tells us that the mask looks upon these ancient Roman gardens as on the "last . . . lapse from Olympus." Christina walks by and so impresses Roderick with her beauty that he sketches her face as Juno's. In *Italian Hours* James writes of the Villa as the home of a woman, known familiarly as Rosina, who was the morganatic wife of King Victor Emmanuel.[14] Access to the gardens was limited by her whim. James laments that the sight of Juno was at the discretion of a lesser queen who could produce no "relevant" heirs, no stable line. As Christina dominates Juno's face, "becoming" Juno in Roderick's sketch, James's imagery of the fall from Olympus and the potential expulsion from the gardens by a modern queen begins to establish what will be a repetitive theme: the reenactment of the fall from past to present, from Olympus to Edenic garden, to the modern world as a passage made happy by the artist's ability to revive ancient beauty by giving it a modern face.

James's motif of the fall, combining both pagan and Christian themes, enables a vision of creation, destruction, and recreation as religious, historical, and aesthetic processes controlled by an artist-God. Roderick's *de facto* abandonment of the idea of sculpting a "more idealistic" Christ for a bust of Christina Light results in a work virtually everyone perceives in religious terms. For Mr. Leavenworth, she is Diana or a comparable deity, pagan and pure. By Christian standards, she is tarnished and fallen. Miss Blanchard finds her half like a "madonna" and half like a "ballerina." Gloriani compares her to Salome, a woman capable of demanding and receiving human sacrifice: the head of John the Baptist. For Rowland, she inspires religious fear: the bust is unsafe, so destabilizing in its beauty that it seems willing to "draw down a too confiding spirit into some strange underworld of unworthy sacrifice, not unfurnished with traces of others of the lost; . . . she struck him not only as preying possibly on the faith of victims, but as ready to take on occasion, her own life in her hand."[15] In brief, the bust embodies the "sacred terror" that conflates sanctity, violence, and beauty.

Roderick Hudson uses multiple versions of the fall in the service of a larger theme: the promise of self-creation through losing or obliterating one's former self. Roderick and Christina are each in search of an ideal they do not encounter in the real world. Roderick believes that he perceived this ideal before his birth; Christina seeks it in a man who possesses "the sacred fire." Each lives by a Dionysian ethic prizing fearlessnesss of risk, failure, or death; each believes in self-transformation. Both take their positive qualities of spontaneity and passion to the point of cruelty—Roderick in his treatment of Mary, and Christina in that exercise of do-gooding, in dropping Roderick, that makes her virtues seem more dangerous than her vices. Roderick banks all on inspiration and genius; Christina on her flights of persuasive and self-persuasive imagination. Neither respects the concept of moderation.

Roderick and Christina play roles redolent with religious meaning. He sees himself as an artist-God bent on pure creation. Christina's bust is not only referred to as a religious object, but she herself is treated as a fetish by her mother, whose capacity for worship, maternal instinct, and social ambition, James tells us, are entirely invested in her. Christina regards her mother, who has raised money on her beauty, as a Judas who will extract her thirty pieces of silver when she auctions her off to the prince. Christina treats herself as a shrine: she has little feeling for nature, but adorns herself with dozens of white rosebuds she demands of Assunta while both are in church. She is sought after, but feels chronically displaced and restless in the "real" world of society as if hoping for a home in the sacred fire, in art itself.

The ultimate seduction in the novel is not Christina's effect on Roderick, but James's seduction of the reader into seeing religious, social, and moral life in aesthetic terms. James succeeds in shifting all forms of discourse toward aesthetics. James seems to have constructed the novel as a dialectic in which sharp dualities prevail: Roderick, the artist as genius versus Singleton, the artist as craftsman; Christina, woman as seductress versus Mary, woman as nurse; Northampton, the "humane community" devaluing art, versus Rome, the city of art; Catholic ritual versus Puritan simplicity, or the thematic conflict between art and passion. Yet James's substitution of an aesthetic standard enables success or failure to be measured by qualities of creativity and style. What endangers beauty, endangers all. What makes the novel fascinating is James's use of Italy and the American mind to subsume dualities as they encounter a common threat: the erosion of sensibility.

The challenge to art in *Roderick Hudson* has generally been seen as deriving from sexuality and the life of passion. Yet Roderick creates sculpture of disturbing charm out of his dissipations. Moreover, this art more closely aligns his Dionysian impulses with his productions, frankly celebrating excess. The greater threat to art derives from a dissociation of that synthesis of power, belief, and genius that characterizes the texture of papal Rome and permits a vision of the artist as traveler through history, creating through resurrecting or resynthesizing past and present. The novel's political theme (extended further in *The Princess Casamassima*) explores the relationship between art and society in terms of a threat to sensibility experienced by both Italians and Americans.

Radicalism poses a challenge to the web of tradition that sustains Roman sublimity. It enters *Roderick Hudson* explicitly in the words of Mrs. Light, who has thought through politics as it affects the maintenance of style. She fears placing her daughter on a throne that might prove unstable:

Since the overturning of the poor King of Naples and that charming queen, and the expulsion of all those dear little old-fashioned Italian grand-dukes, and the dreadful radical talk that's going on all over the world, it has come to seem to me that with Christina in such a position I should be really very nervous. Even in such a position she would hold her head very high, and if anything should happen to her she would make no concessions to the popular fury. The best thing, if one would be prudent, seems to be a nobleman of the highest possible rank short of belonging to a reigning stock. There you see one striding up and down, looking at his watch and counting the minutes till my daughter reappears![16]

Although Rowland Mallet's disdain for Mrs. Light's calculating greed and lifetime of frivolity diminish the impact of her statement, it coincides with James's own assessment of the political scene sullied by the rising demand for popular, secular freedom. In his description of the Roman May of *Italian Hours* James reports a populace stirred by news of the pope's illness and the Religious Corporations Bill. He describes a crowd of protestors shouting in unison "Abbasso il ministero!" and murmuring "Al Quirinale! Al Quirinale!"[17] Although on arriving at the Quirinal the crowd was easily dispersed, James recognizes that it represents the "seeds of revolution" that threaten the "stillness of mind" associated with the papal city so adept at absorbing within itself its pagan past.

In James's Rome, in the Rome he bestowed on Roderick, there is no need to yell "Abbasso!" at anything, for all can be sustained in sublime composition: the "legendary wolf" rests in a grotto and "draws apparently as powerfully as the pope himself."[18] The Emperor Marcus Aurelius extends his bronze arm in benediction and, James notes, "one may call it singular that in the capital of Christendom, the portrait most suggestive of a Christian conscience is that of a pagan emperor."[19] The insurgent crowds, the newsstands featuring unexpurgated news, and the cry for self-determination reflect a future lacking all reverence and any redeeming qualities of "style."

James's Naples discloses a radicalism all its own, lodging its challenge to the ideal of eternally creative Rome. James's use of

Naples and a Neapolitan prince reflects his profound ambivalence over a region that was stable but without the "style" or spirituality of papal Rome. James saw Naples as both seductive and "fallen." He seems both charmed and appalled by the intimate terms on which Neapolitans live with their church and saints. In his description of feast days in Anacapri, he recalls visiting near Sorrento "a wayside chapel that seemed the scene of every function of domestic life, including cookery and others. . . . It is barbarous to expectorate in the temple of your faith, but that is doubtless an extreme case. Is civilization really measured by the number of things people do respect?"[20] Describing a group of bedecked Italians in a procession in honor of St. Antony, James remarks on "the absence of any approach to our notion of the posture of respect and this among people whose manners in general struck one as so good and in particular as so cultivated. The office of the saint—of which the festa is but the annual reaffirmation—involves not the faintest attribute of remoteness or mystery."[21] For James, Naples embodied the triumph of physicality over the sublime; or, more benignly, a vision of the sublime rooted in daily, domestic concerns. James found in this perspective much to amuse but little to admire. The outlook of "the South" appeared to be entirely at odds with his sense of mystery, sublimity, or the superiority of the element of the "ideal."

In *Roderick Hudson*, Naples is a place of shame and excess. It appears in the novel first in a cautionary tale told by Madame Grandoni, who compares Roderick's work to that of Herr Schafgans, who, having the misfortune to fall in love with an earthy model, escaped his embarrassment over marrying her by fleeing with her to Naples. There the spirituality of his art collapsed under the pressure of meeting her demands and he fell so far as to use his talent to paint Vesuvius on "tourist boxes."[22] Roderick, in the course of his fall, Rowland tells us, "has taken to riotous living and has just been spending a month at Naples—a city where amusement is actively cultivated—in very bad company."[23]

The Prince Casamassima adds another dimension to Neapolitan materialism. With his magnificent estates, his hereditary diamonds for his princess, his titles, wealth, decency, and dullness, he virtually embodies riches without spirit. One of the prince's titles is that of *grandee d' espagne*, a fact linking him with the Spain that James considered secure in the embrace of convention, resting on its "fatal past." The prince's reverence for his family and his rigid courtesy toward Christina suggest a sense of ritual expressed primarily through the mundane. For Christina and perhaps for James, he represents a region in which religious and aesthetic emotion have been invested in mediocre concerns. His pride in his name and in the intelligence of his prelate uncles suggests that he inherits a tradition of equating respect for "civilization" with family loyalty.

And yet something is wrong. The prince's very desire to marry Christina makes him suspect. His longing for her beauty even at the price of marriage suggests a decline in the discipline and control of the aristocracy itself. His family is correct to oppose the marriage and advocate his traditional choice of a bride among his own peers instead of his following his instincts. His marriage serves as a socially disruptive force since it will tie him forever without prospect of divorce to a woman who shares none of his values. The prince has defied his family on the strength of his desire. In his dullness he has discovered and acted on the modern ethic of self-gratification.

Roderick Hudson provides a radical perspective on modern life. The carefully structured contrasts between Northampton and Rome collapse under the pressure of a modernism that James equates with the fracturing of aesthetic vision and social convention. The novel culminates in a sense of the derangement of art, religious sentiment, and society. Christina abandons her quest for sublimity to marry the prince, and Roderick, unable to create, cannot resurrect himself through art. The failures of Christina and Roderick may constitute a critique of the Dionysian wish to live in the "sacred fire" or "sacred terror." Dionysian sentiment cannot establish a synthesis between self and society, or protect against the power of circumstance or the artist's inevitable recognition of his own humanity. Thus the Dionysian ends by turning on itself in the self-important appetites of the prince, in the romantic death of the uncreative artist, and in Christina's poisonous declaration of her dead soul at the novel's end. Yet papal Rome remains for James the place, perhaps the only one, where the personal quest for the sublime through art and social order were in harmony with each other. Not surprisingly, Christina and the prince leave Rome immediately after marrying; it is in the mountains of Switzerland where Roderick dies and where Christina resolves to go for "delight."

Christina Light expresses James's vision of the modern spirit as a *femme fatale*. Her portrait crystallizes his darkest fears about the Italian and American future. Her Italian-American heritage offers the promises and pitfalls of both cultures. Christina has the charismatic, hypnotic beauty that James associates with Italy. Born in the shadow of St. Peter's and a Catholic of sorts, she knows the rituals associated with redemption and grace but has found no comfort in them as spiritual or aesthetic experiences. She displays the worldliness and sophistication of Roman society to excess: although she is most frequently dressed in white and cast in the role of marriageable *jeune fille*, she exploits rather than plays the part. Even her feeling for animals is unnaturally socialized. She uses her overpampered, oversubdued dog, Stentorello, to put down other contenders for her affection by negative comparison to him. When learning of her illegitimacy, she acts with predictable self-interest and marries the prince. And yet something is wrong here, too.

The Americanness of Christina Light surfaces in an atavistic yearning for sublimity that is constantly at odds with the urbane European society in which she was raised. Its severity shows in the unsparing harshness of her moral judgments of herself. She considers her worldliness "corrupt, corrupting, corruption." She is the only one who considers her marriage to the prince in other than economic terms, weighing her dislike of him against her attraction to everything he has. Her admiration for Mary Garland's meat-cleaver moral sense has elements of a genuine wish to be able to reject high living for high thinking. Her desire for self-transcendence drives her not only to seek a man with the "sacred fire," but also to ask Rowland for books on history to help end her ignorance of larger issues. Her roving, creative imagination ties Emersonian notions of possibility to her own performances—her power to create multiple selves.

Can the American dream of sublimity be tied to a Roman sensibility? Through Christina, James creates a vision of irreconcilability. Christina's hybrid heritage, expressed in that constant shift in attitudes that makes Madame Grandoni call her capricious, oscillates between a quest for sublimity and a quest for social position and wealth. Her Italianate feeling for beauty and American yearning for sublimity serve to undermine rather than reinforce each other; she can reach a sustaining accord with neither culture. She is unable to feel a reverential joy in the harmony of art and spirit represented by papal Rome. She cannot, with *pietas*, integrate her social position as princess into its rightful place in the historical tapestry of Italian life. Her quest for sublimity is virtually doomed by her inability to love any one or any principle with sufficient force to overpower her sharp, ironic intelligence. Driven back on herself, her notions of sublimity become tied to self-rejection and rejection of all forms of stability. Always changing, always outraging expectations, she is the quintessential *déracinée* who makes mutability her fixed principle. Her disruptive impact as a *femme fatale* contains James's most pointed comment on culture and character. She is, James fears, the future. She dramatizes those derangements of self, society, art, and religious sentiment that flow from irreverence and alienation. She indicates a feared direction of the modern self: the discovery of pleasure in sheer discord.

The Princess Casamassima is generally not considered one of James's Italian novels. Set in London and, James wrote in the preface to the New York Edition, the product of his walks through its slums and sorrows, the novel is generally considered his attempt at Dickensian realism. Yet it also derives from James's inability to let either Italy or Christina Light alone. Italy is alive in the novel as memory, as experience, as a crucible for changes in aesthetic and political sensibility. The twinned themes of politics and art that emerged in *Roderick Hudson*, and the use of different regions of Italy for expressing specific attitudes, survive in heightened form. The opposing claims of Christina's role as the Princess Casamassima and her American yearnings reach a far higher pitch.

If becoming a princess enabled Christina to conceal the humiliation of her illegitimacy in opulence, it has, as Madame Grandoni says, also forced her into "ill-starred connection with an ignorant and superstitious Italian race whom she despised for their provinciality, their parsimony and their futility."[24] In the scanty account James offers of their life, he tells us that her relations with his family . . . and what she had had to suffer from their family tone, their opinions and customs . . . , had evidently planted in her soul a lasting resentment and contempt; and Hyacinth gathered that the force of reaction and revenge might carry her very far, make her modern and democratic and heretical à outrance—lead her to swear by Darwin and Spencer and all the scientific iconoclasts as well as by the revolutionary spirit.[25]

The rebellious princess has consorted with anarchists in Naples and become a revolutionist.

The presiding atmosphere of the novel is one of ideological materialism. The structure of opposites that shaped *Roderick Hudson* is politicized as class conflict replaces art as a controlling principle. Hyacinth Robinson and Millicent Henning, in sensibility and beauty, are the novel's noble savages, representing the best aesthetic products of the lower classes. Muniment, the shrewd, impoverished chemist's assistant and his lively, crippled sister represent different forms of coercive intelligence claiming either power or help. The marriage of the prince and princess embodies how the class war and the sex war can intertwine.

Out of the power struggle between the prince and princess, James evolves a statement of the personal as political. Life on the prince's family estate has made the princess acutely aware of the subordinate position of a bride in an established family. She is "nailed" into their conventions. Yet her "crucifixion," as her marvelous name implies, is light, if not rosy. She has learned to use her humiliation for her own benefit. The novel takes her up three years after her marriage. She has made the prince feel "like an ass." She has aroused such extraordinary frustration in her long-suffering and passive husband that he has pushed her into the garden. Unpleasant in itself, his act has produced an amazing benefit: she used it to separate from him with a great settlement, and now possesses enough of the wealth she had always considered the most interesting thing about him. Life as a victim has taught her to make victimization work for her so well that she has victimized him far beyond her own inconvenience. Her own "Darwinian" struggle for resources in the social jungle of his estates, and her vision of a Spencerian world ruled by mechanical principles have enabled her to elaborate her desire for power into a worldview.

The Princess's vision of class conflict is more than a commitment to social justice. Through her attempt to become a terrorist, to commit a political murder, she is seeking a form of self-transcendence. She wishes to eliminate her uprootedness by eliminating the idea of social order, to dismantle the stable institutions that exacerbate her sense of displacement. More profoundly she wishes through the murder of some grandee to kill that greedy part of herself that betrayed her yearning for the sublime by marrying the prince. The quality of her feeling extends James's view of her Italian-Americanness.

The Italian-American theme discloses large inversions of the values that guided *Roderick Hudson*. If creativity was the ideal in that novel, destructiveness is the ideal in this. If the Italianness of the princess was evident in her affinity for beauty, it is now evident in her adoption of an inverted aesthetic of ugliness. She wishes to see the worst, most horrible hovels. She rents progressively uglier homes, storing away her elegant furnishings in preference for hideous, rented objects. She retains a sense of the power of place and setting: from the choice of the country house Medley to express her love of things made beautiful by the accumulation of time, to the house at Madeira Crescent in its barrenness, Christina demonstrates the use of objects to express a new, anti-aethestic.

Christina's Americanness is reflected in an inversion of her thirst for sublimity. Her reforming spirit and drive for change rise to the pitch of violence. She is determined in her inverted social climbing to reach the heights of the depths, to be in touch with those who go farthest. In her desire to kill or die for a noble cause she suggests that dictum of John Brown that Edmund Wilson found definitive in his critical study *Patriotic Gore*: "without the shedding of blood, there is no remission of sins." It is not social justice that Christina craves, but redemption. To kill is, paradoxically, to sacrifice, to expiate one's own guilt. Thus her "vendetta" against the prince and her sense of retributive justice can be satisfied. Her quest for proximity to those who commit murder also reminds one of Brown, who is said to have killed no one himself at Pottawatomie, but organized the raid and supervised its progress. Her wish to play a trusted role in "the movement" suggests her willingness to be an architect as well as an agent of violence. The one form of social behavior she is seen wishing to construct on her own is an act of annihilation, an act so entirely at odds with her own material self-interest as to rule out venal motives and to make every violent assertion of self synonymous with self-denial.

The perversity of Christina is thus far more complex than has generally been thought. Not simply a victim of the excesses of an American will, nor merely the Jamesian heroine in her "ugly" aspect, nor even only the creature of caprice Madame Grandoni calls her, Christina opens up moral paradoxes in which destruction can be seen as a creative act, murder and suicide are one, and victim and victimizer are the same. In a sense, *The Princess* both fulfills Gloriani's vision of morally relativistic art and validates Rowland's distaste for it. The oxymoronic "sacred terror" of art, and the "sacred fire" of paradoxical Dionysian creation/destruction are elaborated in this novel in terms of raw power: the conflict of classes and the war between the sexes. The Eternal City of art has been abandoned by the princess for a London dominated by materialism and the historical moment.

James celebrates Italian sublimity as the antidote to the poison of English circumstance. Through Hyacinth Robinson, James pays tribute to the power of aesthetics to function as a force for redemption. Illegitimate child of a Frenchwoman who murdered his father, an English lord, Hyacinth shares with Christina a dark ancestry and a hybrid heritage. Moved by his mother's death in prison, his abandonment by his father, and his poverty, Hyacinth offers his life to the revolutionary cause by expressing his willingness to undertake a suicide mission of assassination. His exposure to Venice precipitates a recoil from political action and an infatuation with art.

James's Venice is a city viewed through his reading of Ruskin's *Stones of Venice* and his own enthusiasm for the city as a work of art. As such, it embodies the power of art and architecture to resist the tides of nature and even of rising secularism and social unrest. As James writes in *Italian Hours*,

It takes a great deal to make a successful American, but to make a happy Venetian takes only a handful of quick sensibility. The Italian people have at once the good and the evil fortune to be conscious of few wants; so that if the civilisation of a society is measured by the number of its needs, as seems to be the common opinion to-day, it is to be feared that the children of the lagoon would make but a poor figure in a set of comparative tables.

Not their misery, doubtless, but the way they elude their misery, is what pleases the sentimental tourist, who is gratified by the sight of a beautiful race that lives by the aid of its imagination."[26]

James's vision of the Piazza San Marco as "the drawing room of all Europe" (one of the few to which one does not need an invitation) enabled him to use Venice as the crucible in which Hyacinth Robinson's revolutionary tendencies are ground up. From Venice, Hyacinth writes to the princess:

want and toil and suffering are the constant lot of the immense majority of the human race. I've found them everywhere but haven't minded them. Forgive the cynical confession. What has struck me is the great achievements of which man has been capable in spite of them—the splendid accumulations of the happier few, to which doubtless the miserable many have also in their degree contributed. . . . They seem to me inestimably precious and beautiful and I've become conscious more than ever before of how little I understand what in the great rectification you and Poupin propose to do with them. The monuments, and great treasures of art, the great palaces and properties, the conquests of learning and taste, the general fabric of civilization as we know it, based if you will upon all the despotisms, the cruelties, the exclusion, the monopolies and the atrocities of the past, but thanks to which all the same, the world is less of a bloody sell and life more of a lark.[27]

As Christina misuses her beauty in the service of ideological seduction, Hyacinth discovers the reverse: liberation from the limits of ideology into the transcendent perspective provided by art. Through aesthetic sensibility, Hyacinth finds a perspective on political personalities. Once impressed by Hoffendahl as a brilliant strategist of revolution, Hyacinth now evaluates him by a different standard: sensitivity to beauty. By this measure Hoffendhal is a comic absurdity, too limited to see the power or value of aesthetic achievement. Hyacinth sees him as capable of such folly as cutting "up the ceilings of the Veronese into strips, so that everyone might have a little piece."[28]

Underlying Hyacinth's accusation is his new fusion of morality and aesthetics, his fear that revolutionary drives might originate in the ugliness of envy. In rejecting what he delicately calls, "the grudging attitude," Hyacinth writes to the princess: "I don't want everyone to have a little piece of anything and I've a great horror of that kind of invidious jealousy which is at the bottom of the idea of a redistribution." In condemning envy of fortunes "higher" and "brighter" than one's own, he hopes that he may not die with that "stain upon his soul."[29]

Just as the opposites of *Roderick Hudson* were displaced by the overriding fascination with art, so too the class conflicts that shape *The Princess Casamassima* collapse into an aesthetic question. Hyacinth increasingly articulates the view that equality is an insufficient guiding principle if it means a redistribution of power and possessions among people equally without sensibility. The key social issue for James is not equality of power but increasing access to beauty and to art for those with the sensibility to revere them. It is the princess who articulates James's evident sympathy when she murmurs to Hyacinth: "Fancy the strange, the bitter fate: to be constituted as you're constituted, to be conscious of the capacity you must feel, and yet to look at the good things of life only through the glass of the pastry cook's window."[30]

Venice, as the embodiment of the long Italian experience of patience with obstacles, with its open-air drawing room and magnificent buildings, is the city where the goddess of art deals most lavishly with the poor, simply by enduring. Hyacinth is its spiritual child, discovering there a nurturing route to self-transcendence. His love of art and beauty, which draws him to Christina, gives him hope that in addition to fabricating beautiful covers for books he may one day write himself and lay more direct claim to the world of art.

As Venice has offered Hyacinth a glimpse of the sublimity of creativity, so London's anarchists have offered him a taste of the negative sublime: self-transcendence through destruction. Even after turning from the cause, he reveals what drove him to offer his life. Hyacinth believes

that the flood of democracy was rising over the world; that it would sweep all the traditions of the past before it; that, whatever it might fail to bring, it would at least carry in its bosom a magnificent energy; [. . .] he was afraid the democracy wouldn't care for perfect bindings or for the finer sorts of conversation. The Princess gave up these things in proportion as she advanced in the direction she had so audaciously chosen; and if the Princess could give them up it would take very transcendent natures to stick to them. At the same time there was joy and exaltation in the thought of surrendering one's self to the wash of the wave, of being carried higher on the sun-touched crests. . . . That vision could deepen to ecstasy; make it indifferent if one's ultimate fate, . . . were not almost certainly to be . . . dashed to pieces on immovable rocks.[31]

Hyacinth and Christina are pushed by Muniment toward their own demise. Driven by an oceanic wish to extinguish themselves in a cause, they are rendered vulnerable to the calculating, unsentimental cruelties of the man who betrays Hyacinth's friendship and capitalizes on Christina's delusion that she will be trusted. Muniment arouses passion and trust while feeling nothing. Both Hyacinth and Christina consider him "remarkable" or "first rate" for his ability to endanger or wound them. The princess's sexual liaison with him adds an erotic dimension to her need to expiate her guilt through destruction and self-destruction. She is purging her guilt over worldliness in masochism. Able to arouse in her, as no one has in years, tears of rage, Muniment serves as an agent of retributive justice, the Nemesis of the *femme fatale*. His power to exploit her pain is less important than what he symbolizes. For James, the essence of revolution is precisely the spirit of brutal utility.

Placing her trust in Muniment, the princess loses on all fronts: the prince cuts off her money, the poor mistrust her as a champion, while Muniment fails her as a revolutionary contact and disposes of her as a lover with a few, cruel words. In her willingness to commit political murder and suicide, the princess aimed for purgation and sublimity only to encounter a far more bitter guilt and humiliation than those she had tried to dispel. Hyacinth, the one poor man Christina has explicitly set out to save, is ironically the one to whose suicide she contributes. As she stands by his dead body, she seems a soul as tormented as she is tormenting. The novel's closing words belong to Schinkel, who reduces the tragedy of Hyacinth's death to concern for the revolver that "would certainly have served much better for the Duke." What has died is sensibility. And in her own longing for purgation and sublimity through suicidal violence, Christina has helped to pave the way for a soulless future.

The stark, utilitarian materialism of James's London world redeems the Italian south from James's censure. An odd celebration of the Italian sensibility is expressed through his tragicomic portrait of Prince Casamassima, that man much condemned for his reverence toward his ancient name and family. James treats him as the stock figure of Italian farce: the snubbed suitor of *Roderick Hudson* becomes the dull husband so afflicted with jealousy that he drives his wife toward the result he most fears. Spying and following her in London, he cannot understand the depth of his wife's rejection of him or of the traditions of privilege that he embodies. He is entirely ethnocentric, attributing social unrest in England to the absence of "the true faith" that helps one bear adversity. He questions whether no one gives alms. Even after Madame Grandoni convinces him that the princess wishes to hurt not only him, but also the "sacred institutions" of society, he continues to suspect that her concern for the poor and talk of revolution are only covers for her adultery. He is, we are constantly reminded, stupid, stupid, stupid. Yet to him James grants the wormy apple of truth.

Only through the prince's surveillance do we learn of Christina's affair with Muniment. By then the prince has become an oddly sympathetic figure, redeemed from his faults and limitations by the sheer power of his devotion to his wife. Only when his honor is unquestionably wounded does he act. The Catholic view of marriage as a sacrament enables a view of the affair as the violation of a sacred trust so that adultery may serve as the archetypal model for all transgression. Spurred, the prince acts with a sharp, practical intelligence. He bypasses the princess, writes directly to Muniment, and informs him that Christina's allowance is to end and that she will be unable to supply him with any more money. As Christina waits for him to dismiss the importance of money compared to her assets of intelligence and competence, Muniment delivers the humiliating blow: "I've no intention whatever of saying anything harsh or offensive to you, but since you challenge me perhaps it's well that I should let you know how inevitably I *do* consider that in giving your money—or rather your husband's—to our business you gave the most valuable thing you had to contribute."[32] The prince has judged him correctly to be more of a user than a lover.

The Princess Casamassima and *Roderick Hudson* document James's use of Italy as the land where sublimity has been incarnated. In the cities of art, papal Rome and Venice, James finds the aesthetic sublime interwoven with the institutions of the church, and the daily texture of a present "made classic" by a history visible in the living composition woven from millennia of architecture, painting, and sculpture. If James saw that that cohesiveness was losing out to a democratic cry for change that threatened to destroy what he valued, he nevertheless found in Naples a lesser but more durable talent for translating the reverence for beauty into personal life. He bestowed upon his prince a gift for finding, in simply beholding his wife's perfect face, joy. In that Neapolitan capacity to feel pleasure despite tribulation, to accept the imperfection of soul but continue to admire what can be revered, James offered, even from English gloom, a tribute to that Italian sunlight that was like no other.

Notes

1. Henry James. *Italian Hours* (New York: Grove Press, 1959), 354.
2. Henry James, "Preface," *Roderick Hudson* (New York: Harper Torch-books, 1960), 9–10.
3. Ibid., 16–17.
4. Ibid., 14.
5. Leon Edel, "Introduction to the Torchbook Edition," *Roderick Hudson*, by Henry James (New York: Harper Torchbooks, 1960), viii.
6. Philip Rahv, "The Heiress of All the Ages," in *Literature and the Sixth Sense* (Boston: Houghton Mifflin, 1970), 111.
7. James, *Italian Hours*, 136–37.
8. James, *Roderick Hudson*, 74–75.
9. Ibid., 83.
10. Ibid., 89.
11. Ibid., 88
12. Ibid., 62.
13. Ibid., 74.
14. James, *Italian Hours*, 193, 211.
15. Ibid., 130.
16. James, *Roderick Hudson*, 170–71.
17. James, *Italian Hours*, 196.
18. Ibid., 141.
19. Ibid., 142.
20. Ibid., 352–53.

21. Ibid., 352.
22. James, *Roderick Hudson*, 91.
23. Ibid., 195.
24. Henry James, *The Princess Casamassima* (New York: Penguin Books, 1982), 203.
25. Ibid., 214–15.
26. James, *Italian Hours*, 3–4.
27. James, *The Princess Casamassima*, 352.
28. Ibid., 353.
29. Ibid., 354.
30. Ibid., 298.
31. Ibid., 428.
32. Ibid., 525.

FIVE Henry James's American Girls in Darkest Rome: The Abuse and Disabuse of Innocence

DANIEL MARK FOGEL

COMMENTING on the use of the Roman setting in *The Marble Faun*, Henry James remarked that Hawthorne "incurs that penalty of seeming factitious and unauthoritiative, which is always the result of an artist's attempt to project himself into an atmosphere in which he has not a transmitted and inherited property. An English or a German writer . . . may love Italy well enough, and know her well enough, to write delightful fictions about her; the thing has often been done. But the productions in question will, as novels, always have about them something second-rate and imperfect."[1] The thirty-six-year-old writer who penned this magisterial, not to say condescending, critique of his greatest American predecessor had already set in Italy the tale that had made him an international sensation, *Daisy Miller* (as well as five other tales and the novel *Roderick Hudson*), and he had under way, moreover, his first masterpiece, *The Portrait of a Lady*, the latter two-thirds of which is set in the Eternal City. Given that Henry James could claim little more of "a transmitted or inherited property" in Rome than Hawthorne, and given his forcefully articulated view that a novel set in Rome without this essential "property" must perforce be "something second-rate and imperfect," we are justified in interrogating the Master's ghost thus: Why did you set your great early tales of American Innocence Undone in a locale that would seem to condemn you, by your own precept, to the second-rate and the imperfect? After all, didn't you write, on your first visit to Rome,

that the "Italian tone . . . lies richly on my soul and gathers increasing weight, but it lies as a cold and foreign mass—never to be
absorbed and appropriated"?[2] Notwithstanding your avowal seven
years later, on your fourth visit to Rome, that the city seemed
"common-place and familiar" because you had thoroughly "enjoyed and appropriated it in former years," we put it to you that
there is a considerable inconsistency between the settings you chose
for your own fiction and your strictures on other practitioners of
the art of the novel.[3] But of course we cannot hope that Henry
James will reply to any such possibly impertinent interrogations. If
he will speak at all, it must be through all of us who read him,
making our own minds chambers in which the reverberations of his
great voice are reawakened, renewed, and interpreted.

And so in reply to the question of why James condemned Hawthorne's use of the Italian setting to which he himself had come
inveterately to resort, I imagine that he would reply—from the
ghostly vantage point of today—that in contrast to Hawthorne he
was committed from early on not to an American but to a cosmopolitan experience and perspective, so that Rome on repeated and
prolonged acquaintance became as much his "property" as his native New York. But I do not think he would have put it that way in
1879. He was too close to the time when he felt, as he told his
brother William, that he might sojourn forever in Italy only to "feel
more and more my inexorable Yankeehood."[4] Rather, I think he
would have said that no one was more aware than he that, as he
wrote in 1875, "Italian scenery and manners have come to be a
rather threadbare resource in romance." Still, he confessed "to a
sneaking kindness for the well-worn theme," and he was quite
ready to risk the penalties Hawthorne had in his view incurred
because doing so enabled him to give the strongest, most dramatic
accent to his great theme of American Innocence Undone in a
strange land.[5] His aim was not, after all, to "write delightful fictions about" Italy, but to set in Italy unsparing fictional anatomies
of the meaning of the American character, with the Old World
serving as the contrast medium against which his immitigable
Americans would most distinctly show.

This chapter will focus on two of James's great treatments of the abuse and disabuse of innocence in darkest Rome, *Daisy Miller* and *The Portrait of a Lady*, with some reference to other pertinent works, especially *The Golden Bowl*. We may begin by observing that by the late 1870s James not only had a considerable personal experience of Rome—four visits during which he logged a total of nearly eleven months in the city—but also a rich literary experience, an inheritance drawn from the Italian writings of numerous authors in addition to Hawthorne, notably Goethe, Byron, Stendahl, George Eliot, and Robert Browning, not to mention John Ruskin's celebrations of Italian civilization and art. Foremost among the literary experiences that come into play in the two works with which I am principally concerned are the Byronic associations of the Castle of Chillon and the Colosseum in *Daisy Miller;* James's Eliotic revelation, in Rome and after an unnarrated interval, of the unhappiness of Isabel Archer's marriage, a close parallel to the Roman discovery of Dorothea Brooke's miserable disillusionment with Casaubon; and the Browningesque elements in the characterization of Gilbert Osmond.

This last point seems, by the way, to have been insufficiently appreciated, despite the recent publication of Ross Posnock's book devoted to the James-Browning relation and William Buckler's brilliant essay on James's reading of *The Ring and the Book.*[6] Only Sandra Djwa, among commentators on *The Portrait of a Lady*, has picked up on its relation to "My Last Duchess."[7] Clearly James had in mind Browning's dramatic monologue as he wrote one of the most telling passages about Gilbert Osmond in *The Portrait of a Lady*. I am thinking of the last paragraph of chapter 28: we are in Rome (and not, as Djwa unaccountably says, in Florence at the Uffizi), where Lord Warburton has just taken his leave after having met Isabel in the gallery of the Capitol, before the statue of *The Dying Gladiator*, and Osmond is reveling in his consciousness that he may succeed where Warburton has failed:

We know that he was fond of originals, of rarities, of the superior, the exquisite; and now that he had seen Lord Warburton, whom he thought a very fine example of his race and order, he perceived a new attraction in the idea of taking to himself a young lady who had qualified herself to figure in his collection of choice objects by rejecting the splendid offer of a

British aristocrat. Gilbert Osmond had a high appreciation of the British aristocracy—he had never forgiven Providence for not making him an English duke—and could measure the unexpectedness of this conduct.[8]

Twice here James echoes key words from the closing lines of Browning's poem. First, as Djwa notes, James's "rarities" recalls Browning's "Notice Neptune, though,/Taming a sea-horse, thought a rarity"; more ominously, in an echo overlooked by Djwa, Osmond's notion that Isabel might "figure in his collection of choice objects" picks up on the chilling use of the word *object* by Browning's duke, who, with an unwitting *double entendre*, assures the count's emissary that "his fair daughter's self, as I avowed/At starting, is my object." Much later in the novel, when Osmond, in order to cool his daughter's ardor for Rosier, consigns Pansy to the convent (the fate to which Browning's duke may have consigned his last duchess, though I incline to the view that he simply had her killed), we learn that Osmond regards Pansy in the same way, "as a precious work of art" (*PL*, 739). In associating Osmond with Browning's Renaissance Italian duke at the moment when we see that Isabel's suitor is capable both of envying and of savoring his triumph over an English duke, James makes clear the heinous wickedness that underlies Osmond's devotion to taste. Osmond, like the duke, prefers a thing, an *objet d'art*, to a warm, spontaneous human being, prefers, in short, the portrait of a lady to the lady herself. As Djwa points out (p. 81), what unleashes the tyranny of Browning's duke and of Osmond alike is the recognition that the lady in each case "has a mind and spirit of her own." This tyranny is what Adeline Tintner seems to overlook in her otherwise highly instructive study of Pater's influence on James, for, in arguing that Osmond's Paterian notion of success in life is "to avoid competition and to concentrate on one's own personal impressions of great art," Tintner ignores that Osmond's overriding intention is in fact viciously competitive, that he does not finally appreciate art for art's sake but for the pleasure of making others see that he is better and more exclusive than everyone else.[9] Ralph knows long before Isabel that "under the guise of caring only for intrinsic values" (the true Paterian stance), "Osmond lived exclusively for the world" (*PL*, 597), and when Isabel at last makes this out for herself in chapter 42, her recognition that Osmond lives in order to extract from the "base, ignoble world" "some recognition of one's own superiority" is concomitant with her realization that "he would have liked her to have nothing of her own but her pretty appearance" (*PL*, 632, 634).

Osmond's obsession with appearance leads me to what I believe is the thread that runs through *Daisy Miller* and *The Portrait of a Lady*, unifying the Italian elements in each of these works and justifying the risk that Henry James underwent in taking both of his heroines, like Hawthorne's Miriam and Hilda, to Rome. Beneath James's sense of the beauty of Italian art and civilization, beneath his knowledge of the almost unimaginable accretions of Italian history and tradition, beneath his appreciation of the way the very air of the country ministered to sensibility and to the gathering of impressions, there lay like a serpent in a bank of flowers—if I may borrow a memorable comparison from *The Portrait of a Lady*—a sense that nowhere else was convention so entrenched and so likely to be, if not a mask for treachery, duplicity, and intrigue (matters long associated, in Anglo-American literary tradition, with Italy), at least a force unsurpassed in its stultifying, life-denying power. For Daisy Miller's tragedy follows from her inability to recognize the conventions that govern behavior in the community of Italian-ate Americans in Rome, and then from her unwillingness to conform to those conventions once they have been made clear to her; and, as James summed up for himself in his notebooks what he was aiming at with Isabel Archer, "[t]he idea of the whole thing is that the poor girl, who has dreamed of freedom and nobleness, who has done, as she believes, a generous, natural, clear-sighted thing, finds herself in reality ground in the very mill of the conventional."[10] This last phrase is repeated in the novel by Ralph Touchett, who exclaims to Isabel in their moving last interview, "You wanted to look at life for yourself—but you were not allowed; you were punished for your wish. You were ground in the very mill of the conventional" (*PL*, 785).

That Henry James should have seen Italy as more thoroughly embued with convention than the other countries that he held in imaginative possession—for example, France, England, and America—may be explained in part by its antiquity, by his sense that Italy was more thoroughly layered with history and tradition than any other land. The burden of history in Rome was immense. "And now as for this Rome," he wrote in 1869, "it seems a sadly vain ambition to attempt to give you any idea of its affect upon the mind. It's so vast, so heavy, so multitudinous. . . . At every step in some guise or other History confronts you."[11] Similarly, in 1873 he wrote from Rome that "what one feels and inhales, naturally and easily, with every breath, is the importunate influence of tradition of *every* kind—the influence of an atmosphere electrically charged with historic intimations and whisperings. Practical profit from so huge an influence as this must disengage itself shortly."[12] In *The Golden Bowl* James records, in his account of Prince Amerigo, the consequence of seeing oneself as the inheritor and vessel of such a deep and thickly accreted history: "There are two parts of me," Amerigo tells Maggie; "[o]ne is made up of the history, the doings, the marriages, the crimes, the follies, the boundless *bêtises* of other people. . . . But there's another part, very much smaller doubtless, which, such as it is, represents my single self, the unknown, the unimportant—unimportant save to *you*—personal quality."[13] Amerigo's history constitutes the larger part of his identity; his traditions—familial, cultural, religious, and national—form and inform a highly evolved and characteristically passive selfhood, and the smaller portion, "the personal quantity," is nearly crowded out.[14] He himself illustrates the contrast between this historical and impersonal formation of identity and the American character in his witty comparison of himself to "a chicken, at best, chopped up and smothered in sauce; cooked down as a *crème de volaille*, with half the parts left out" and of Adam Verver to "the natural fowl running about the *bassecour*. His feathers," the Prince tells Maggie, "his movements, his sounds—those are the parts that, with me, are left out."[15] Amerigo's being is cooked; Adam's is not merely raw, but alive and squawking. The personal element of identity in the Italian prince is submerged and belittled by the impersonal, historical, conventional elements, whereas the American sense of identity is absolutely personal, unconditioned by custom, usage, and the past. This American sense of the uncompromised autonomy of the self is most purely expressed, perhaps, by Isabel Archer when she tells Madame Merle, "I don't know whether I succeed in expressing myself, but I know that nothing else expresses me" (*PL*, 398). James knew, finally, that English and French social relations were governed by a myriad of conventions absent in American life, but Italy, by virtue of its greater antiquity, by virtue of its longer and more intricately entangled political, social, familial, and religious history, was the epitome of European convention, and London and Paris, by contrast with Rome, seemed to him thoroughly modern metropolises.[16]

Daisy Miller's defiance of social convention begins in the first half of her story, in Vevey. Even in that gayer, freer atmosphere, resembling, as James notes at the outset, "an American watering-place," Daisy's behavior draws the disapprobation of Winterbourne's aunt, Mrs. Costello, and the puzzlement of Winterbourne himself.[17] Daisy enters into conversation with Winterbourne without formal introduction or the presence of a chaperone; she extracts from him an offer to take her rowing by moonlight (which she declines to do once she has gotten everyone—the courier Eugenio and her mother, who disapprove, and Winterbourne, who would like to go out in the boat with her—to make the fuss for which she has been hoping); and she agrees to go to the Castle of Chillon alone with Winterbourne. At Vevey, hearing that Daisy has agreed to this last expedition, Mrs. Costello pronounces her "a dreadful girl" (*DM* I, 688). This phrase is revised in the New York Edition to "a horror," which Frederick Newberry plausibly suggests is misheard by Winterbourne as "a whore."[18] We may suppose that Daisy is scarcely aware of any violations of propriety in Vevey, but in the darker, more repressive atmosphere of Rome, when she has scandalized the American community by walking the streets unchaperoned with the presumed Italian fortune hunter Giovanelli (and one notes, incidentally, that her street walking is germane to the implicit imputation that she is a whore), she is apprised of her transgressions by Mrs. Walker. When Mrs. Walker urges Daisy to leave Giovanelli, with whom Daisy has been walking on the Pincio, and to get into Mrs. Walker's carriage lest Daisy be "thought a very reckless girl," Daisy refuses, declaring that "[i]f this is improper . . . then I am all improper, and you must give me up."[19] Daisy, like Isabel, is an "Americana," a young woman who embodies the American ideals of social independence and personal liberty. How much Isabel, in the early stages of her adventure, resembles Daisy in this regard may be suggested by the *Daisy Miller*-like dialogue with which

chapter 7 of *The Portrait of a Lady* closes. "You can't," Mrs. Touchett says, "stay alone with the gentlemen. You are not—you are not
at Albany, my dear." "I wish I were," Isabel replies, and she goes
on to say that "I always want to know the things one shouldn't do."
"So as to do them?" Mrs. Touchett asks. "So as to choose," says
Isabel, reserving to herself the same right that Daisy exercises on
the Pincio (*PL*, 258–59).

James provides Daisy Miller with settings that emphasize that
hers is the struggle of an innocent and unquestioning devotion to
personal liberty against oppressive authority. Byron had firmly established for the nineteenth-century mind the status of the Castle
of Chillon and of the Colosseum as shrines to freedom. Motley
Deakin provides an excellent account of the meaning of these places,
and of other locales in *Daisy Miller*, for James's readers of 1879. The
thematic pattern that Deakin reads in the settings of the tale seems
complete, he observes, when Daisy "is buried in that cemetary
fitting for those who 'protest,' a cemetary appropriately small and
hemmed in by an old, imperial Roman wall equally symbolic of the
forces the rebel confronts."[20] As we recall, the role assigned the two
Italian characters in *Daisy Miller*, Eugenio and Giovannelli, is very
small. James concentrates his attention on American society in
Rome, which he had condemned in a letter of 1873 as "a very poor
affair indeed. Limited and isolated, without relations with the place,
or much serious appreciation of it, it tumbles back upon itself and
finds itself of meagre substance."[21] In the tale, the ostracism to
which the American community in Rome subjects Daisy is designed
to impress Italian society by the completeness with which the
Americans could and would mimic European conventions, doing in
Rome as the Romans do. "They ceased to invite her," James writes,
"and they intimated that they desired to express to observant Euro-
peans the great truth that, though Miss Daisy Miller was a young
American lady, her behavior was not representative—was regarded
by her compatriots as abnormal" (*DM* II, 61). It is of course a great,
and oft-noted, irony that the one character who appreciates and
attests to Daisy's unsullied innocence is the "subtle Roman" Giovanelli (*DM* II, 67). Only when Giovanelli assures Winterbourne that
Daisy was "the most innocent" young lady he ever saw does Winterbourne realize how erroneously he has judged her and how much

he has justified his aunt's earlier observation that he has "lived too long in foreign parts" (*DM* II, 67). For Winterbourne, too, in a curious way, is a victim of convention—he fails to see Daisy as she is because he is incapable of breaking out of the conventional categories with which he ceaselessly tries to interpret her. All of my quotations from *Daisy Miller* are drawn from the original text in the *Cornhill*, but I would observe that in the New York Edition revision James provided Winterbourne for the first time with a middle name, Forsyth, and that this provision of a flower name to match Annie P. Miller's *Daisy* may point to the blighting of both of their natures by the deathly chill of convention. Although Winterbourne sees in the end that he has misread Daisy—"I was booked to make a mistake," he tells his aunt (*DM* II, 67)—there is no evidence that he recognizes his own possible role in Daisy's death. His declaration to her at the Colosseum that "it makes very little difference whether you are engaged or not," elicits Daisy's dismal reply: " 'I don't care,' said Daisy, in a little strange tone, 'whether I have Roman fever or not!' " (*DM* II, 65). Her statement makes it plausible for us to see a willed element in Daisy's succumbing to the fever, akin to the willed element in Milly Theale's death in Venice: in both cases there is undoubtedly a lethal disease, but in both the doomed young ladies effectively turn their faces to the wall because of the profound injustice of the wounds that hoped-for lovers have dealt to their self-esteem.

Daisy Miller is clearly a case of the abuse of innocence. In Isabel Archer we have a far richer, more complex case, one entailing not only the abuse but also the disabuse of the innocence of an Americana. Of special interest is that the tragedy of Isabel's life and the triumph of her at last seeing through her earlier delusions are intimately entangled with the machinations of two Italianate Americans, Madame Merle and Gilbert Osmond, and with Italy itself, particularly with Rome.

From the very first time that he is mentioned, Osmond is associated with his adopted land. When they are still in England, at Gardencourt, Madame Merle mentions Osmond to Isabel as an example of American men who have no occupation abroad: "The worst case, I think, is a friend of mine, a countryman of ours, who lives in Italy (where he also was brought before he knew better),

and who is one of the most delightful men I know. Some day you
must know him. I will bring you together, and then you will see
what I mean. He is Gilbert Osmond—he lives in Italy; that is all
one can say about him" (*PL*, 393). Some time later, before Isabel
meets Osmond but after she has been installed with her Aunt
Touchett in Florence, Madame Merle gives her to understand that
"[o]ne should not attempt to live in Italy without making a friend
of Gilbert Osmond, who knew more about the country than any one
except two or three German professors" (*PL*, 442). Osmond is linked
with Italian figures, notably when his sister, the Countess Gemini,
lists his "favourite subjects" for Isabel: "One is Machiavelli, the
other is Vittoria Colonna, the next is Metastasio" (*PL*, 457). When
he tells Isabel of the "two or three people in the world I envied,"
the ascending order takes him from "the Emperor of Russia" to "the
Sultan of Turkey" to "the Pope of Rome" (*PL*, 463). When Osmond
joins Isabel on her first "pilgrimage to Rome" (*PL*, 481), moreover,
he finds himself "happier than he had perhaps ever been in his life,"
and he celebrates his mood in a "correct and ingenious" sonnet
titled "Rome Revisited," which he presents "to Isabel, explaining
to her that it was an Italian fashion to commemorate the pleasant
occasions of life by a tribute to the muse" (*PL*, 502). When Isabel
has returned from her tour of the East and she and Osmond are
about to be married, he likens their future to "the latter half of an
Italian day—with a golden haze, and the shadows just lengthening,
and that divine delicacy in the light, the air, the landscape, which
I have loved all my life, and which you love to-day." Osmond
determines that, once married, they will live in Italy, for "It was in
Italy that they had met, Italy had been a party to their first impressions of each other, and Italy should be a party to their happiness"
(*PL*, 553–54). As for Madame Merle, Osmond's partner in villainy,
her Italian associations are also strong, though they are less heavily
emphasized in the text. Although she is almost a professional house
guest of her wealthier friends, her home base is her apartment "on
the third floor of an old Roman house" (*PL*, 559). After the Countess
Gemini names Machiavelli, Vittoria Colonna, and Metastasio as
Osmond's favorite subjects, she replies to Madame Merle's statement that "with me . . . Osmond is never so historical" by exclaiming, "you yourself are Machiavelli—you yourself are Vittoria Co-

lonna!" (PL, 457). Finally, early on, long before Isabel glimpses the
dark side of either of these old lovers, Osmond and Madame Merle,
she comes to associate both of them with convention. At Gardencourt, during the early stages of Isabel's friendship with Madame
Merle, Isabel decides that if "she had a fault, it was that she was
not natural . . . her nature had been too much overlaid by custom
and her angles too much smoothed. She had become too flexible,
too supple; she was too finished, too civilised." Even so, Isabel
makes allowances, affirming to herself that Madame Merle's "nature spoke none the less in her behaviour because it spoke a conventional language. 'What is language at all but a convention?' said
Isabel" (PL, 388). And Osmond, just after he has first declared his
love for Isabel, toward the end of that initial Roman "pilgrimage,"
tells her that she "will discover what a worship I have for propriety." "You are not conventional?" Isabel asks. And Osmond replies,
"No, I am not conventional: I am convention itself" (PL, 511). In
retrospect, when we assess the ruin of Isabel's happiness as the
result of her having been "ground in the very mill of the conventional," these become ominous words indeed!

Isabel Archer enters Italy with her American idealism and innocence unblemished—and with her misplaced pride and untenable
self-reliance never having been seriously challenged. Her initial
responses to the land are the stock responses of the nineteenth-
century American traveler. They bear, in addition, a striking resemblance to some of the first responses to Italy recorded by Henry
James in his letters home, though Isabel is more idealistic than
James was and more sentimental. At San Remo, she finds herself on
"the threshold of Italy—the gate of admirations. Italy, as yet imperfectly seen and felt, stretched before her as a land of promise, a
land in which a love of the beautiful might be comforted by endless
knowledge" (PL, 420). In Florence for the first time, "She performed
all those acts of mental prostration in which, on a first visit to Italy,
youth and enthusiasm so freely indulge; she felt her heart beat in
the presence of immortal genius, and knew the sweetness of rising
tears in eyes to which faded fresco and darkened marble grew dim"
(PL, 444). Her first response to Rome, like James's, is to take it as a
massive infusion of history: "She had always been fond of history,
and here was history in the stones of the street and the atoms of

sunshine. She had an imagination that kindled at the mention of great deeds, and wherever she turned some great deed had been acted" (*PL*, 485).

These responses to Florence and Rome bespeak the noble temper of Isabel Archer's innocence. But no sooner does Isabel enter Italy than James begins to let us in on the forces at work to despoil her of that innocence. Isabel's first Italian stop is at San Remo in chapter 20. In chapter 21, we advance to Florence; the first paragraph describes Osmond's portentous house, with its "incommunicative character. It was the mask of the house; it was not its face" (*PL*, 423). We move in this chapter from Osmond's discussion with the nuns who have brought Pansy home from the convent in Rome to his conversation with Madame Merle, in the course of which she induces him to turn his attention to Isabel Archer with the assurance that "there is no doubt whatever about her fortune" (*PL*, 439). No less chilling, I think, is what I would mark as the first symptom of the decline of Isabel's innocence and freshness, as well as the first unwitting setting of the pattern for her relations with Osmond. Isabel finds herself very tired in the course of her first visit to Osmond's house in Florence, and we read that

[a] part of Isabel's fatigue came from the effort to appear as intelligent as she believed Madame Merle had described her, and from the fear (very unusual with her) of exposing—not her ignorance; for that she cared comparatively little—but her possible grossness of perception. It would have annoyed her to express a liking for something which her host, in his superior enlightenment, would think she ought not to like; or to pass by something at which the truly initiated mind would arrest itself. She was very careful, therefore, as to what she said, as to what she noticed or failed to notice—more careful than she had ever been before (*PL*, 461).

Surely for Isabel, as for Daisy before her, the disposition to speak freely and unselfconsciously has been a hallmark of her innocence; her new fear of expressing herself freely, as soon as she enters into social relations with Osmond, is the beginning of her fall from innocence.

What the alert reader, or rereader, must apprehend at this juncture is that Isabel's guardedness about what she says in front of Osmond is the first step toward the inexpressiveness that is one of Osmond's own most salient and sinister traits. We have noticed that the front of his house is like a mask. We know that the role he plays, that of a man of supreme taste indifferent to the vulgar world, is a pose, masking his obsession with the impression he makes on others. As he says to Pansy early on, with unintended irony, and as his name, too, indicates, he is very much "of the world" (*PL*, 431). Indeed, connected with his devotion to propriety and his determination to uphold appearances is a systematic repression of the outward signs of his inner being, a methodical concealment of his intentions, thoughts, and feelings. This concealment is connected with his pride and also with many of the Italianate aspects of his character, notably his apparent exaggeration of the fatalistic passivity James associated with Italy and embodied later in Prince Amerigo and his Borgia-like, Machiavellian penchant for intrigue and duplicity. Even his "Italian" fatalism is a mask, for, as Maves points out, Osmond has not, despite his claims, been "content to lead a quiet life" and to "take things as they came" (*PL*, 455); "his discontent," says Maves, "has turned him vicious."[22] A good example of the emphasis James lays on Osmond's inexpressiveness occurs in the description of the "vacant . . . countenance" with which he takes Warburton's announcement of his second departure from Rome, which dashes Osmond's hopes that the English lord will ask for Pansy's hand in marriage: "It was indeed a part of Osmond's cleverness that he could look consummately uncompromised. His present appearance, however, was not a confession of disappointment; it was simply a part of Osmond's habitual system, which was to be inexpressive exactly in proportion as he was really intent" (*PL*, 683). This trait, furthermore, is shared by Madame Merle, who cultivates the appearance of propriety as assiduously as Osmond: "Her great idea," the Countess Gemini tells Isabel, "has been to be tremendously irreproachable—a kind of full-blown lily —the incarnation of propriety. She has always worshipped that god" (*PL*, 753). The only break in Madame Merle's maintenance of the inexpressive mask comes when she realizes that Isabel has discovered how Madame Merle and Osmond have deceived and used her, and that break lasts only for a "moment. Then the conscious stream of her perfect manner gathered itself again and flowed on as smoothly as might be to the end" (*PL*, 759).

As I have already indicated, Isabel begins to shed her innocence, and her illusions, very early in her relation with Osmond. For instance, in the same paragraph that we are told that she and Osmond are determined to live in Italy, we read that her old "desire for unlimited expansion had been succeeded in her mind by the sense that life was vacant without some private duty which gathered one's energies to a point" (PL, 554). Alas, the "private duty" Isabel envisions is the conventional Victorian duty of wifehood: "There was explanation enough in the fact that he was her lover, her own, and that she was able to be of use to him" (PL, 554). How bitterly ironic this last phrase appears once we have digested with Isabel the knowledge that she is a woman who, as her sister-in-law puts it, "has been made use of" (PL, 754), or who, in Isabel's own mental image, has been "a dull un-reverenced tool" (PL, 759)! Isabel begins to harden into a social mask. When we meet Isabel after her marriage, in 1876—ironically, the centennial year of American independence—we see that the independent American girl has vanished, or, rather, been vanquished: as Ralph puts it to himself, "[t]he free, keen girl had become quite another person; what he saw was the fine lady who was supposed to represent something. . . . she represented Gilbert Osmond" (PL, 597). When Rosier sees her "framed in the gilded doorway" the first time the novel takes us to one of the Osmonds' Thursday soirées, she strikes him "as the picture of a gracious lady" (PL, 570). Isabel had once defended Osmond against Ralph's attacks by avowing that he "is simply a man—he is not a proprietor" (PL, 550), but as the "picture of a gracious lady" who "represented Gilbert Osmond" she has become his property just as the portrait displayed in "My Last Duchess" is the duke's.

As Osmond's property, Isabel becomes more and more like him in her guardedness, particularly and most poignantly in relation to Ralph, from whom she feels she must conceal her unhappiness. The final dialogue between Ralph and Isabel, which Joseph Wiesenfarth has aptly called the "great love scene" of the novel, comes as an enormous relief because in it Isabel tells Ralph the truth about her marriage, because "the only knowledge that was not pure anguish" was that at last "they were looking at the truth together" (PL, 785).[23] Isabel practices the same policy of concealment with Caspar Goodwood, and the images with which he takes this in strike me as particularly interesting. He finds her "imperturbable, impenetrable" (*PL*, 713), and he laments to her, "I can't understand, I can't penetrate you! . . . I am told you are unhappy. . . . But you yourself say you are happy, and you are somehow so still, so smooth [in the New York Edition, James adds "so hard" after "so still, so smooth"]. You are completely changed. You conceal everything. . . . You are perfectly inscrutable, and that's what makes me think you have something to hide" (*PL*, 717). I submit that this imagery of the smooth, the hard, and the impenetrable associates Isabel with Madame Merle, whose own icon for herself is the chipped porcelain cup kept from sight in the cupboard (*PL*, 389). Moreover, Caspar Goodwood's impression of Isabel is remarkably like the metaphoric pagoda that figures Maggie Verver's situation at the beginning of the second half of *The Golden Bowl*. The pagoda is plated with "hard bright porcelain," and, indeed, virtually every term used in Caspar's images of Isabel's inexpressiveness—*smooth, impenetrable, inscrutable*, and the New York Edition *hard*—appears in the opening paragraph of volume 2 of *The Golden Bowl*.[24] The pagoda figures the arrangement of the lives of two couples, Maggie and Amerigo, and Charlotte and Adam; what is inscrutable to Maggie, what she cannot penetrate, is the truth of the relations between Charlotte and Amerigo, whose as yet unconsummated adultery is developing behind the smooth, hard facade of their perfect manners, their exquisite behavior, their mastery, in short, of all of the conventions that their positions in life entail and that their training as Italianate American and as Roman prince make easy for them. To master this situation herself, Maggie is forced to become, like Isabel before her, a wearer of masks, an inexpressive and even duplicitous mistress of shades; she is forced to play parts and to learn the rules of the intricate games that seem second nature to the others.

Poor Isabel! She had dreamed of "infinite expansion" and had avowed that only she expressed herself, that her clothes most certainly did not do so—though she had no rejoinder to Madame Merle's question, "Should you prefer to go without them?" (*PL*, 398) —and yet in the end she is thickly, almost stiflingly, muffled in the "social drapery" she finds lacking in Caspar Goodwood's self-presentation (*PL*, 691). As Isabel is more and more "ground in the very mill of the conventional," the image of Rome darkens. We recall

her realization that her dwelling—Osmond's mind and metonymi-
cally the Palazzo Roccanera—had become "the house of darkness,
the house of dumbness, the house of suffocation" (PL, 633), and this
puts us in mind of some of her other impressions of Italian buildings,
of her sense of Mrs. Touchett's Florentine Palazzo Crescentini "as a
sort of prison" (PL, 444), and of her view of Pansy's convent, when
Isabel makes her last visit there, as like one of the "great penal
establishments" the effect of which is "the surrender of a personality" (PL, 761). (I want to note, incidentally, in view of Osmond's
use of the socializing, normalizing power of the convent to bring
Pansy to heel and also in view of my emphasis on the tyranny of
convention in The Portrait of a Lady, that the words convent and
convention are etymologically identical). Warburton, rebuffed by
Isabel, walks "through the tortuous, tragical streets of Rome" (PL,
497–98), and Rosier thinks of the Palazzo Roccanera as "a dungeon"
where Pansy is "immured in a kind of domestic fortress, which bore
a stern old Roman name, which smelt of historic deeds, of crime
and craft and violence" (PL, 566). Isabel herself comes to think of
the Roman world around her as atuned to her own pain: "in a world
of ruins the ruin of her happiness seemed a less unnatural catastro-
phe. . . . She had become deeply, tenderly acquainted with Rome.
. . . she had grown to think of it chiefly as the place where people
had suffered" (PL, 723–24). Finally, at Gardencourt, "at a distance,
beyond its spell, she thought with a kind of spiritual shudder of
Rome" (PL, 789). And yet, as Henrietta Stackpole tells Caspar
Goodwood on the last page of the novel, Isabel has "started for
Rome" (PL, 800).

I used to think, as I have argued elsewhere, that Isabel's return
to Rome and to Osmond "is a return on a higher level to her original
idealism," and I also concurred in the widespread view that Isabel
returns in large part to help Pansy.[25] I cannot utterly dismiss this
old "romantic" and affirmative reading of the novel, or my belief
that James did intend for his readers to maintain to the end the
view of Isabel "more tender" than "scientific" that he recommends
in chapter 6 (PL, 242), but I must confess that my present sense of
the novel has darkened like Isabel Archer's vision of Rome. Perhaps
I should add that this darkening effect may be the result of my
reliance on the 1881 text for the present discussion, whereas my

previous, more affirmative reading was based on the revision of 1907. Perhaps, too, the rise of feminist criticism has made it harder to argue that Isabel's return to a psychologically abusive husband is uplifting. In any case, I am led to wonder whether Isabel's old desire that "[h]er life should always be in harmony with the most pleasing impression she should produce" (*PL*, 242) does not make it impossible for her to break with convention, even though her life with Osmond is a species of death-in-life. The return to Rome seems to me particularly ominous as an embrace of death-in-life in view of a parallel I have noted between the seductive vision Isabel has of death as "a cool bath in a marble tank, in a darkened chamber, in a hot land" (*PL*, 769) and Henry James's first letter home from Italy, of 31 August 1869, in which he writes, "I had a cold bath in a great marble tank."[26] Isabel's image of easeful death and James's report of his first night in Italy are disturbingly close here. At the same time, I am more than ever impressed with the power and beauty of this great novel. Doubtless James's knowledge of Italy was not as superficial as Hawthorne's, and what he made of it as the setting for *Daisy Miller* and, far more impressively, for *The Portrait of a Lady*, amply disproves his own precept that the Italian fiction of non-Italian writers would inevitably be "second-rate and imperfect."

Notes

1. Henry James, *Hawthorne*, in *Literary Criticism: Essays on Literature, American Writers, English Writers*, ed. Leon Edel and Mark Wilson (New York: Library of America, 1984), 445.
2. *Henry James Letters, vol. 1, 1843–1875*, ed. Leon Edel (Cambridge: Harvard University Press, 1975), 137.
3. *Henry James Letters, vol. 2, 1875–1883*, ed. Leon Edel (Cambridge: Harvard University Press, 1975), 141.
4. *Letters*, 1: 137.
5. *Literary Criticism: Essays on Literature, American Writers, English Writers*, 1011.
6. Ross Posnock, *Henry James and Robert Browning* (Austin: University of Texas Press, 1986); William E. Buckler, "Rereading Henry James Rereading Robert Browning: 'The Novel in *The Ring and the Book*.' " *Henry James Review* 5 (1984): 135–45.
7. See Sandra Djwa, "*Ut Pictura Poesis*: The Making of a Lady," *Henry James Review* 7.2–3 (1986): 72–85, especially pp. 80–81.

8. Henry James, *The Portrait of a Lady*, in *Novels 1881–1886: Washington Square, The Portrait of a Lady, The Bostonians*, ed. William T. Stafford (New York: Library of America, 1985), 501, hereafter cited parenthetically as *PL*. This edition reprints the Houghton Mifflin text of 1881.

9. Adeline R. Tintner, "Pater in *The Portrait of a Lady* and *The Golden Bowl*, Including Some Unpublished Henry James Letters," *Henry James Review* 3 (1982):85.

10. *The Complete Notebooks of Henry James*, ed. Leon Edel and Lyall H. Powers (New York: Oxford University Press, 1987), 13.

11. *Letters*, 1:162–63.

12. Ibid., 324.

13. Henry James, *The Golden Bowl*, vols. 23 and 24 of *The Novels and Tales of Henry James* (New York: Scribners, 1909), 1:9.

14. For a helpful discussion of Amerigo's passivity, see Carl Maves, *Sensuous Pessimism: Italy in the Works of Henry James* (Bloomington: Indiana University Press, 1973), 138–39.

15. *The Golden Bowl*, 1:8.

16. See, for example, *Letters*, 1:323, where James writes from Rome "that in coming here with a mindful of Parisian memories, one seems to have turned one's back on modern civilization."

17. Henry James, *Daisy Miller: A Study, Cornhill Magazine* 37 (1878):678, hereafter cited parenthetically as *DM* I.

18. *Daisy Miller*, in *The Novels and Tales of Henry James* (New York: Charles Scribner's Sons, 1909), 18:25; Frederick Newberry, "A Note on the Horror in James's Revision of *Daisy Miller*," *Henry James Review* 3 (1982):229–32.

19. Henry James, *Daisy Miller: A Study, Cornhill Magazine* 38 (1878):53, hereafter cited parenthetically as *DM* II.

20. Motley Deakin, "Two Studies of *Daisy Miller*," *Henry James Review* 5 (1983):16; all of the first of Deakins's two studies, "Daisy Miller and Baedeker," pp. 2–17, is germane to the present discussion.

21. *Letters*, 1:331.

22. Maves, *Sensuous Pessimism*, 75.

23. Joseph Wiesenfarth, "A Woman in *The Portrait of a Lady*," *Henry James Review* 7.2–3 (1986):24.

24. *The Golden Bowl*, 2:3.

25. Daniel Mark Fogel, *Henry James and the Structure of the Romantic Imagination* (Baton Rouge: Louisiana State University Press, 1981), 54.

26. *Letters*, 1:129.

SIX *Rococo Venice, Pietro Longhi, and Henry James*

ADELINE R. TINTNER

LTHOUGH it did not become intense until after 1900, James had a real interest in Venetian rococo art of the eighteenth century as we can see by his inclusion of it in his fiction. We all know about his presentation of the High Renaissance figures of Venetian painting, Titian, Veronese, and Tintoretto. They are pervasive throughout his tales and novels, beginning with the 1870 guidebook story, "Travelling Companions," climaxing with the Titian *Young Man with the Torn Glove* in *The Ambassadors* (1903), and tapering off to the Titian reference in "The Velvet Glove" of 1909. Even the unfinished *Ivory Tower* has an episode in Dresden where the Venetian Renaissance masters play an important role in the drama. The eighteenth century punctures the stories only every now and then, but in a very important way that shows that James enjoyed and respected it when few others did. One must remember that James had avant-garde taste in art. He was the first critic in England to appreciate Burne-Jones. His 1877 appraisal is still quoted in books on that artist. He introduced Vermeer into *The Outcry* even before Proust did in *A la recherche du temps perdu* and his focusing on a portrait by Bronzino in *The Wings of the Dove* brought the reader's attention not to a High Renaissance master but to a master of mannerism. Bronzino was practically unknown in England at this time and it was only during the year when *The Wings of the Dove* was published, 1902, that the first monograph on Bronzino in English appeared. James had carefully chosen this painter of the courts with his icy, greenish palette to personify his own princess, Milly, condemned to early death. In *The Golden Bowl* Verver is shown to be adventurous as a collector, for at that time his association of Bernardino Luini with Prince Amerigo, hardly noticeable today, showed again an advanced taste, since Luini was at that time confused with Leonardo da Vinci. The one canvas by Luini then in the National Gallery in London was attributed to da Vinci, and this was before James knew Berenson.

But Luini and Bronzino did not fare as badly as did Italian rococo art (or any rococo art) which is finally getting accepted today, although, in the introduction to her recently published book on Fragonard, Dore Ashton claims that she always runs past the eighteenth-century wing of art in galleries and museums and is only making an exception for Fragonard, an artist more or less ignored until today. But James never shared this extreme antipathy.

The best way to dramatize the change in attitude to the rococo is to compare the entry under rococo in three different editions of the *Encyclopedia Britannica*. In the edition of 1911 we read "Everything, indeed, in the Rococo manner is involved and tortured. A debased style, at best essentially fantastic and bizarre, it ended in extravagance and decadence. The word came eventually to be applied to anything extravagant, flamboyant or tasteless in art or literature. The very exuberance of the rococo form is, indeed, the negation of art which is based on restraint. There is something essentially Italian in the bravura upon which the style depends, yet Italy has produced some of the worst examples."

Twenty years later, in 1932, the Encyclopedia has changed its point of view somewhat. The style is no longer called debased and its basis in rock work is "one of the features of its absolute freedom and irregularity of rhythm, the twisted curves of a shell being the standard. . . . For the grave and pompous style of Louis XIV, the rococo substitutes playfulness and exquisite gracefulness and charm."

In the 1967 edition the tide has changed yet again. "The design of rococo might be shaped in asymmetric fashion, but it always was balanced and closely related to the overall pattern." There is now a bibliography of a few books to refer to, notably Fiske Kimball's, and the catalog of the Munich rococo show of 1958, but what is oddly ignored is the one book that had been published on Venetian painting of the eighteen century, Michael Levey's of 1959. In it, however, Levey feels Pietro Longhi has recently been exaggerated in value,

that he was a lazy painter of a lazy people, which clearly shows
that he does not know how to read a Longhi picture. As so many
others have had their strategy of viewing ruined by impressionism
and the need to step away from a picture, he never gets close
enough to understand a Longhi. One has to get on top of it.

Henry James's appreciation of Venice in its eighteenth-century
manifestation was a gradual discovery.[1] Eighteenth-century Italian
art of any region was not highly esteemed by Ruskin, who determined what the cultivated Anglo-American tourist was to admire
in Europe. "Travelling Companions" (1870), a short story, was the
first fictional fruit of the solo trip to Italy James took in 1869 and it
proceeds to follow closely the monuments that Murray, the guidebook of the time, decided one should look at. It is in Venice that
Mr. Brooke declares his love for the heroine, and it is before *Sacred
and Profane Love* by Titian, the master of Venetian painting, that
they plight their troth. However, the eighteenth-century ambiance
of Venice enters the story in a crucial way through the imagination
of George Sand, whom James in his youth admired greatly. Even
before the heroine has been compromised by missing the train back
to Venice, so that the two young people are forced to remain unchaperoned overnight in Padua, she mentions one morning how she
has been reading George Sand's *La Dernière Aldini*.[2] The first part of
that novel takes place in the last years of the eighteenth century
and the plight of its hero and heroine is exactly that of James's
couple. Countess Aldini and her talented low-born gondolier have
declared their love on the Lido sands among the Jewish tombs, as
had James's couple, and they stay out all night as innocently as the
American pair had. The next day they are believed to have spent a
night making love, as Charlotte Evans's father believed his daughter
had. Sand's novel is filled with the customs of Venetian eighteenth-
century life relevant to James's tale, for which reason he undoubtedly mentioned it.

Venice then ceases to interest James in print for over ten years,[3]
although in 1872 he wrote a travel sketch about the city included in
his 1875 *Transatlantic Sketches*, a nonfictional recapitulation of the
tour made in "Travelling Companions." Even before his first long
essay on Venice in 1882, in which the life of the city and the

pictures of Tintoretto excited James, he had been exposed to the
Venice of the eighteenth century without leaving England. Through
the furnishings of that period it enters his consciousness when he is
first invited to Mentmore in 1880. This was the country house of
Lord Rosebery, who had inherited through his wife Baron Meyer de
Rothschild's house, furnishings, and huge fortune, a house at which
James was to be a frequent guest during the 1880s. Writing to his
mother while there as a weekend guest, James calls the place a
"huge modern palace, filled with wonderful objects. . . . All of them
are precious and many are exquisite. They are at afternoon tea in a
vast gorgeous hall . . . and the chairs are all golden thrones, belonging to the ancient Doges of Venice."[4] These "thrones," made around
1700, were owned by eighteenth-century doges, and the huge lusters
or lanterns that contribute to the "glittering scene" came from the
eighteenth-century Bucentaur, the barge of the doges.[5] The young
James is reminded of "Paul Veronese's pictures," but the furnishings
are those of the eighteenth century. The entire house was filled
with wonderful eighteenth-century chairs made somewhat later
than the set of early eighteenth-century great armchairs.[6] He mentions "the gilded lanterns," so focal an element in the great hall, in
1887 when, on another visit to Mentmore, he writes about them to
Charles Eliot Norton.[7] It was during his stay there that he learned
to respond to the art and furnishings of that period. In addition,
Mentmore also had acquired a Guardi "view" painting, which am-
plified its Venetian *settecento* note.

In 1884 James had increased his Rothschild acquaintance to include Baron Ferdinand de Rothschild, the Cambridge chum of Edward VII and builder of Waddesdon Manor, a house not far from
Mentmore in Aylesbury, Sussex, which was to become a monument
to French art of royal provenance from the prerevolutionary period.[8] But in the midst of these exquisite pieces of French eighteenth-century art the main gallery leading from the dining areas
to the social rooms is dominated by two huge "view" paintings by
Francesco Guardi, a painter whom James as a young art critic had
called the "Tiepolo of landscape." However, he had never seen very
large and important Guardis of the stature of the Waddesdon "views,"
The Bacino di S. Marco with the Molo and the Doge's Palace, a
view taken from San Giorgio Maggiore and *The Bacino di S. Marco*

with S. Giorgio and the Salute. Neither great view encompasses the
Grand Canal. That is left for James to do himself in a remarkable
essay written in 1892 and reprinted in *The Great Streets of the World*
the same year, for in it he adopts his point of view from the "view"
painters. The view or Veduta painters of Italy painted for aristocrats
on their grand tour. The view paintings were dispersed in England,
Poland, etc., but the view itself was Venice. In a letter James wrote
in 1902 to the Curtises, the owners of the Palazzo Barbaro, when
the campanile fell in the Piazza, he said, "for the Campanile *WAS*
Venice . . . the great chiselled and embossed cup of the Piazza . . .
the Campanile of centuries of art, of all *THE* Views, the great
uplifted identifying head. It's a decapitation. . . . I advocate re-
building . . . to bring the view back to the picture—*the* picture."[9]
Venice was *the* view above all.[10]

The stance of the narrator, which now becomes so pervasive in
his fiction, James seems to have learned after writing his 1882 essay
about Venice. "When I hear the magical name I have written above
these pages . . . I simply see a narrow canal in the heart of the
city."[11] In the National Gallery he saw four Guardis concentrating
on views of Venice from the canal and the bay. His gondola became
his "point of view," the point of view during his trip of the spring.
His interest in Venetian things aroused by his 1882 travel piece, he
buys during the next year an eight-volume set of the *Mémoires de
Jacques Casanova de Seingalt*[12] and his signature appears in volume
one, "H. James, New York. August 21st 1883." He sailed from New
York on 22 August "and this suggests," writes Leon Edel in a note
to a one-time owner of the book, Lord David Eccles, "that he took
aboard with him the eight volumes of Casanova perhaps for ship-
board reading."[13] The books have all been handled frequently and
indicate more than one reading of each.[14]

The important Venetian experience had begun inauspiciously in
February 1887, when James was a guest at Mrs. Katherine DeKay
Bronson's Ca'Alvisi. Her small house on the Grand Canal, right
opposite Santa Maria della Salute, had an attached wing that had
sheltered Robert Browning, as well as an improvised theatre where
Mrs. Bronson used to put on plays, living a life which seemed to
revive the time of Goldoni and Casanova a hundred years later.
(James had seen at least one Goldoni play on an earlier trip.)

There, having contracted jaundice, he was confined for sixteen stormy days,[15] and later as a guest of the Daniel Curtises in the Palazzo Barbaro he was penetrated by the art and ambiance of the Venetian rococo period through the impact that the house had on him. The effect on James's fiction of the "flicker of the canal" on its "gilded roof" had to wait for *The Wings of the Dove* (1902), but the house's garden, cultivated by his host, Daniel Curtis, was to play an important part in the plot of *The Aspern Papers* (1888), that tale of a "publishing scoundrel" who competes with Casanova in an intrigue to obtain possession of the papers of a famous American romantic poet still kept by his aged mistress. And Casanova's presence is maneuvered by James into his tale through the effect that the gossip of Miss Bordereau's niece, Tita, has on the narrator. (She will later bargain for the papers that the narrator wants by asking, in Casanovian terms, for marriage in return. "If she had not been so decent," the narrator figures, "her references would have seemed to carry one back to the queer rococo Venice of Casanova."[16] This is the only literary reference in a tale in which every part has been carefully planned and where every name mentioned is redolent with history. Invited by the Curtises for ten days, his visit lasted five weeks, during which time he sopped up the *settecento*. The Barbaro's salons had originally contained four famous Tiepolos now dispersed through the museums of the world after having been sold in the 1870s[17] before James visited, but their spaces had been filled with work contemporary with Tiepolo. James wrote that he worked in a room with a "pompous Tiepolo" overhead but it was only a copy. He probably used the word in its first meaning—full of pomp, or magnificence, characteristic of a Tiepolo fresco. The last part of *The Aspern Papers* reflects in other ways the splendor of the Barbaro rooms with their "gilded roof" and gilded chairs which we can see not only in John Singer Sargent's academy picture (1899),[18] a painting of the Barbaro Salon, but also in photographs taken during the period James was there.

The last few pages of the tale are animated with two metaphors for the Piazza San Marco. There are at least six metaphors for the Piazza in James's fiction, each one slightly different while epitomizing the feelings James had for that magical corner of Venice. One of them is as follows: "the place has the character of an immense

collective apartment, in which the Piazza San Marco is the most
ornamented corner and palaces and churches, for the rest, play the
part of great divans of repose, tables of entertainment, expanses of
decoration." He follows that immediately with:

And somehow the splendid common domicile, familiar, domestic, resonant, also resembles a theatre, with actors clicking over bridges, and in
straggling processions, tripping along fondaments. As you sit in your gondola the footways that in certain parts edge the canals assume to the eye
the importance of a stage, meeting at the same angle, and the Venetian
figures, moving to and fro against the battered scenery of their little houses
of comedy, strike you as members of an endless dramatic troupe.[19]

Here appear the drawing room and the theater, the *loci* and *foci* of
his stay both at the Barbaro with all the splendor of its Tiepolo-
dominated interior and also at the Ca'Alvisi, home of theatrical
performances and of a hostess who lived the life of an eighteenth-
century Venetian, enjoying relations with members of all classes
that remind one constantly of Goldoni. They establish a familiarity
of the *settecento* in Venice which after 1891 James enfolds in three
short stories.

To return to *The Aspern Papers*, other signs of the eighteenth
century make themselves felt in the "green shade" that Juliana
Bordereau wears and the lacey "everlasting curtain that covered
half her face,"[20] approximating under different conditions the Venetian mask worn publicly during earlier times. The opening paragraph inaugurates the scheme of the narrating scholar, and the
world of Casanovian intrigue is immediately ushered in as the reader
is prepared for the extremes to which someone will go to obtain the
personal papers of a great poet. But the price demanded by the
American spinster, Tita, now thoroughly changed to a Venetian
intrigante, is one which even the "publishing scoundrel" is not
prepared to pay.

For James in 1882 "all Venice was both model and painter" and a
place where "Tintoret, Carpaccio and Bellini" were "the dazzling
Venetian trio," with Ruskin's blessing. But ten years later, in 1892,
when James makes his own great "view" painting of the Grand
Canal—improving, he must have thought, on the many different
versions of this theme at the hand of Canaletto (for he accuses him
at the end of the essay of falsifying one part of that view)—his

tastes have changed. James's appreciation of the eighteenth century, fostered by the Barbaro's interior, has made the Piazza San
Marco now suggestive of the great *settecento* art form, the opera.
"Piazza San Marco," he now writes, "is the lobby of the opera in
the intervals of the performance," and there is another painter he
almost shamefully announces that he now enjoys. In writing of his
visit to the Museo Civico, he admits that "of its miscellaneous
treasures I fear I may perhaps frivolously prefer the series of its
remarkable living Longhis, an illustration of manners more copious
than the celebrated Carpaccio, the two ladies with their little animals and their long sticks."[21] The Longhis are now in the Rezzonico,
once the home of Pen Browning through "his rich American wife"
—a quotation from a letter by James, who visited it.

We can almost date James's interest in Longhi. The latter, who
was at that time not appreciated at all, had been the subject of an
article by John Addington Symonds (with whom James was in
correspondence) which appeared in 1889 and was reprinted in Symonds's *The Memoirs of Carlo Gozzi* (1890), the eighteenth century
playwright for whom James has not left any evidence of interest.
But he had the book in his library probably as soon as it was
published. As Symonds wrote to a friend, this book "contains a
vivid picture of Venetian life in the last century . . . including a
criticism of the almost unknown painter Longhi."[22] These memoirs,
along with the Casanova volumes, would reinforce the interest
James took in Casanova. Since the piece on Longhi is one of the first
serious attempts in English to assess that painter's work, it prepared
James, when he came to write his Grand Canal article two years
later, for the abundance of Longhi's work in Venice. The very house
in which he was living, the Barbaro, contained a typical Longhi
scene. In it the somewhat sly manservant passing around cakes
to the little girls "visiting grandmama," as the picture is called,
is a brother to all the other manservants who appear in so many
Longhi pictures and who function as observers as well as servitors
within the painted world. He must have impressed James enough
to make him insert a clause in the revised version (1908) of *The Portrait of a Lady*, a year after his last trip to Venice, describing the
servant in the Osmond household when Isabel Archer first visits
there.

The shabby footboy, summoned by Pansy—*he might, tarnished as to livery and quaint as to type, have issued from some stray sketch of old-time manners, been 'put in' by the brush of a Longhi or a Goya*—had come out with a small table and placed it on the grass, and then had gone back and fetched the teatray; after which he had again disappeared, to return with a couple of chairs. Pansy had watched these proceedings with the deepest interest, standing with her small hands folded together upon the front of her scanty frock.[23]

The two little girls in the Curtis Longhi who are not looking at the footman, although the footman is looking with amusement at them, may have suggested to James the relation between little Pansy and her footman. Like the little girl to the left, her hands are folded on the front of her dress. Surely such footmen appear with amusing frequency in Longhi's small scenes, much more than in Goya's, whom James links with the Italian painter as if he felt that the reader might not be familiar with Longhi. In *The Visit to Grandmama* there is a little drama taking place between Grandmama and her manservant, a certain complicity. She is restraining the taller granddaughter apparently from reaching for the doughnuts as she looks toward the manservant, whose glance, amused and understanding, is on the side of the children as well as on the side of their grandmother and his mistress. The signals that pass between the lady and her servant are a sign of the energy that, in these little panels, is generally transmitted by the servant alone. We see the sense of intelligent interplay on the canvas as well as the establishment of the elements of rococo design, the triangles off center and the many diagonals, in rather complicated variations. We see it operating rather intensely where the servant offers the guest a cup of chocolate, the guest who points to the invalid as if meaning, well, he'll probably need another cup after he downs the one he has. The invalid is pointing to the cup given to the young lady. What results is a fairly energized oval, another rococo form, in a counterclockwise movement. There is a whole mute conversation created by gesture, and socially meaningful gesture, not the thrusts, passionate and erotic, which we see throughout the Fragonard oeuvre. In *The Dressmaker*, the sleeping servant à la Vermeer points out of the canvas but also establishes the air of secrecy and silence as well as a rococo imbalance. *The Temptation* or *Milord's Visitor* in the

Metropolitan again is a tiny triumph of design and of muffled intrigue, as well as interrupted boredom, where the servant once more coming directly from *our* space into the center unites the two groups; the first, where Milord, who is eating and being shaven, looks as if this was the wrong time to be offering him a young courtesan, and the second created by the girl who is eagerly presented by her duenna or companion. The latent energy is perceived only under deliberate scrutiny. It exists but is barely seen in the tiny embroidered slipper peeping out from under the tablecloth of Milord. On it are painted little flowers in an accurate and specific fashion. The servant comes in from the left and, in another canvas, we see the faithful family retainer in his old age being waited on by his three young mistresses. Longhi turned a blind eye to the condition of the poor and to the prevalence of vice and corruption in Venice, unlike Hogarth in London, but he surely understood the rapport between the trusted house servant and the decayed aristocrats utterly dependent on him. Other canvases show how the visitor of the old lady Adriana Barbarigo is the intruder in one painting; the servant alone with the lady is on a more intimate relationship with her.

When later in 1909 James wrote *The Outcry* as a play and then as a novel (1911), which had as its theme the drain of artworks from England, he felt his readership would have heard of Longhi by this time. He features as one of the great events indicating this drain the sale of "Lady Lappington's Longhi" for eight thousand pounds. Attention is given to details. The questioner, though, finds Longhi an unfamiliar name: "Her Longhi?" "Her great Venetian family group," the answer is, "the What-do-you-call-'ems . . . seven full-length figures, each one a gem."[24] There are probably a number of sources for this picture. One is the bad and confused portrait of the Pisani family by Pietro's son, Alessandro, which Symonds wrote was on "the wall of Mme. Pisani's drawing room in the Palazzo Barbaro on the Grand Canal in Venice,"[25] but there are only six adult figures in this group, not seven. There are other family pictures, but the more probable source is another family group, the very fine *The Sagredo Family* by Pietro Longhi, because the family had some connection with the Barbaro family. It contains seven figures, although three of them are of small children and one is of a servant carrying a tray, the accessory necessary to a Longhi picture, as James had remarked in his *The Portrait of a Lady* revision. After James's 1890 visit to the Barbaro there seems to be a sign of the effect of Symonds's essay on Longhi on a piece of James's short fiction. In 1891 James wrote a tale called "Brooksmith" about a manservant who was so fascinated by the conversation made in his master's salon that when his employer dies the servant never can find a milieu like the one he had enjoyed, so he simply fades away. The Longhi picture called *The Conversation*, now in the Stanford University Museum, looks as if it might have started James thinking about such a subject, for the servant in the front of the picture is listening in rapture, as are the other guests, to the Voltairian figure lecturing to them. The aristocratic talker and the enthralled listening servant are equally emphasized and put opposite each other in the same frontal picture-plane. The relation is chiefly between these two, the master and the appreciative servant, as it is in "Brooksmith," which also metaphorically includes eighteenth-century references to Voltaire.

The next long visit James paid to the Barbaro in 1892 not only produced the Grand Canal essay of 1892, in which he pays tribute to the palace as well as the Ca'Alvisi, but it also affected his fiction. Even before that visit "The Pupil" (1891) has a storm scene in Venice, recalling the February storms in 1887 when James stayed at the Ca'Alvisi. The metaphors for the lying and cheating family of Moreens include calling them "adventurers," and the mother and daughter of the "Great Moreen Troupe" are likened to painted actresses living in a cold prisonlike palazzo as if on a temporary Venetian stage. "The scagliola floor was cold, the high battered casements shook with the storm, and the stately decay of the place was unrelieved by a particle of furniture.. . . . [A] blast of desolation, a prophecy of disaster and disgrace, seemed to pass through the comfortless hall."[26] Mrs. Moreen locks up Morgan, her son, and then "liberates" him after having tried to borrow money from his tutor. This language of imprisonment and talk of their "escape" together, which extends even beyond the palace confinement, echoes the account of Casanova's imprisonment in the Leads, which was part of the ducal palace.

Also in the wake of *The Aspern Papers* is "The Chaperon," a short story of 1891, with an episode in Venice in which a cosmopolitan group of English socialites reenact eighteenth-century mores by attempting matchmaking on a boat—not on a gondola but a yacht. But since these are very conventional people they look only at art recommended by Ruskin, such as the Gianbellini in San Giovanni in Bragora. Another story written just after James's return from his long visit to the Barbaro in the summer of 1892, "Collaboration" (1892), is a tale of the cosmopolitan collaboration between a French poet and a German musician which opens under the protection of a "distant Tiepolo in the almost palatial ceiling,"[27] not in Venice but in the Paris studio of a cosmopolitan painter who represents in his salon, also equipped with "Italian brocade on the walls," an "air" that is "international." Having been working under a Tiepolo ceiling himself at the Barbaro, James invokes the greatest representative of plastic art of Venetian cosmopolitanism of the eighteenth century when all of Europe enjoyed its humanizing influence. "My studio in short is the theatre of a cosmopolitan drama."[28] Tiepolo watches over the "talk."

The Venetian element in James's fiction reappears with Pantaloon in *The Sacred Fount* (1901). This novel of an intellectual treasure hunt followed James's next important visit to Venice in 1899, again as a guest in the Palazzo Barbaro. If one views *The Sacred Fount* as a comedy of masks one can understand why James called it a "fantasticality" and why he introduces the narrator as a "pantaloon," as well as describing the face of the young man in the portrait as that of some "whitened old-world clown." The "old-world" designation reads like Violet Paget's use of those words to describe this period in her *Studies in the Eighteenth Century in Italy* (1880), which James owned and which may have been a source for *The Aspern Papers*. The importance of the mask, which the young man—dressed as a typical Venetian would have been in the eighteenth century, in a black costume "fashioned in years long past"—holds, is that it is an object which "appears a complete mask, such as might have been fantastically fitted and worn,"[29] such as we see in Longhi's *The Rhinoceros* in the National Gallery and especially in his *The Meeting of Dominoes* in the Rezzonico.

James's trip to Venice in 1899 was as creatively productive for him as the 1890 and 1892 trips, and in it he consolidated the material he had absorbed chiefly from the rococo world of the eighteenth century. Tiepolo, whose name was only mentioned in "Collaboration," now appears in the substance of a figure of speech in "Two Old Houses" (1899), a travel sketch where James describes his impression of the Barbaro once more without mentioning its name. The passage refers to the water-steps we see in Coburn's photograph of the Palazzo, which was to figure in volume two of the New York Edition of *The Wings of the Dove:*

The high doors stand open from them to the paved chamber of a basement . . . from which . . . mounts the slow stone staircase. . . . (If) a lady . . . scrambles out of a carriage, tumbles out of a cab . . . she alights from the Venetian conveyance as Cleopatra may have stepped from her barge.[30]

James writes that she makes "the few guided movements" on getting out of the gondola by leaning on "the strong crooked and offered arm." This is an accurate description of the famous Tiepolo painting in the Palazzo Labia of Cleopatra being helped by Antony as she disembarks. Sargent had painted a wonderful picture of the outside of this palace.

James tells us that, using the Barbaro as a touchstone, he "clung to his great Venetian clue—the explanation of everything by the historic idea. It was a high historic house, with such a quantity of recorded past twinkling in the multitudinous candles."[31] This is the house which becomes the Palazzo Leporelli in *The Wings of the Dove*. All of what eighteenth-century Venice gave to James is enfolded within the pages of the second volume of that novel, after Milly rents her palace and James uses images of the main social rooms of the Barbaro to describe his heroine's stage:

The high florid rooms . . . where the sun on the stirred seawater . . . played over the painted "subjects" in the splendid ceilings—medallions of purple and brown . . . embossed and beribboned . . . all flourished and scalloped and gilded about, set in their great moulded and figured concavity (a nest of white cherubs, friendly creatures of the air . . .)[32]

This description, coincides with the appearance of the great Barbaro *sala* and the words *rococo, shell, scalloped*, etc., are the earmarks of Venetian eighteenth-century decoration. James wrote in September 1903 to Daniel Curtis that when Mr. Curtis went back to the Barbaro, his home, "it affects me as if you lived in a bouquet or a chandelier or a fountain or a piano—that is, in some incredible ornamental thing. . . . Sit tight therefore in your chandelier." These

are all parts of an interior which reached their perfection in the
eighteenth century. The fountain is a rococo icon as is the piano,
and especially as is the chandelier, as James seemed to know. The
"mask" of the period, so obvious in the small paintings of Longhi,
appears when Milly and Kate "wearily put off the mask." Their
"puttings off of the mask" occurred when alone; they "flourished
their masks" when on public view.[33] The duplicity of Kate, her
scheme for marrying Densher to the dying Milly, is intrigue worthy
of the eighteenth century, Casanova reframed within the romantic
Edwardian drama. The role of Eugenio, the Venetian upper servant,
so intimate and knowing, is modeled on the servant of Goldoni and
Longhi. Densher's flat, the other house, contains the atmosphere of
"the quaint, the humblest rococo, of a Venetian interior in the true
old note,"[34] a modified tribute to the Ca'Alvisi. The Piazza San
Marco again provokes James's metaphors: "A great social saloon,
smooth-floored, blue-roofed chamber of amenity, favourable to
talk,"[35] suggestive of *The Conversation* by Longhi, and, again, he
calls it "the splendid Square, which had so notoriously, in all the
years, witnessed more of the joy of life than any equal area in
Europe."[36] Mrs. Stringham appreciates the historic note and although she sees them all as a Veronese picture, the drama played
out of intrigue involving cheating and lying is the note that history
has attributed to the age of Casanova. The bargain Kate makes with
the giving of her body for the financial security of her and Densher's
future is the note of the *settecento*. The great storm of Venice in
"The Pupil" serves as the natural symbol for disorder. In *The Wings
of the Dove*, the Piazza "was more than ever like a great drawing
room, the drawing room of Europe, profaned and bewildered by
some reverse of fortune." The men in the street "resemble melancholy maskers."[37] Densher's seeing Lord Mark at Florian's, an eighteenth-century institution, gives him, like Casanova, "[a] sense of
relief . . . a sense of escape,"[38] for Casanova had escaped in just that
part of Venice. But "neither relief nor escape could purge of the
smack of the abject."[39] Because Lord Mark thought Densher up to
" 'some game . . . [t]o some deviltry. To some duplicity,' "[40] he is
imprisoned in his guilt as Casanova had been in the Leads. This
guilt prepares him for his ultimate escape from his immoral pact
with Kate. The "multitudinous candles" of the Barbaro reappear in

the Palazzo Leporelli (whose name suggests the eighteenth-century libretto of *Don Giovanni*, which Casanova was supposed to have collaborated on with Da Ponte) "where even more candles than their friend's large common allowance . . . lighted up the pervasive mystery of Style."[41]

James's last piece on Venice was written as a toast to the eighteenth century itself, as personified by Mrs. Bronson. As a Longhi picture was small, intimate, and the opposite of pompous, so Mrs. Bronson, living in a "small house" in a "city of palaces," loved "the small, the domestic and the exquisite" and would have "given a Tintoretto or two . . . for a cabinet of tiny gilded glasses or a dinner-service of the right old-silver."[42] He admired her ability to "place people in relation and keep them so, take up and put down the topic, cause delicate tobacco and little gilded glasses to circulate, without ever leaving her sofa cushions." Thus she resembled the lady in Longhi's *The Morning Cup of Chocolate*. The "wonderful Venetian legend had appealed to her from the first," and about her water-steps "the ghost of the defunct Carnival . . . still played some haunting part,"[43] and the Carnival was pure *settecento*. She seemed to be an incarnation of Goldoni, for "she put together in dialect many short comedies," and made a theater out of one of her drawing rooms "permanently" where members of her "circle" plus "children of the Venetian lower classes" took part.[44]

In addition, elements of the opera appear in a figure of speech, for the Ca'Alvisi itself "played . . . the part of a friendly private box at the constant operatic show, a box at the best point of the best tier, with the cushioned ledge of its front raking the whole scene and with its withdrawing rooms behind for more detached conversation."[45] The same year, Edith Wharton published her first novel, *The Valley of Decision* (1902), strongly influenced by Violet Paget's *Studies of the Eighteenth Century in Italy*. James read it and, immersed as he now was in the Venice of the period, he wrote the young novelist a detailed letter (unfortunately now lost).[46] He also praised it to Wharton's sister-in-law and years later singled it out for mention in his essay, "The New Novel" (1914).

Nor was James's interest to falter as time went on, for he acquired Horatio Brown's *In and Around Venice* which appeared in 1905,[47] and when two years laters in 1907 he made his final trip to Venice, he felt that "never has the whole place seemed to me sweeter, clearer, diviner." It was also at that time that he inserted in *The Portrait of a Lady* the Longhi reference and wrote *The Outcry* with Lady Lappington's Longhi playing a star part among the other distinguished pictures. Of James's great novels one would say that, of those written after 1900, four had eighteenth-century Venetian material folded into them, with an interest which went beyond current tastes and really anticipated rather than reflected the growing appreciation of that period. *The Sacred Fount, The Wings of the Dove*, the revised *The Portrait of a Lady*, and *The Outcry* bear witness to James's growing fascination with the rococo Venice of the previous century.

To conclude, I want to compare Fragonard's version of the contemporary rococo made in France with that of Pietro Longhi through a similar iconographic exercise, the painter in his studio painting a young woman.[48] Through this comparison we can see how easy it was for James to accept the Italian exponent of the style and not the French. In Fragonard's studio the situation is frankly erotic. The mother or duenna bares the bosom of the young woman, and the young painter picks up her skirt with his walking stick. You can be sure that painting the model is not going to be the only activity in this studio. But in Longhi's picture the attitude of the painter to his painting, which is actually going on, is workmanlike, and he is interested in only that aspect of his beautiful young model. And you can be sure that he will maintain that attitude because the young woman's protector is guarding her. The erotic element is there, muffled and just suggested, because of the presence of the man in a mask who is clearly in some intimate relation to the girl. The masked man is only partially masked here but the mask is not completely off. It will be put on as soon as the cavalier leaves the studio. He, at any rate, is leading a secret life. The painter, with his back to the spectator, reminds us of Vermeer's famous portrait of the artist at work which crept into one of James's prefaces. Even the rococo design elements are very different from Fragonard's violent diagonals, thrusts, and expressions of sexual energy. In Longhi, the painter is subsumed under the shape of the portrait he is working on, his head absorbed into the oval of the girl's head. He is making a portrait only of her head, and the forms of that oval and the triangle of the girl's outline are duplicated in miniature on the right-hand wall in the hanging palette and the violoncello, somewhat off center.

The point I want to make is that James's insertion in the *Portrait of a Lady* revision of the description of Osmond's shabby servant and his relation to Pansy suggests that James was very sensitive to one of the dominant notes of Longhi's genius. It was the inclusion of the faithful servant tenderly supplying the wants of a decaying nobility, not for gain but for sentimental reasons. He is shown even doing his thinking for him, for over one-quarter of Longhi's little panels contains a servant as an important part of the picture drama. In 1760 there were over 12,000 domestics wearing their master's cut-down clothes. The comment is delicate, not savage, like Hogarth's. The delicacy may have been determined by the need to avoid censorship by a police state during that period. Longhi, therefore, used a kind of secret form of pictorialism, showing a hidden private life, known only to the household servants. Secrets always appealed to James, and we see during this period, when he was a constant visitor to the Palazzo Barbaro, a reflection of this in the 1901 *Sacred Fount*, which is a kind of commedia del'arte tale, where Pantaloon is mentioned and the secret relations of people wearing masks, figuratively, and where a painting in the house is wearing a mask, actually, populate the novel, and where the secrets of their erotic relationships are being pried into by the narrator. But, like Longhi's dramatis personae, outsiders cannot know what these relationships are. In Longhi's work lapdogs join the servants in caring for and being cared for by the family members. In a picture called *The Concert* only a little poodle is listening to the music; the others are playing cards and are inattentive. Incidentally, also in the revised *Portrait*, poodles and lapdogs enter where ordinary dogs were before. The chairs are not overturned as in Hogarth's *Progresses* nor are the trees uprooted as in a Fragonard landscape. Passions do not leave their marks on the canvas but the little footstools are seen in triangular positions and the little lap dogs come up from the angles of the canvas or the book on the table is placed in an irregular position. But although a trio of people are decorously sitting on stable chairs, there is, as Rumpole of the Old Bailey might say, a certain amount of hanky-panky going on, but well hidden from the casual, in-a-hurry spectator.

What we can say about James's discreet use of eighteenth-century painters—especially Longhi, who, after all, does appear in two of the late novels and, for James, that is a lot of attention—is that he has put his finger on the essence of Longhi's genius. For the faithful servant, whom James selects for his attention, is the cornerstone of the society to which he belongs. The servant is the consciousness of the value of the old families. He keeps them going, for they need his help and he gives it willingly. He also establishes the rococo elements in the pictures: he builds the triangles, he energizes the scenes with his brisk walk across the canvas carrying food or coffee cups of chocolate which they seem to drink all day long. He brings in the doughnuts or crullers, the only solid food they seem to eat. In James's second reference to Longhi, to Lady Lappington's family picture, he puts his finger on the other aspect about the society Longhi paints which is really part of the first, the continuing importance of family pride. We see it in the centered pictures of the illustrious doges in their family, but we see it especially in the big family pictures, where their only remaining pride is in the one thing left (since money has disappeared), the continuing of the family line in their children, themselves, and their faithful servants, so often included in family pictures, those servants who keep them from falling apart. The servants are but an extension of the family, a continuity and a support. The Venetian aristocrats are different from Lady Lappington, who is selling what seems to be a family portrait of her own through inheritance. The Countess Pisani took her family group, after she lost her own home, to her new rooms in the Barbaro. James seems to suggest in *The Outcry* that the British aristocracy has lost this family feeling and will sell anything to the highest bidder. I think we can say with confidence that James's two references to Longhi in 1908 and in 1910–11 show that James had a keen sense of appreciation and understanding of the foremost rococo portraitist and painter of sophisticated life in Venice of the eighteenth century.

Notes

1. *Henry James Letters*, vol. 1, 1843–1875, ed. Leon Edel (Cambridge: Harvard University Press, 1974), 136. "Taine, I remember, somewhere speaks of Venice and Oxford—the two most picturesque cities in Europe. I personally prefer Oxford, September 25th (1869)." The editor adds a note to the effect that "HJ later changed his mind and preferred Venice" (p. 144).

2. *The Complete Tales of Henry James*, ed. Leon Edel (Philadelphia: Lippincott, 1961–64), 2:194. "I have been reading two or three of George Sand's novels. Do you know *La Dernière Aldini?* I fancy a romance in every palace." Mr. Brooke answers, "The reality of Venice seems to me to exceed all romance. It's romance enough simply to be here."

3. *Henry James Letters*, vol. 2 1875–1883, ed. Leon Edel (Cambridge: Harvard University, 1975), 318.

4. Two thrones in the manner of Andrea Brustolon, circa 1700, "covered with crimson velvet, from the Doge's Palace at Venice." Another set of six Venetian armchairs by Brustolon, like the ones he made for the Ca'Rezzonico, are also distributed in the great hall of Mentmore. (From the catalog of the sale of the contents of Mentmore, held 18–20 May 1977.) *Mentmore, Volume One, Furniture* (London: Sotheby Parke Bernet, 1977).

5. "Three Venetian Gilt Lanterns 12 feet high, circa 1700," which "reputedly surmounted the stern of the Bucentaur, the state barge of the Doge of Venice. The two smaller flanking ones are surmounted by pennants each with the lion of St. Mark." (*Mentmore Furniture Catalogue*, No. 820, 258).

6. "A Set of Ten Venetian Rococo giltwood Armchairs, six covered in stamped green leather and four covered in Genoese velvet, circa 1745" (*Mentmore Furniture Catalogue*, No. 820, 239). There is another set of seven Venetian giltwood chairs covered in stamped leather and two in Genoese leather, circa 1730.

7. To Charles Eliot Norton, 17 September 1887, "From the far-away roof depend three immense and extraordinary gilded lanterns that were part of the fit-up of the Bucentaur." (Unpublished letter, courtesy Leon Edel.) James also described in this letter more carefully the great armchairs, "talking to someone who is lolling in a kind of golden throne, one of a set of similar wonders, scattered over the hall—the property of I forget which most significant of the Doges."

8. See my "Waddesdon Manor and *The Golden Bowl*," *Apollo* (August 1976): passim, or chapter 12 in my *The Museum World of Henry James* (Ann Arbor: UMI Research Press, 1986).

9. Letter to Daniel Curtis, [1902], Dartmouth College.

10. The Palazzo Barbaro was a fourteenth-century building whose rooms

had been last decorated in the eighteenth century. It was bought by the Daniel Curtises, who were originally from Boston. James spent his first visit there from 25 May to the beginning of July, although he had only expected to spend ten days there. (See Leon Edel, *Henry James: The Middle Years* [Philadelphia: Lippincott, 1962], 227–31.)

11. Henry James, *Italian Hours* (New York: Grove Press, 1959), 13.

12. *Mémoires de Jacques Casanova de Seingalt*, 8 vols. (Paris: Garnier, n.d.), signed by James. Author's collection.

13. Letter from Leon Edel, 3 December 1962 to the Viscount David Eccles which has been attached to the flyleaf of volume one of the eight-volume set of Casanova's *Mémoires*.

14. Notation in the catalog compiled by Lord Eccles of his collection of Henry James French books at Lamb House, Rye.

15. Edel, *Henry James: The Middle Years*, 212.

16. *Complete Tales*, 6:318–19.

17. The Barbaro contained the following paintings by Tiepolo until they were sold in 1874: a ceiling with *The Apotheosis of Francesco Barbaro* (now in the Metropolitan Museum, New York) and four overdoors. 1. *The Betrothal*, Museum Copenhagen; 2. *Tarquin and Lucretia*, Museum Augsburg; 3. *Gifts Offered to Cleopatra*, Necchi Collection, Paris; 4. *Timoclea and the Thracian Commander*, Washington National Gallery.

18. John Singer Sargent, *An Interior in Venice*, presented as a Diploma Work before the Royal Academy of Arts, Gordon, in 1899. The Daniel Curtises and their son, Ralph, with his wife appear in it. Sargent was a working guest there often, having known the Curtis family as a boy.

19. *Complete Tales*, 6:379.

20. Ibid., 362.

21. James, *Italian Hours*, 51.

22. John Addington Symonds, *The Letters of John Addington Symonds*, Herbert M. Schueller and Robert L. Peters (Detroit: Wayne State University Press, 1969), 3:364. In a letter to Henry Graham Dakyns, 27 March 1889, Symonds speaks of his book on Count Gozzi which is about to appear.

23. Henry James, *The Portrait of a Lady*, ed. Leon Edel (Boston: Houghton Mifflin, 1963), 226.

24. Henry James, *The Outcry* (New York: Scribners, 1911), 17–18.

25. *The Memoirs of Count Carlo Gozzi*, trans. John Addington Symonds (New York: Scribners and Welford, 1890), 2:355.

26. *Complete Tales*, 7:447.

27. Ibid., 8:407.

28. Ibid., 408.

29. James, *The Sacred Fount* (New York: Scribners, 1901), 55.

30. James, *Italian Hours*, 66.

31. Ibid., 67.

32. Henry James, *The Wings of the Dove* (New York: New American Library, 1964), 309.
33. Ibid., 314.
34. Ibid., 341.
35. Ibid., 349.
36. Ibid., 351.
37. Ibid., 398.
38. Ibid., 400.
39. Ibid., 402.
40. Ibid., 419.
41. Ibid., 351.
42. James, *Italian Hours*, 78.
43. Ibid., 79.
44. Ibid., 81.
45. Ibid., 78.
46. Cynthia Griffin Wolff, *A Feast of Words* (New York: Oxford University Press, 1977), 97.
47. Leon Edel and Adeline R. Tintner, *The Library of Henry James* (Ann Arbor: UMI Research Press, 1987).
48. Pierre Rosenberg, *Fragonard* (New York: Metropolitan Museum, 1987), fig. 150; and Teresio Pignatti, *Longhi* (London: Phaedon, 1969), fig. 49.

SEVEN *The Force of Revelation: Receptive Vision in Henry James's Early Italian Travel Essays*

BONNEY MACDONALD

*I*N THE early life of Henry James, the 1860s are unique for marking a decade of domestic calm and stasis in an otherwise well-traveled and cosmopolitan youth. By 1860, James had toured Europe three times, lived in Manhattan twice, attended numerous European and American academies, and had, after a fascinating but peripatetic "sensuous education,"[1] taken up a quieter residence in Newport, Rhode Island. In 1864 the James family moved from Newport to Boston and, in 1866, made their permanent home in nearby Cambridge. From 1860 to 1869 James lived with his family in New England—in Newport and the Boston area—for a longer period of time than he had yet remained in any one place.[2] In these formative and relatively peaceful years, James followed the path of many Eastern men of letters.[3] He was known and published by James T. Fields at the *Atlantic*, by James Russell Lowell and Charles Norton at the *North American Review*, and by E. L. Godkin at the *Nation*. In short, during the 1860s, Henry James displayed the talent, social finesse, and, seemingly, the ambition of a future Boston man of letters.

Toward the end of this successful decade at home, however, James became constructively restless. Despite impressive literary success and social ease, he longed for more stimulating company and unfamiliar landscapes. James had outgrown his surroundings and was ready to move on. "You may imagine," as he wrote to T. S. Perry during a hot New England August, "that existence here has not been thrilling or exciting. I have seen no one and done nothing—. . . I like Cambridge very well, but at the end of another year, I'm sure I shall have had enough of it."[4]

Eighteen months later the prediction was realized when, on 17 February 1869, James sailed to England to begin his first unaccompanied tour of Europe. The departure marked, for the rest of James's life, a fully saturated and determining event, a moment to which he would return repeatedly in his essays, letters, and fiction. As he recalled years later in the autobiography, his long-awaited and foggy arrival in Liverpool teemed with a sense of promise, youthful ecstasy, and personal destiny:

I found myself, from the first day in March 1869, in the face of an opportunity that affected me then and there as the happiest, the most interesting, the most alluring and beguiling, that could ever have opened before a somewhat disabled young man who was about to complete his twenty-sixth year.[5]

During these first days in England, James reveled in his "exposure to appearances, aspects, images, [and] every protrusive item almost, in the great beheld sum of things." Receptive, eager, and in search of revelatory impressions, James submerged himself in British details. "Wherever I looked . . . I sank in up to my nose. . . . Recognition . . . remained, through the adventure of the months to come, the liveliest principle at work."[6]

However, if in the early spring of 1869, James "uncapped his throbbing brow in the wild dimness of [Oxford's] courts,"[7] revered the verdant splendor of England's countryside, and explored the "dusky vistas" of Dickensian London, his senses were overwhelmed when, in September of the same year, he descended the alpine slopes of Switzerland into northern Italy. If his responses to England were stately, reverent, and appreciative, his reactions to Italy were filled with runaway enthusiasm and energetic rapture. England, as he wrote back to Cambridge, was a "good matron," and Switzerland, where he had traveled that summer, was a "magnificent man"; but Italy, as he reported in newly impassioned prose, was a "beautiful dishevelled nymph."[8] James's five-month Italian tour carried him through the northern Alps to Lake Como, and then on to Milan, Venice, Florence, and, by November, to Rome. His journey, as he wrote of his memorable descent down the Simplon Pass into

Isella, was a "rapturous progress thro' a wild luxuriance of corn and vines and olives and figs and mulberries and chestnuts and frescoed villages."[9]

In near-Whitmanian relish for listing the seen and felt objects of the world, James significantly could not total the sum of his Italian pleasure, name enough sights, nor find the words to convey his newfound delights. "If I might talk of these things," he wrote to William, "I would talk of *more* and tell you in glowing accents how beautiful this month in Italy has been and how my brain swarms with pictures and my bosom aches with memories. I should like in some neat formula to give [you] the 'Italian feeling' . . . ."[10] As the travel essays and letters attest, however, James's love of Italy remained *beyond* the reach of words, lending the Italian writings— for James as well as his readers—much of their magic. As implied in the fiction and stated in the preface to *Roderick Hudson*, "the loved Italy was the scene of my fiction—so much more loved than one has ever been able, even after fifty efforts, to say!"[11]

These travel works of the early 1870s are part of James's growing fascination with European travel and the international theme.[12] But, while critics have explored the theme of Americans abroad in the fiction, and while biographers have agreed on the importance of European travel in James's formative years, few have closely examined the travel essays. Perhaps this gap in criticism is generated by the form itself, since travel writing generally constitutes a genre which is difficult to define. The travel essay, after all, is neither biography, nor fiction, nor wholly factual account, but some combination of the three. It constitutes, as Paul Fussell has remarked in his work on twentieth-century travel, a "sub-species of memoir in which autobiographical narrative arises from the speaker's encounter with . . . unfamiliar data, and in which the narrative—unlike that in a novel or a romance—claims literal validity by constant reference to actuality."[13] Moreover, literary accomplishment is not always expected from travel writing. We may "know" that travel literature is rich in content but, as H. M. Tomilson rightly notes, we too often relegate it to the territory of light or "background reading."[14]

James's early travel essays, then, offer a valuable tool for readers of James. Combining narrative structure with attention to visual and factual detail, they illuminate artistic as well as epistemological concerns which culminate in the later fiction. They are, as Carl Smith claims, "tales of a sort" which underscore James's interest in the "traveler as perceiver."[15] In addition to portraying scenes of travel, these essays reveal James's developing ideas on perception and the artistic process. They not only offer "portraits of places" and accounts of travel, but also exhibit a theoretical probing of aesthetic experience—an exploration of visual perception and thought, as well as the related issues of seeing and knowing which inform the later novels.

That James explores such issues in his fiction is well established; that he does so in the travel writings, and that he accomplishes the task so directly is not as widely recognized. The travel essay, according to Fussell, traditionally incorporates a "gross physicality [and] a tie to the actual"[16]—characteristics often attributed to travel writing but rarely associated with James's work itself. In contrast to the abstraction of the late style, James's early travel essays focus on direct impressions and "felt" experience in the Italian landscape. Their point of view, as Edel has suggested, "is empirical; its interest lies in places and persons." James is concerned "with things his eyes can rest upon, . . . [and] [a]t every turn [he] invites us to look; and through sight we are asked to charge our other senses."[17] Unlike much of James's early fiction, and certainly unlike many of the late works, James's travel pieces *directly* display the texture of the seen and felt world which structures James's Italian experience. Through their attention to receptive sight, tactile vision, and picturesque impressions, these essays chart James's developing visual and artistic stance, and trace the revelatory force of the visible world as it reveals itself during James's early years in Italy.

Depicting a scene to which James would return in memory and fiction, "The Old Saint-Gothard" recounts James's cherished descent into northern Italy. The journey begins at dawn in Lucerne where James boards a steamer to Flüelen. Here in the Alps—watching the porters load the south-bound coaches—James describes the receptive and wondrous mood that characterizes his travel essays. Finding himself "on the threshold of Italy" before the Simplon Pass,

James "surrender[s] to the gaping traveller's mood, which," he tell-
ingly adds, "surely isn't the unwisest the heart knows":

I don't envy people . . . who have outlived or outworn the simple sweetness
of feeling settled to go somewhere with bag and umbrella. . . . In this
matter wise people are content to become children again. We don't turn
about on our knees to look out of the omnibus-window, but we [do] indulge
in very much the same round-eyed contemplation of visible objects.[18]

Bound for Italy by coach, James thus begins his descent and engages
in the pleasures of the innocent and receptive eye, "sucking in the
gladness of gaping" (OSG, 100), and taking delight in the surrounding landscape. In the visual drama which follows, his "traveller's
mood" remains one of receptivity and leisurely pleasure. He must
"ignore the very dream of haste," and proceed slowly and "very
much at random" (CC, 237).

Along with this unhurried pace, James's emerging portrait of the
traveler incorporates an overall receptive stance. The Italian essays
abound with portraits of the flâneur who, in hours of receptive
delight, "roam[s] and ramble[s]"[19] through Italian cities. James
"stroll[s] among Florentine lanes; sit[s] on parapets . . . [and] look[s]
across at the Fiesole or down the rich-hued valley of the Arno."[20]
Continuing with the receptive verbs that characterize these essays,
he finds himself "pausing at the open gates of villas, and wondering
at the height of the cypresses and the depth of the loggias" (IR,
124). At Arezzo he "lounges away the half-hours . . . under a spell"
(CC, 245), and in Perugia his stance is nearly Whitmanian as he
relishes the chance to

lie aloft there in the grass with silver-grey ramparts at one's back and the
warm rushing wind in one's ears, and watch the beautiful plain mellow
into the tones of twilight . . . (CC, 235)

With an affection for lounging and loafing not often associated with
the upright and meticulous observer, James immerses himself in the
pleasures of "aimless contemplation" (AF, 121). He is never weary,
he reports, of "staring into gateways, of lingering by . . . half-
barbaric farm-yards, [or] of feasting a foolish gaze on sun-cracked
plaster and unctuous indoor shadows" (RR, 160). In contrast to the
focused and appropriative vision often associated with James's artistry, the author of these sketches is an unhurried and "musing

wanderer" who enjoys his impressions as he finds them. In Rome he rides on the Campagna, and takes in the "strong sense of <u>wandering</u> over boundless space, . . . hardly knowing whether it is better to gallop far and drink deep of air and grassy distance . . . or to <u>walk</u> and <u>pause</u> and <u>linger</u>, and try and grasp some ineffaceable memory of sky and color and outline" (RR, 165–66).

Whether in the open air of the Campagna or the hushed atmosphere of a gallery, James frequently finds himself exhausted by the sheer multiplicity of sight, sound, and sense, claiming that he has "received more impressions than [he] knows what to do with,"[21] and that Italian sights and "details overwhelm" him.[22] These protests, however, are short-lived. For if Italy abounds with an unmanageable number of pictures and impressions, it is that very undefined multiplicity and uncontained grandeur of place that James also treasures. Every observed detail, in this "ever suggestive part of the world" (IR, 112), not only holds *specific* meaning, but also resonates with the unseen beauty of its context. Thus, when walking outside the Villa Borghese on a sunny March afternoon, James is struck by the immediately visible scene of Italian schoolboys playing in the sun while a young priest looks on, but he is also carried away by larger, unseen, and undiscovered reverberations as well. The specific scene, he notes, may "sound like nothing, but the *force behind* it, . . . the setting, the air, the chord struck, make it a *hundred* wonderful things (RR, 170).[23]

These "hundred" reverberations and relations, however, remain unnamed in James's early sketches. The penumbra of relations resonates with the undefined and *undefinable* nature of Italy's magic. Thus, a moment's impression is not merely singular, but informed by a host of surrounding details, associations, and what William James calls "vague," "fringe," or relational meanings.[24] The observed scenes of Italy, to recall Henry's term, are thus "ever-suggestive" because they resonate, like overtones in music, with unseen but present meanings and associations. After the initial impression, the drama of any one observation becomes saturated with a fund of associations, impressions, and expectations which—like William James's famous "stream of thought"—are multiple and continuous. The "unbroken continuity of impressions," Henry thus writes, is an

example of the intellectual background of all enjoyment in Rome. . . .
[Y]our sensation rarely begins and ends with itself; it reverberates, com-
memorates, [and] resuscitates something else. *(RR, 161)*

This multiplity of impressions influences not only the way in which
James *sees* Italy, but the style of his Italian essays as well. Throughout, James expands his vision to meet the magnitude of his surroundings. Italy's multiplicity of sound and sense prompts not only
perpetual delight but an enthusiastic and consciously nonhierarch-
ical vision reminiscent of Whitman. Without attention to an or-
dered or selected progression, James takes in as much as his senses
will allow, and "pray[s] *not* to grow in discrimination."[25]

The multiplicity of Italian impressions generates a nonhierarchi-
cal catalog of the visible landscape and inspires a Whitmanian
rapture in cataloging the objects viewed. James attempts to name
the objects of his impressions as they come to him, without selection and without "discrimination." The magic of the northern lakes,
as he writes of his journey from Bellinzona to Como, "lay before me
for a whole perfect day":

[it gleams] in the shimmering melting azure of the southern slopes and
masses; in the luxurious tangle of nature and the familiar amenity of man;
in the lawn-like inclinations, where the great grouped chestnuts make so
cool a shadow in the warm light; in the rusty vineyards, [and in] the
littered cornfields and the tawdry wayside shrines. But most of all it's the
deep yellow light that enchants you and tells you where you are. *(OSG,
104)*

In this account of the drive to Como, James is unable to name or
list all of the delights of the land, and his catalog—like that in
"Song of Myself"—seems at once to note the limitations of language when faced with the rapturous multiplicity of experience, as
well as to take simple delight in the passing scenes of life and
landscape.

James's catalog passage, however, evokes not only a delight in
multiplicity but an overall reverence for the seen and "accessible"
world as well. The Italian landscape, as James wrote of Perugia,
"continually solicits his wonder and praise," prompts "worshipful
gazing" and "helpless wonderment," and indulges him in countless
hours of "romantic *flânerie*" *(CC, 237, 233)*. Sheer joy in perception
permeates his descriptive accounts of Italian cities, so that visual

experience becomes a full-time pursuit. "The mere use of one's eyes" as James wrote of Venice, "is happiness enough" (*V*, 54).

If much of Italy became a delight to James's receptive vision, it was in Rome that this instinctive and consciously embraced reverence was most pronounced. Under what Nathalia Wright has called "unpremeditated rapture,"[26] James wandered through the city "at random" (*RH*, 147), visiting galleries and back streets and, in the following passage, St. Peter's basilica. James's account of the church not only registers his receptive stance and the multiplicity of his impressions, but an overall reverence for the sheer magnitude of St. Peter's grandeur and Italy's splendor.

Walking across the threshold, James is brought to "an immediate gasping pause" by the overwhelming size and beauty of the church. Describing his receptive glance, he insists that no projection of the imagination is needed, and adds that "[he] only ha[s] to stroll and stroll and gaze and gaze" at the vaulted interior for its magic to take hold. Continuing his exploration, James lingers as the beauty of the basilica transcends his conscious attention. And in the midst of this magnitude he records not only the receptivity of his vision and the multiplicity of his impressions, but a distinctly Jamesian reverence for a grandeur that is larger than himself. Watching

the glorious altar-canopy lift its bronze architecture . . . [and] its collossal embroidered contortions, like a temple within a temple, [you] feel yourself, at the bottom of the abysmal shaft of the dome, dwindle to a crawling dot. (*RH*, 150)

Responding to the magnitude of the church, here, James instinctively and consciously reveres the vast interior which overwhelms his vision. Reverence in this passage (as elsewhere in the essays) is less a religious stance than an aesthetic experience charged and structured by religious emotion. In the receptive and reverent vision inspired by Italy, James treasures and records those visual moments during which the grandeur and multiplicity of the tangible Italian world not only delight the senses but also lead the viewer (as in religious experience) to a reality which transcends the present moment and stands larger than the self.

If James delights in the multiple and suggestive sights of Italy, he also stands in awe of the tangible and tactile nature of those Italian impressions. Visual impressions, in these early Italian essays, seem to carry substance and weight, and *present themselves* to the viewer as if animated from within. In James's flights of descriptive reverie there reigns an implied insistence on the physical impact of visual experience so that "every glance is a *sensation*." A sensuousness of place and impression shapes the Italian essays and suggests that visual perception—as William James knew well—is not limited to the mind; rather, it is tactile in nature, and evokes sensation as well as thought.

This tangible nature of impressions first emerges with Henry James's 1869 arrival in Rome, when Italy leaves the realm of preconception and imagination to become a fully actualized presence and reality. Italy's atmosphere, James wants to suggest and confirm, carries substance, and its "tone . . . lies richly on my soul and gathers increasing *weight*."[27] "Languishing beneath the weight of Rome's impressions,"[28] James makes a phenomenological observation on the *tangible* nature of imaginative and visual experience: "The aesthetic," as he writes in an essay on Rome, "is so intense that you should live on the taste of it, should extract the nutritive essence of the atmosphere" (*FRN*, 197).

Visual perception, in this comment, becomes imbued with the warmth and immediacy of sensorial experience. Gazing, looking, and glancing at Italy, Henry James bears witness to William James's claim that acts of perception and imagination are "more like a process of sensation than like a thought."[29] And although mental association may later take over, all acts of imagination and cognition, William suggests, begin in "sensorial vividness."[30] Before the mind grasps an object or scene in its larger or relational context, vision is stunned into a moment of pre-associative receptivity in which the object of vision is revealed in its tactile immanence. Sensations, as William thus writes in the *Principles*, are the

starting point of cognition, thoughts the developed tree. . . . [T]he objective presence of reality known about, [and] the mere beginning of knowledge [are most often] named by the word which says the least. Such a word is the interjection, as lo! there! ecco! [or] *voilà!*[31]

Together, William's account of perception and Henry's narrated experience suggest that "knowledge about" an object (a cathedral, for instance) begins in a receptive moment of visual awe. Acknowledging the distinct beauty or "thisness" inherent in an object or scene, the viewer awakens, as the *Principles* suggests, "to the consciousness of something there [which] has [an] objectivity, unity [and] substantiality"[32] independent of the viewer's mind or imagination. In opposition to the Berkeleyan idea that the realities of visual perception (such as spatiality, density, or depth) are a result of intellectual association and projection, William and Henry James each suggest that perception of substance, depth, and beauty is rooted in primary experience in the seen and tactile world.

In addition to having substance and weight, the objects of James's receptive vision seem to take on, as it were, a life of their own. Throughout the early Italian essays, they vibrate with a seemingly independent force and with what Merleau-Ponty has called "internal animation."[33] Italy functions, then, not only as a tangible presence, but as an active agency which solicits response and commands attention. "At every step," as James wrote of Rome's "weighty" historical presence, it *"confronts* you, and the mind must make some response."[34] It speaks to the viewer, solicits a response, and invites him into an exchange. Florentine scenes, as James thus writes, do not merely await the interested gaze, they actively recruit the viewer's attention and *"force"* themselves into view. In Florence, James continues, "the scene *itself,* the mere scene, shares with you such a wealth of consciousness" (*IR*, 129, 124)[35] that you feel the unmistakable "genius of the place" in all its substantial and active presence (*AF*, 273).

Thus, when Henry James is brought to an "immediate gasping pause" on the threshold of St. Peter's, or when he "surrenders to the gaping traveler's mood [in] . . . round-eyed contemplation of accessible objects," he not only absorbs the scenery with pleasure and delight, but also engages in a phenomenologically structured visual moment. Viewing the wide open space of the Campagna, or the grandeur of St. Peter's, James immerses himself in all that Italy has to offer. In addition, that is, to seeking out scenic beauty, he allows the actualized splendor of Italy to *reveal itself* to him. The object of vision, as Pierre Thévanez has written in "What Is Phenomenology?" is not "constructed by consciousness, [but] gives itself" to the viewer.

A phenomenological reading of James's travel sketches, then, highlights what James himself suggests: that Italian scenes actively *impress themselves* upon the viewer with a vividness that surpasses the mind's ability to create and project images, and that the seen world of Italy comes to the viewer with a distinct and animated presence. A visual phenomenon, Thévanez claims, is "that which gives itself and [stands] immanent to consciousness." It is not a matter of simple realism or of "making an object appear in its factual reality," Thévanez continues, but of rendering it "in its immanent reality to the [viewing] consciousness."[36]

With an emphasis on receptive vision, multiplicity of impressions, tactile experience, and the "gestalt of the picturesque," Henry James gives voice to the concrete and tactile nature of full consciousness—to the "worldliness," as William James wrote, "of thought."[37] James's Italian sketches suggest that the sensorial world actively participates in acts of imagination and thought, and that the whole felt and lived world generates meaning and artistry. Focusing on moments of direct experience and perception (as in the above accounts of St. Peter's, a Florentine afternoon, or Italian schoolboys at play), phenomenological consideration of the travel sketches highlights James's seldom-noted reverence for the felt life in its "total and concrete density."[38]

Through this reverence for the seen, felt, and tactile world, Henry James implicitly concurs with what Bruce Wilshire calls a central doctrine of phenomenology. All states of consciousness, Wilshire claims, "are intrinsically referential and worldly, [and] cannot be specified in isolation" from the material and sense world. Phenomenology, he continues, is an "exercise in seeing" and offers, moreover, the insight that all acts of thought and imagination are rooted in the concreteness of the seen and felt world.[39] With their repeated reference to "locatable"[40] scenes and local textures, James's Italian essays reveal the "intrinsic referentialness of mind"[41] central to a phenomenological account of visual experience. Consciousness is "referential" or "intentional," and does not operate in isolation from lived experience. Consciousness, as phenomenology suggests, is always *of* something—it refers, points, or "intends" toward some object.

With these premises in mind, the reader approaches a fuller understanding of William James's explicit claim that cognitive and mental acts begin in primary "sensorial vividness"; but more important, he also approaches a better understanding of Henry James's implicit suggestion that acts of imagination similarly engage the world of seen and tactile experience. In this light, moments of visual impression in the Italian essays can be seen to illustrate what Merleau-Ponty has called "primary perception." By the words, the "primacy of perception," he explains,

we mean the experience of perception . . . at the moment when things, truths, values are constituted for us. . . . It is not a question of *reducing* human knowledge to sensation, but of assisting at the birth of this knowledge to make it as sensible as the sensible and . . . to define a method for getting closer to present and living reality.[42]

Gazing at the glory of Roman ruins, at the beauty of the Arno, or at the magnitude of St. Peter's, Henry James is brought by the "*scene itself*" to an "immediate, gasping pause" (see above). During these moments of receptive vision and direct impression, James not only retraces the rapture of travelers before him, he seizes it as his own, and in so doing evokes Merleau-Ponty's account of visual wonder. Rather, consciousness is also structured by primary visual experience and thus remains eternally open to the actual and the visible.

From an exploration of James's receptive stance and the tactile nature of his visual experience in Italy, a pattern begins to emerge. James's Italian essays not only convey his visual stance and the character of his impressions, but the *structure* of those impressions as well. In addition to being sensorial and tactile, James's Italian perceptions are structured by his understanding of the "picturesque." Visual impressions of Italy—whether of St. Peter's or of a work by Tintoretto—are received by the eye as fully formed, unified, and self-contained. As William James and phenomenologists have claimed, we "see in wholes." Thus the beauty of a cathedral or painting does not enter our vision through an association of separately perceived images, but—as Henry James wrote of Sargent's paintings—as a "whole, . . . a scene, and a *comprehensive* impression."[43] Arriving in Rome, Henry James happily reported to William that "for the first time I know what the picturesque is";[44]

it means, as he defined it elsewhere, "simply the presentation of a picture, *self-informed* and *complete.*"[45]

If Henry James first comprehended the picturesque upon his arrival in Rome, he had nonetheless come across the concept before: first, through William Morris Hunt's teachings in Newport and, among others, through those of William James. Studying art with Hunt in 1861 along with William, Henry James learned a great deal about *seeing* as well as about painting and drawing.[46] He came to learn how a painting can, as it were, speak for itself. During his "hours of Art" in the Newport studio, James pored over Hunt's collection and listened to instruction on drawing and painting. And although James does not record the specifics of this instruction, Hunt's *Talks on Art* offers a reliable source for understanding the lessons that James must have received from this "genial and admirable master."[47] A painting, Hunt claims, must "instantly *seize* and hold the attention." For this reason, as he advised young painters, a picture must "keep the first impression . . . [and] seize you as forcibly as if a man has seized you by the shoulder! It should impress you," Hunt insists, "like *reality*."[48] In order to achieve this forceful impression of reality, Hunt further claims, a painting must be perceived and offered as *unified* impression. While drawing, he advises his students, "see what the shape of the whole thing is [and] establish the fact of the *whole*, [for] it is [that first] impression of the thing that you want to get."[49]

Like Hunt, William James also claims that visual impressions are structured by an initial unity. Although the visible world is multiple and filled with unrelated phenomena, thought and perception are nonetheless "sensibly continuous."[50] And though, after an initial sensation, we do associate images and meanings in order to comprehend an object in all its relational or "fringe meanings," our initial impression is structured by a unified and "single pulse of consciousness."[51] No matter how complex, William thus writes, an object "is at any moment thought in one idea." Perception, he thus insists, "is one state of mind or nothing,"[52] so that our impressions of the world, no matter how complicated, always arrive in consciousness—as in Henry's definition of the picturesque—self-informed and unified. They "vibrate," William explains, not as a series of separately perceived details, but as a "systematic whole."[53]

With this definition of visual impressions in mind, the reader can now find new meaning in James's remarks on Italian art. Sitting amidst the glories of St. Peter's, for instance, James notes that the "constituted beauty" cannot be defined simply by describing the beauty of Michelangelo's *Pietà* of the rich interior of the cathedral. Similarly, as James claims in "Venice: An Early Impression," Tintoretto had an unequaled distinctness of vision for his ability to convey the whole pictorial unity of a scene. When Tintoretto conceived a painting, he did not compose a scene solely from his imagination. Instead, "it *defined itself* to his imagination with an intensity [and] amplitude . . . which [make] one's observation of his pictures seem less an operation of the mind than a kind of supplementary experience of life."[54] Tintoretto's work does not merely give the viewer a visually interesting display of separate colors and images. Visual scenes in his works are the product of unified impressions, so that "you get from [Tintoretto] the impression that he *felt*, pictorially, the great, beautiful and terrible spectacle of human life" (*V*, 59):

It was the whole scene that [Tintoretto] seemed to have beheld in a flash of inspiration intense enough to stamp it ineffaceably on his perception; and it was the *whole scene, complete*, peculiar, individual [and] unprecedented that he committed to canvas with all the vehemence of his talent. (*V*, 59)[55]

In painting, then, James admired an artist's ability to capture that fleeting moment when the visible world reveals itself in its pictorial unity—when the painter's artistry conveys what Merleau-Ponty has called the "coming-to-itself of the visible."[56] But if James admired a painter's ability to convey the picturesque, he was equally impressed by a writer's ability to capture that same pictorial unity. "I'd give a great deal," he thus proclaimed after viewing Tintoretto in Venice, "to be able to fling down a dozen of his pictures into prose of corresponding force and color."[57]

These comments on visual perception offer clues to the way in which James organized visual experience. In recording his impressions in the Italian sketches, James *shapes* visual experience according to a consistent aesthetic of perception by which visual impressions become a source of revelatory knowledge and transformation. Visual perception in James's Italian essays—whether of a cathedral or a painting—is not only receptive in its stance and tactile in effect, but unified and self-informed in structure. As James wrote of a Tintoretto canvas, it *"defines itself* to the imagination" and makes a "stamp" or impress on perception.[58] Indeed, as it emerges in James's Italian essays, visual experience resonates with the physicality and force associated with the words "impress" or "impression."

As "impress" describes a characteristic stamp or mark (as in printing), so the act of "impressing" suggests some application of pressure to produce that mark. But in addition to describing this physical action, "impress" carries a military connotation. To "impress," in this definition, is to "enlist, force or press into duty"—or, as the *O.E.D.* notes, "to take or *seize*" a person for military or public service. Similarly, "impression" connotes transactions of force and power. It describes an influence or pressure from an external force, a "charge,"as the *O.E.D.* continues, "in some *passive* subject by the operation of an external cause." As in the military account which suggests a "charge, attack, or assault," a perceptual definition includes a similar physical pressure. Impressions are those "perceptions which enter with [the] most *force* and violence."[59]

As James's travel essays indicate, impressions arrive in the senses not only with the charm of local scenes, the tactile nature of vision, and the unity of the picturesque, but with a full physical "force." The act of perception thus reveals the artist, as the phenomenologist Herbert Speigelberg notes, as "not only projecting the world, but as having been *taken over* by the world."[60] In James's essays, the visible world of Italy is sufficiently forceful to overtake and "enlist" its viewer. It not only delights the eye but, in bringing the viewer to an "immediate gasping pause," impresses and—to recall Hunt's term—"seizes" him with the force of reality. Thus, whether viewing a church or a canvas, James is not only drawn to beauty, but compelled by its power as well. The impact of Italy's beauty in the essays is thus not so different from a dramatic "charge" or "onset." Italy makes its colorful, tactile, and picturesque stamp or impress on its receptive viewer at every turn. The scenes and objects of the visible world are often beyond and more forceful than the descriptive power of language—as, indeed, James had hoped they would be.

For these reasons, James's Italian sketches often insist that the glory of Italy is "more lovely than words can tell" (*IR*, 108), and that the whole, picturesque impression of Italy's splendor surpasses description. The "charm of certain grassy surfaces in Italy, over-frowned by masses of brickwork that are honeycombed by the suns of centuries," as James is eager to discover, "is something that I hereby renounce once for all the attempt to express" (*V*, 55). And the grandeur of the Colosseum, he continues, "is a thing about which it is useless to talk, [although] as a piece of the picturesque . . . it is thoroughly and simply delightful."[61] Under the "spell" (*CC*, 245) of the surrounding landscape, James—in keeping with his understanding of the picturesque as internally animated and self-informed—attempts to discover and confirm the possibility that the power of Italy is greater than that of his emerging craft. "Do what we will," he thus announces and projects, "there remains in all these deeply agreeable impressions a charming something we can't analyze" or define (*OSG*, 99).

With its colorful, picturesque, and impressive force, James's Italy remains—to cite Bernard Berenson's term—"life enhancing" be-cause it generates not only beauty but revelatory force as well. The seen world of landscape, architecture, and art impels its viewer into a state of enchantment and rapture; the visible world, as Berenson knew, can convert or change its viewer, and enlist him, as it were, in a newly heightened state of perceptual consciousness. For years, as Berenson recalled, he had known this feeling of being trans-formed by visible beauty, but had not been able to identify it. But, as he writes in *Aesthetics and History in the Visual Arts*,

then one morning as I was gazing at the leafy scrolls carved on the door jambs of St. Pietro outside Spoleto, suddenly [the] stem, tendril and foliage became alive [and] . . . made me feel as if I had emerged into the light after long groping in the darkness of initiation. I felt as one illumined, and beheld a world where every surface was in living relation to me and not, as hitherto, in a merely cognitive one. Since that morning, nothing visible has been indifferent or even dull.[62]

On his Italian travels, as the essays and early letters attest, Henry James experienced a similar discovery of the picturesque and the "radiation of the visible world."[63] James associates visual impressions of Italy with an experience of conversion, joy, and revelatory power similar to that described by Berenson. In a passage worth quoting in full for its uncontained enthusiasm and sense of revelatory conversion, Henry James writes to William of his first day in Rome and the "excitement of [his] first hour[s]."[64] His delight in the surroundings speaks for itself:

At last—for the first time—I live! . . . I went reeling and moaning thro' the streets, in a fever of enjoyment. In the course of four or five hours I traversed almost the whole of Rome and got a glimpse of everything—the Forum, the Coliseum (stupendissimo!), the Pantheon . . . [and] all the Piazzas and ruins and monuments. The effect is something indescribable. For the first time I know what the picturesque is. . . . Even if I should leave Rome tonight I should feel that I have caught the keynote of its operation and the senses. . . . In fine, I've seen Rome, and I shall go to bed a wiser man than I last rose—yesterday morning.[65]

In 1869 James left America in search of inspiration, drama, and the picturesque sights of Italy, with a desire to be "deeply impressed by some *given* aspect of life."[66] What he sought and found was material for a lifetime's work—an "arrangement of things hanging together," as he recalled of his arrival in Europe, "that had the force of revelation."[67] On his Italian tour, James learned to recognize and receive what he would later call a "direct impression of life,"[68] and learned to utilize the impact and structure of that impression—learned to employ an uncanny union of perception and thought, of seeing and knowing, which would inform his writing in the years to come. On his Italian travels James discovered the joy of receptive vision, and the sheer pleasure and force of visual impression. And, by returning to these visual moments again and again in his work, as well as to the Italian setting which generated them, he would later demonstrate how the moment of visual "revelation" itself could become an implicit and powerful source for his art.

Describing the sights of Italy on this first "passionate pilgrimage," Henry James began to work with a creative tension between receptive sight on the one hand and the power of the creative imagination on the other. The essays that grew out of these early Italian travels suggest that while art may well "make life," the opposite may also be true. Life, to reverse James's famous claim, may also "make art." The early Italian travel writings display moments of this very transformation. Here, the seen and felt world of Italy generates sufficient "romantic rightness" and revelatory "force" to overtake its young and receptive observer, so that when the artist, as Rilke has written, has "the right eyes . . . the sight transforms the seer."[69] Although James would indeed go on to transform much of his world through the power of his remarkable craft, the early Italian essays record those resonant and influential moments in which the world transforms its viewer. In these moments of vivid impression, James has the "right eyes" and thus stands expectant, receptive, and willingly transformed by the wondrous sights and felt life of the surrounding Italian landscape.

Notes

1. For background on Henry James's education, see Leon Edel, *Henry James: The Untried Years* (New York: Avon Books, 1953), 81–166; F. O. Matthiessen, *The James Family* (New York: Alfred A. Knopf, 1947), 69–101.
2. The exception to James's extended residence with his family in New England is his brief period at the Harvard Law School in 1862–63.
3. James began to publish in the mid-1860s. In 1864, an unsigned review of Nassau Senior's *Essays on Fiction* appeared in the *North American Review*; later that year, "Tragedy of Errors," an unsigned short story, was printed in *Continental Monthly*; and, in 1865, "The Story of a Year," James's first signed work of fiction, was published in the *Atlantic*.
4. Henry James to T. S. Perry, 15 August, 1867, *Henry James Letters*, vol. 1, *1843–1875*, ed. Leon Edel (Cambridge: Harvard University Press, 1974), 1:71–72.
5. *Henry James: Autobiography*, ed. Frederick W. Dupee (Princeton: Princeton University Press, 1983), 548.
6. Ibid., 548–49.
7. Henry James to William James, 26 April 1869, *Letters*, 1:110–13.
8. Quoted in Edel, *The Untried Years*, 295.
9. Henry James to Alice James, 31 August 1869, *Letters*, 1:128–29.
10. Henry James to William James, 25 September 1869, *Letters*, 1:142.
11. Henry James, Preface to *Roderick Hudson*, in *The Art of the Novel* (Boston: Northeastern University Press, 1984), My emphasis.
12. The travel pieces first appeared in magazines. Later collections of the sketches were published in *Transatlantic Sketches* (1875), *Portraits of Places* (1883), and *Italian Hours* (1909). Although the latter was pub-

lished in 1909, with essays from that year, most of the pieces in the volume were written in the 1870s.

13. Paul Fussell, *Abroad: British Literary Traveling Between the Wars* (New York: Oxford University Press, 1980), 203.

14. Ibid., 214.

15. Carl Smith, "James's Travels, Travel Writing and the Development of His Art," *Modern Language Quarterly* (1977): 367–80. Smith makes the argument that James's travel writings illuminate his intellectual development, and that themes which are implicit in the fiction can be found in more obvious form in the essays. In addition, he rightly notes that the travel works are concerned with epistemology and point of view. I tend, however, to disagree with his main thesis, which suggests that the point of view foreshadowed by the travel essays is one of detachment. Where I understand James, especially in these early essays, to stand receptive, immersed, and in awe, Smith sees James to be a detached and distant observer.

16. Fussell, *Abroad*, 214.

17. Leon Edel, *Henry James, The Conquest of London: 1870–1881* (New York: Avon Books, 1962), 54–55.

18. Henry James, "The Old Saint-Gothard," in *Italian Hours* (New York: Grove Press, 1979), 100. All further references to essays from *Italian Hours* will be indicated by essay abbreviation and page number in the text in parenthesis. The following abbreviations will be used for the essays:

"Venice: An Early Impression"	*V*
"The Old Saint-Gothard"	*OSG*
"Italy Revisited"	*IR*
"A Roman Holiday"	*RH*
"Roman Rides"	*RR*
"Roman Neighborhoods"	*RN*
"From a Roman Notebook"	*FRN*
"A Chain of Cities"	*CC*
"The Autumn in Florence"	*AF*

19. Henry James to Alice James, 31 August 1869, *Letters*, 1:127.

20. My emphasis. James frequently italicizes emphasized words in his text. In order to distinguish his emphasis from my own, I have used underlining instead of italics to indicate all my own emphasized passages or words within quotations.

21. Henry James to John LaFarge, 21 September 1869, *Letters*, 1:134.

22. Henry James to Henry James, Sr., 14 January 1870, *Letters*, 1:191.

23. My emphasis.

24. William James, *The Principles of Psychology* (New York: Dover Publications, 1950), 1:221.

25. Henry James to William James, 22 September 1872, *Letters*, 1:300.
26. Nathalia Wright, *American Novelists in Italy: Allston to James* (Philadelphia: University of Pennsylvania Press, 1965), 214.
27. Henry James to William James, 25 September 1869, *Letters*, 1:136. My emphasis.
28. Henry James to Alice James, 6 October 1869, *Letters*, 1:145.
29. William James, *Principles*, 1:223.
30. Ibid., 2:301–5.
31. Ibid., 1:222. See also Ibid., 2:8.
32. Ibid., 2:8.
33. Maurice Merleau-Ponty, *The Primacy of Perception* (Evanston: Northwestern University Press, 1964), 182.
34. Henry James to Alice James, 7 November 1869, *Letters*, 1:162.
35. My emphasis.
36. Pierre Thévanez, "What is Phenomenology?," in *What is Phenomenology*, ed. James Edie (London: Merlin Press, 1962), 44–46. In this chapter, I am indebted to Paul Armstrong's thorough study on *The Phenomenology of Henry James* (Chapel Hill: University of North Carolina Press, 1983). Using the phenomenological concept of intentionality, Armstrong discusses how impression is a "way of knowing" in James's work. My thesis differs from Armstrong's in its attempt to show that Henry James's early work does not so much "project" a whole" (my emphasis), on the basis of a single impression, as illuminate an act of perception in which the impression so seizes the viewer that it seems itself to arrive already whole. In Armstrong's reading of Husserl, "no act of perception can deliver more than incomplete access to anything" (p. 42). While I would agree that perception in James often entails a leap of faith by which we project a whole from a partial impression, I would add that it can also display an aesthetic moment in which the viewer receives and stands transformed by the whole impression.
37. Cited in Bruce Wilshire, *William James and Phenomenology* (Bloomington: Indiana University Press, 1968), 19.
38. Thévanez, "What is Phenomenology?," 29.
39. Wilshire, *William James*, 8, 6.
40. Fussell, *Abroad*, 214.
41. Wilshire, *William James*, 8.
42. Merleau-Ponty, "The Primacy of Perception," in *The Primacy of Perception*, 25.
43. Henry James, *The Painter's Eye* (Cambridge: Harvard University Press, 1956), 222.
44. Henry James to William James, 26 October 1869, *Letters*, 1:160.
45. Henry James, "Lake George," *Nation* 11 (25 August 1870); 119–20. Emphasis mine.
46. *Autobiography* (1983), 286. My emphasis.

47. Ibid., 275.
48. William Morris Hunt, *Talks on Art* (Boston: Houghton, Osgood, 1880), 2–3. My emphasis.
49. Hunt, *Talks on Art*, 8, 61.
50. William James, *Principles*, 1:239.
51. Ibid., 1:405.
52. Ibid., 2:45, 80.
53. Ibid., 2:83.
54. My emphasis.
55. My emphasis.
56. Merleau-Ponty, *The Primacy of Perception*, 182.
57. Henry James to William James, 25 September 1869, *Letters*, 1:139–40.
58. My emphasis.
59. See entries for "impress" and "impression" in *The Compact Edition of the Oxford English Dictionary* (New York: Oxford University Press, 1971). My emphasis.
60. Herbert Spiegelberg, *The Phenomenological Movement* (The Hague: Nijhoff, 1960), 1:305. My emphasis.
61. Henry James to Alice James, 7 November 1869, *Letters*, 1:163.
62. Bernard Berenson, *Aesthetics and History in the Visual Arts* (New York: Pantheon Books, 1948), 72.
63. Merleau-Ponty, *The Primacy of Perception*, 182.
64. Henry James to Alice James, 7 November 1869, *Letters*, 1:162.
65. Henry James to William James, 30 October 1869, *Letters*, 1:160–61.
66. Edward Hale, "The Impressionism of Henry James," in *Faculty Papers of Union College* (Albany: Frank H. Evory) 2, no. 1 (January 1931): 11. My emphasis.
67. *Autobiography* (1983), 549.
68. Henry James, "The Art of Fiction," in *Partial Portraits* (London: Macmillan, 1968), 384.
69. Quoted in Howard Moss, review of Rainer Maria Rilke's *Letters on Cézanne*, *The New Yorker*, 7 July 1986, p. 80.

EIGHT *Alice James and Italy*

MARIA ANTONIETTA SARACINO

A NY ENCOUNTER between a complex personality, full of curiosity, such as that of Alice James, and a country such as Italy—rich in history and culture, a country that many nineteenth-century upper-middle-class American women dreamed of—would be potentially alive with stimulating new impressions and observations. Alice James's encounter with Italy, however, due to the particular life of the woman, came about in an unusual and partial manner; but with the intelligence, the perspicacity, and analytic bent of the protagonist, it was bound to have a rich and unexpected outcome.

The eminence of Henry James and his vast literary production have for decades occupied a prominent place in Italian literary criticism, as can be seen in the abundant existing bibliography. The same cannot be said—and understandably so—of Alice James. The youngest child and only girl in the James household, Alice was known, even in America, only through biographical works—mostly devoted to the best-known members of her family—until the complete edition of her diary, edited by Leon Edel, was published in 1964.[1] Welcomed by critics as "one of the neglected masterpieces of American literature,"[2] the diary revealed itself to be much more than a mere *journal intime* or a commonplace book like many others kept by women in the late nineteenth century. If at first the work might have attracted some critics' attention, thanks mostly to its author's name, a closer reading of those pages soon revealed that the book had a specific and considerable value in itself. It opened up in front of its readers a rich blend of feelings and desires, comments on life and death, on politics and culture and on rising feminism, seldom to be found—and in such variety—in writings generally centered upon the author's private world. Moreover, it soon became clear that the book also cast a new and unexpected light on all the members of the James family—particularly on Henry— and on their mutual relationships, offering new interpretative angles even on some of the most famous Jamesian works.

If Henry James at a late stage of his life destroyed part of his private papers in order to protect his image from the curiosity of those who were to come after him—and in one of his *Notebooks* he went as far as to imagine himself fighting a duel with his own biographer[3]—the pages of Alice's diary partially reconstruct some of the fragments of that mosaic, by voicing some of his fears and ambitions, and bringing to light certain moments of private life that he would have preferred not to be revealed.

Any first encounter with a great writer is always primarily with his work, but in time we can acquire a better understanding and new insight by reading about his private life. We delve into his personal world by reading his diaries and papers in an effort to reconstruct the complex network of his family relationships. In some cases our efforts are not particularly fruitful. Sometimes the author in question emerges as an isolated and solitary figure capable of pouring his entire life experience into his writings, to the point where an incursion into his private world can turn out to be disappointing.

Where Henry James is concerned—and this collection of essays is proof of it—quite the opposite occurs. An indefatigable observer of the world around him, he lived in a dense network of family and social relationships, drawing from them an inexhaustible source of creative energy. Henry James's relationship with his family was, perhaps more than for any other of his contemporary writers, primary and fundamental. It is no exaggeration to say that this particular fabric of affections and relationships that accompanied him throughout his life was instrumental in originating the extraordinary literary production that we have today. Even he so regarded himself above all as a son and brother that he entitled part of his autobiographical memoirs—written when he was almost seventy years old—*Notes of a Son and Brother*.[4] If we set out with this assumption, it seems all the more important that we consider the other and less well-known members of the James family and investigate the close bonds between them. We might add that in this case our efforts are particularly fruitful, because few are the families who, like the Jameses, seem to have deliberately wanted to leave so many traces behind them. Indeed, from Henry's vast narrative and critical production to William's scientific works, from their father's philosophical writings to Alice's diary, from their accounts of their travels to their autobiographies, scholars and critics alike have a myriad of paths to follow, which, from one member of the family to another, from one side of the Atlantic to the other, spans almost an entire century of cultural life. What is most fascinating in such an enterprise is that we can embark upon any one of these paths almost at any point, without a preestablished order, and yet find that, although each path leads to all the others in an original and autonomous pattern, each one is fundamental to the structure of the whole.

Here I should like to focus my attention on the figure of Alice James, who only in recent years has emerged from the shadows to fit into the intricate mosaic. She is a much more important piece than was initially thought, an irreplaceable intellectual and emotional reference point in a family nucleus where affections dominated unchallenged. Alice James was a woman who never had a family of her own and never worked, who traveled very little and tired easily, and all she published in her whole life was a short letter to a newspaper. Even so, faithful to the wishes of her father —who wanted all the Jameses "just to *be* something . . . , something unconnected with specific doing, something free and uncommitted, something finer, in short, than being *that*, whatever it was, might consist of"[5]—Alice chose for herself an extreme and transgressive role. To the restlessness of her family she responded with the paralysis of her body, to their writings she responded with words. If the others sought in their lives to keep death away through celebrity, she sought to bring it closer by building up to it—day after day—with the patience of a master craftsman. She attributed to death the same importance as her more famous brothers did to their literary or scientific triumphs. "Within the last year"—she writes in her diary in 1881—"he [Henry] has published *The Tragic Muse*, brought out *The American*, and written a play, *Mrs. Vibert* (which Hare has accepted) and his admirable comedy; combined with William's *Psychology*, not a bad show for one family! Especially if I get myself dead, the hardest job of all."[6]

Endowed as she was with the intelligence of the Jameses, but forbidden as a woman to make her own way in life, one has the impression that—certainly unbeknown to herself—Alice may have wanted to offer part of her self to each of the relatives she loved. To her mother she gave a daughter to care for and nurse all her life. To her father, who as a youth had lost a leg in an accident, she offered the paralysis of her body. (As we know, from the day after her father's death she could no longer walk.) She gave William a subject for his research. (He, in fact, devoted many pages of his *Principles of Psychology* to his sister's nervous disorders.) To Henry she offered a constant and somewhat ambiguous love, and was his confidante; she also provided material for his writings. (We know, for instance, that she inspired some of his novels, including *The Bostonians* and *Princess Casamassima*.) She also ideally dedicated to him her only piece of writing, that diary in which the novelist is constantly a presence. For all of them she represented a kind of mirror in which their experiences would in turn be reflected or diverted, but one in which they would always find a place of their own.

Filtered through this particular human experience, the image of Italy that played such an important part in the Jameses' cultural background appears to our eyes as a multifaceted one. While Henry had a positive and enthusiastic attitude toward Italy which remained constant over the years, Alice's direct or indirect experience of the country was such that her reactions reflect a range of different attitudes. Initially Italy was merely one of those many places that contributed to the forming of their "accidental childhood," as she would define it. Later it was the cradle of a superior artistic civilization, especially when compared to the English culture she was more familiar with. It subsequently represented a dangerous rival in her love for her brother, not only because the attention he devoted to Italy was described in his letters to her in a language

usually reserved for lovers, but also because—away from her—
Henry shared his Italian experience with some women friends who
were meaningful to him and of whom Alice was jealous. Moreover,
Alice James regarded Italy as a country with a monarchy that
reigned in style, particularly when compared to the English monarchy that she defines in her diary as haughty and arrogant. Many
miles away from Italy and confined to her room as an invalid, Alice
turned her attention to an aspect of Italian life—the world of
politics—that Henry perhaps overlooked, being immersed as he was
in the beauty of the country's culture, and attuned to viewing
himself in relation to it.

Alice James was only one year old when her father thought of
Europe for the first time as a place where his children could "absorb
French and German and get a better sensuous education," as he
wrote in a letter to his friend Emerson.[7] She was seven when—in
1855—the family traveled to Europe for the first time: London,
Paris, Geneva, the Alps, then back again to Paris and London. We
know from the family biography that between 1855 and 1859 the
James children had already crossed the Atlantic and back three
times, following their restless father. Italy was not yet on their
itinerary; there was no room for Italy in this first phase of their
"sensuous education." Italy was the land of the grand tour, the
country where their education would eventually be completed, when
they reached adulthood. Nonetheless, their first encounters with
Europe are worth mentioning since they prepare the ground for the
future behavior of the James children with regard to culture as a
whole. Whereas the four boys were encouraged to come into contact with European culture during their schooling, Alice was educated at home by governesses who were not often equal to the task
and who only stayed for brief periods, because—as Henry James
recalls in his autobiography—"the requirements of our small sister
were for long modest enough."[8] It was during her first encounter
with Europe that Alice perceived the meaning of a double standard
in the kind of education she received, and this is not only because
she was the youngest of the five children, but mainly because she
was a girl. Years later, she wrote to William, who was about to
embark on a trip to Europe with his own children:

What enrichment of mind and memory can children have without continuity and if they are torn up by the roots every little while as we were! Of
all things don't make the mistake which brought about our rootless and
accidental childhood. Leave Europe for them until they are old enough to
have *the* Grand Emotion undiluted by vague memories.[9]

But it was precisely in those years—and during their European
experience—that the seeds were sown for that close intellectual
and emotional bond between Alice and Henry James that was to
continue for the rest of their lives. If it is in Europe that William
and Henry begin to form some idea of what they will do in life, Alice
returns to America with the feeling of her inadequacy. The "sensuous education" from which her brothers had so greatly benefited
was for her but a blurred and distant experience. If, on the one
hand, she was encouraged to follow her own inclinations, on the
other she was prevented from accomplishing regular studies. If, on
the one hand, she was expected to practice patience, moderation,
and self-control, on the other the family correspondence refers to
her—somewhat ironically—as "that idle and useless young female
. . . whom we shall have to feed and clothe."[10] Years later, going
back in her memory to this period of her life, Alice wrote in her
diary: "Owing to muscular circumstances my youth was not of the
most ardent, but I had to peg away pretty hard between twelve and
twenty-four, 'killing myself,' as someone calls it, absorbing into the
bone that the better part is to clothe oneself in neutral tints, walk
by still waters and possess one's soul in silence."[11] During this
period the image of Italy reached her mostly through the readings
recommended by her brother, such as Howells's story "Lago Maggiore," written in Italy, where the author lived at that time, and
published in the *Atlantic* in 1866. It was also during this period of
her life that—a victim of frequent nervous breakdowns and incapable of giving real meaning to her life—at the age of nineteen
Alice thought that she was definitely stupid. But she also convinced
herself that her stupidity was somehow a way to compensate for
the intelligence of her elder brothers. "You must excuse the frivolity of this letter," she writes to William in 1867, "if you condescend
to read it, on account of the frivolity and want of intelligence of
the writer. You must remember that this mental baseness is not her
own fault, and that as she is your sister, her having so little mind

may account for your having so much. . . . Your loving, *idiotoid* sister, Alice James."[12]

In 1869, Henry James left for Europe, Italy being one of the countries he intended to visit. He was determined to keep up the close bond that tied him to his only sister. If her poor health forced her to postpone her own journey to Europe, he would be her eyes, he would see in her place, and through his letters he would let her live his experiences. By writing to her, he in a certain manner enabled her to continue—indirectly to be sure—that "sensuous education" that had unfortunately been interrupted years earlier. At the same time, by writing, he relieved the pain of their being apart: "I exhale all my pleasurable emotions by means of inarticulate groans and grunts and sighs. Whenever I see anything very stunning I long for the presence of my lovely sister, and in default of it I promise myself to make the object present to her eyes by means of the most graphic and 'spirituelle' descriptions."[13] It is thus through her brother's letters from Italy that Alice received her first impressions of the country; they are strong images. Using a suggestive language, Henry tried to convey to his sister the same exciting sensations that Italy seemed to stir in him: "Down, down, on on into Italy we went"—he writes to her from Lake Como—

a rapturous progress thro' a wild luxuriance of corn and vines and olives and figs and mulberries and chestnuts and frescoed villages and clamorous beggars and all the good old Italianisms of tradition. . . . The most striking feature in Italian scenery seems to be this same old mingling of tawdriness and splendour—a generous profuse luxuriance of nature and the ludicrous gingerbread accessories of human contrivance.[14]

In these letters Henry described Italy to her in its minutest details: from the prices of food to the furnishings of the cafes, from the itineraries he followed in each town he visited to the paintings he saw in the museums, to the friends he met. As the journey proceeded, even the language he used to write about it became more intense, to the point where—on some occasions—he borrowed tones and accents that would mostly be devoted to someone he was in love with. That is how he spoke of Venice: "[S]he lies like a great dazzling spot of yellow paint upon the backward path of my destiny. Now that I behold her no more I feel sadly as if I had done her wrong—as if I had been cold and insensible—that my eyes scowled and blinked at her brightness and that with more of self-oblivion I might have known her better and loved her more."[15]

But this world of absolute beauty also represented for Henry James "the place of places to enjoy *à deux,*"[16] and his sister Alice was the person he longed for most of all. It is with her that Henry would like to have visited Venice. Consequently, his letters from Italy, interspersed as they are with expressions of deep nostalgia for her, became the *medium* of the intensification of his emotional involvement: "Nothing is wanting but to feel fluttering at my side in the soft Italian breeze, some light muslin drapery of the sister of my soul. . . . [I]t's a shame to be here in gross melancholy solitude."[17]

In 1872 it was Alice's turn to embark upon her grand tour, accompanied by her brother Henry and an aunt. Alice was twenty-three, Henry was twenty-eight. Italy was on the itinerary. Henry returned with his sister to some of the places he knew and that were dear to him. Jean Strouse, Alice's biographer, informs us that none of the letters she sent to her family during those six months has survived. Here again it is therefore Henry's letters home that tell us that "Alice enjoys everything *à merveille.* . . . She is really making a capital traveller and when we have done what she is able to do, we have all pretty well done what we desire to do. In short, her undertaking has already proved a most distinct and brilliant success."[18]

In the eyes of her family, Alice was already chronically ill, and this Italian experience of hers was the last parenthesis of physical well-being before her definitive breakdown on her return. Despite the fact that Henry was only a few years older than she, he helped her and took care of her with fatherly affection, and like a father, and a teacher too, he introduced her to the many works of art that the journey had in store for her. At last, this direct contact with Italian art—up to that moment seen only through books or through other people's accounts—was for Alice a true and proper revelation. She began to realize that she too was endowed with the James's intelligence; the paintings conveyed to her, as to her brother, the same power "to speak." Years later, thinking back on that experience, Alice wrote in her diary: "Imagine the bliss of finding that I too was a 'sensitive,' and that I was not only 'mute before a Botticelli,' but that a Botticelli said an infinity of things to me and this in a flash of mutual recognition, after the years of toil in trying to establish some sort of relation, either of speech or silence, with the Botticelli of Boston."[19]

As the parenthesis closed and this direct encounter—which was to remain for her "a memory to dwell on"[20]—ended, to Alice's eyes the image of Italy changed once more: Italy now came to be seen as the very place that separated her from her brother. Italy became threatening since in Italy lived some of Henry's female friends, of whom she was jealous. Constance Fenimore Woolson was one of them. "Henry has had a light attack of jaundice in Venice"—she writes to her sister-in-law in 1887; "he has an excellent doctor and an impassioned Gondolier taking care of him, Mrs. Bronson in the foreground and Miss Woolson in the background . . . so I think we may have no anxiety about him."[21] And later: "Henry is somewhere on the Continent flirting with Constance."[22] But in spite of the harshness and the irony of such remarks, in writing her final will—the last of the many she wrote over the years—she bequeathed to her brother the only possession of hers that could remind him of a country he had loved so much: a picture of Venice.

In Alice's few letters that have survived from this period, Italy makes only a few and rather blurred appearances. It is a country from which she visibly tried to keep her distance, and whenever she spoke of it, she did so in a somewhat ironic and detached tone. Alice now began to be seriously preoccupied with her future. As her parents were now dead and she had turned herself into a permanent invalid, she chose to move to Europe, where her brother lived. But whereas Henry on landing in Europe had proudly declared: "I take possession of the old world, I inhale it. I appropriate it!"[23] Alice arrived in Europe "suspended . . . like an old woman of the sea round his neck where to all appearances I shall remain for all time."[24] From this moment on she spent her life waiting for death, entrusting to the pages of her diary whatever—day after day—fell within her radius of observation. If her invalid condition prevented her from going outside, toward the social, it was the outside, the social, that came to her, in the form of visits, letters, and readings from books and newspapers. Alice devoted special attention to all that happened around her, and in particular she reflected upon the

world of politics and the world of the social. And it is through this
filter that we find in her diary new and different references to Italy.

In sharp contrast with the haughty attitude of the British monarchy, "the King of Italy seems alone among them all, to have some
imagination, and to get some fun out of his limitations," writes
Alice.[25] She praises the fact that Gladstone knows Italian and can
sing Italian songs in a tenor voice. She quotes several passages from
the *Memoirs* of the Italian statesman Massimo d'Azeglio in order to
point out the difference between democracy and autocracy. And in
sharp contrast with what she sees as "the all pervasive sense of
pharisaism in the British Constitution of things,"[26] she quotes an
amusing anecdote which underlines the behavior of the men who
run the House of Savoy—who "seem alone to have that sense of the
picturesque which lifts them out of the vulgar and flimsy platitude
of contemporary monarchs. As the Duke of Aosta lay dying," Alice
writes, "he told the priest who was standing by his bedside to go
and rest. The old man turned away and a man who was standing
among the others stepped forward and took his hand and said
"Thanks"—the priest then expressed some sorrow and affection for
the duke—when "Thanks" was repeated with much emotion—as
the room was dark the confessor said "I don't know who you are?"
—"I am his brother." In all the five years that I have been in
England," concludes Alice James, "I have never heard or read of a
word said by 'our family' which would give one reason for supposing
that they had the faintest conception of what they represented,
save on its flimsiest side."[27]

In the diary she also makes ironic reference to the way Italians
face life: "as soon as an Italian has a pain . . . he not only sobs, but
the whole household surrounds him in chorus. Lately . . . [the doc-
tor] was called to a gallant colonel and found a large, handsome
man lying on a bed all gorgeous with pink silk and lace draperies,
crying his eyes out because his throat was sore."[28]

The whole of Henry James's work—directly or indirectly, in the
stories he creates, in the metaphors he chooses, as well as in the
language he uses—seems to place at its center the image of the
woman. It is to the female world that he mostly directs his attention as a narrator. In the case of Alice James the opposite seems to

happen. In the way she looks at the world around her, in the judgments she makes on people and situations, in the readings she selects for herself, she seems to be constantly geared to male models. If in talking about Italy Henry James makes use of metaphors mostly drawn from the female world, Alice does exactly the opposite. In spite of all the descriptions of Italy she assimilated over the years from her brother's correspondence, whenever she refers to this country in her diary she does so in connection with the male world, or rather with what is by definition regarded as a male realm: the world of politics.[29] She observes Italy with an attentive eye, but at the same time her attitude toward the country is rather benevolent. And perhaps it could not have been otherwise, given the affection and the happy memories attached to a place where she seems to have lived one of the few really happy experiences of her life.

In Italy, as in America, until recently Alice James was only known through biographical references contained in a number of studies on Henry James. The Italian version of her diary, published in 1985,[30] aroused great interest on the part of critics and scholars alike. The numerous enthusiastic critical reviews—reviews that in a number of instances also considered the diary to be a forgotten masterpiece—show that even in the eyes of Italian critics the literary transcription of Alice's very special life-experience had a value of its own, even while it played an important role in the personal and literary life of Henry James.[31] A year after the book was published, this Italian version was adapted for the stage, as a one-woman monologue, and was praised by the critics.

We know that the diary of Alice James remained in the hands of her dedicated friend Katharine Loring, who lived with her during the entire period of her illness and to whom Alice dictated it during the last months of her life. It was Katharine Loring who recounted in but a few words the end of Alice James's "mortal career": "This dictation of March 4th"—Katharine wrote in concluding her friend's diary—"was rushing about in her brain, and although she was very weak and it tired her much to dictate, she could not get her head quiet until she had had it written; then she was relieved and I finished Miss Woolson's story of 'Dorothy' to her."[32]

The story Katharine Loring had just finished reading to Alice
James shortly before she died was taken from *Dorothy and Other
Italian Stories*.[33] The book was written by Constance Fenimore
Woolson, Henry James's lifelong friend who committed suicide in
1894, perhaps—as Leon Edel suggests—because she had an unreci-
procated love for him.[34] It was obviously sheer chance that made of
this book Alice James's very last reading, a chance that perhaps
could also be symbolically interpreted as one last indirect homage
of Alice James to Italy and to her brother, through the reading of a
book written by another woman who had loved Henry James as she
did, and who, two years after writing it, had died perhaps for him.

Notes

1. *The Diary of Alice James*, ed. Leon Edel (New York: Penguin American
   Library, 1982). A version of the diary had earlier been published under
   the title *Alice James: Her Brothers—Her Journal*, ed. Anna Robeson
   Burr (New York: Dodd, Mead, 1934).
2. Gay Wilson Allen, review of *The Diary of Alice James*, *Saturday Review*, 5 September 1964.
3. Leon Edel, "Introduction," *Henry James: Letters*, vol. 1, *1843–1875*, ed.
   Leon Edel (Cambridge: Harvard University Press, 1974), xiv.
4. *Henry James: Autobiography*, ed. F. W. Dupee (New York: Criterion,
   1956). This volume contains *A Small Boy and Others* and *Notes of a
   Son and Brother*.
5. *Autobiography* (1956), 268.
6. *The Diary of Alice James*, 211. 16 June 1891.
7. Quoted in Jean Strouse, *Alice James: A Biography* (New York: Bantam
   Books, 1980), 32.
8. *Autobiography* (1956), 173.
9. *The Death and Letters of Alice James* ed. Ruth Bernard Yeazell (Berke-
   ley: University of California Press, 1981), 148. A. J. to William James, 4
   November 1888.
10. Strouse, *Alice James*, 83–84.
11. *The Diary of Alice James*, 95. 21 February 1890.
12. Alice James to William James, 6 August 1867. Strouse, *Alice James*,
    125.
13. Henry James to Alice James, 16 April 1869. Ibid., p. 150.
14. Henry James to Alice James, 31 August 1869, *Letters*, 1:128–29. 31
    August 1869.
15. Henry James to Alice James, 6 October 1869, *Letters*, 1:145.
16. Henry James to Alice James, 31 August 1869, *Letters*, 1:130.

17. Ibid.
18. Henry James to his parents, 4 June 1872, *Letters*, 1:292.
19. 11 July 1889, *The Diary of Alice James*, 47.
20. "I am frightened sometimes . . . when I suddenly become conscious of how constantly I dwell on the memory of that summer I spent abroad." Alice James to Ann Ashburner, 28 February 1877, Strouse, *Alice James*, 174.
21. Alice James to Alice Gibbens James, 3 April 1887, *The Death and Letters of Alice James*, 123–24.
22. Alice James to William James, 4 November 1888, *The Death and Letters of Alice James*, 149.
23. Leon Edel, "Introduction," *Henry James Letters*, vol. 2 *1875–1883* (Cambridge: Harvard University Press, 1975), xi.
24. 25 March 1890, *The Diary of Alice James*, 104.
25. 17 May 1890, *The Diary of Alice James*, 115.
26. 17 February 1890, *The Diary of Alice James*, 87.
27. 12 February 1890, *The Diary of Alice James*, 83.
28. 13 September 1890, *The Diary of Alice James*, 136.
29. After reading his sister's diary, two years after her death, Henry James wrote to his brother William: "I find an immense eloquence in her passionate 'radicalism'—her most distinguished feature almost—which, in her, was absolutely direct and original (like everything that was in her); unreflected, uncaught from entourage or example. It would really have made her, had she lived in the world, a feminine 'political force'. . . . She would have been . . . a national glory!" Henry James to William James, 28 May 1894, *Henry James Letters*, vol. 3, *1883–1895* (Cambridge: Harvard University Press, 1980), 482.
30. *Alice James. Il diario. 1889–1892*, ed. and trans. with an introduction by Maria Antonietta Saracino (Milan: La Tartaruga, 1985).
31. Paolo Milano, "Non priva di genio," *L'Espresso*, 4 August 1985; Oreste del Buono, "Caro Diario. Ti racconto la mia fine," *L'Europeo*, 13 July 1985; Fernanda Pivano, "Memorie di un'infelice," *Corriere della sera*, 31 July 1985; Rosaria Guacci, "La morte come opera d'arte," *Paese Sera*, 29 October 1985; Natalia Aspesi, "Alice nel paese del malanno," *La Repubblica*, 30 July 1985; Sandro Portelli, "La casa e il mondo di Alice," *Il Manifesto*, 11 September 1985; Benedetta Bini, "Testimoni della propria morte," *Noi Donne*, October 1985.
32. *The Diary of Alice James*, 232–33. Final entry by Katharine P. Loring.
33. Miss Woolson's story was published posthumously in *Dorothy and Other Italian Stories* (1896).
34. Millicent Bell, "The Essence of the Master," *New York Times Book Review*, 24 November 1985.

NINE The Influence of William James's Pragmatism in Italy

GERALD E. MYERS

ART, literature, history, language, landscape—for these William James thanked Italy. Also, albeit an untrampled fact, he admired nineteenth-century Italian technology. Preparing to leave Rome in the winter of 1900, and apprehensive about a shivering stop in Germany, he wrote: "To me the air tight German stoves and unventilated rooms are an abomination." But in Italy, as he had communicated eight years earlier from Florence, "we live well and are comfortable by means of sheet-iron stoves which the clammy quality of the cold rather than its intensity seems to necessitate."[1] Obviously not the sort of thing a pragmatist overlooks!

For James, however, the dominant Italian impression, a panorama of painted and carved witnesses to tradition's authority, excluded pragmatism. The modesty that is extracted from accepting fuzzily defined truths required James's assertion that pragmatism is only a new name for old ways of thinking, but this tipping of the hat immediately gave way to ardent defenses of pragmatism's love affair with novelty. Insofar as "the new" marked pragmatism's territory and "the old" defined Italy's, philosophical tensions for the pragmatist wandering that country's heritage were inevitable. Since James's tensions in this regard began prior to his official adoption of pragmatism, his relationship to Italy serves to illustrate one of his favorite convictions, that one's philosophy is largely an outgrowth of temperament.

In 1873, having joined his brother Henry in Florence, William wrote to their sister Alice: "This is the place for history. I don't see how, if one lived here, historical problems could help being the most urgent ones for the mind." Always anxious about his late start with a career and about his ability to sustain it, and now temporarily motionless in a "dead civilization," he returned to a mood once expressed in 1879 in a letter to Henry, who was at the time learning to articulate Veronese, Bellini, and especially Tintoretto within his own aesthetic. Don't despair about leaving Italy, he had counseled Henry, because one must have but one intellectual *home*, which for Henry was evidently England, for William definitely America. Yet, from Rome in another 1873 letter to Alice, William could write: "Strange to say, my very enjoyment of what here belongs to hoary eld has done more to reconcile me to what belongs to the present hour, business, factories, etc. etc. than anything I ever experienced."[2]

The past in and for itself left William cold, occasionally heating his interest by making a lightning strike somewhere in the present. His intensely negative reaction to Rome at one point in 1873 is an example. In a letter to his father, he deplored the architecture of St. Peter's, calling it an insolent negation of the religion it was designed to enrich; and, after passing the "wreck-strewed" Forum, he wrote that

when we entered under the mighty Coliseum wall and stood in its mysterious midst, with that cold sinister half-moon and hardly a star in the deep blue sky—it was all so strange, and I must say, inhuman and horrible, that it felt like a nightmare. . . . Anti-Christian as I generally am, I actually derived a deep comfort from the big black cross that had been planted on that damned blood-soaked soil. I think if Henry had not been with me that I should have fled howling from the place.[3]

Left like that, the experience would have forever dismissed Rome and its history for William, but that history in fact altered the experience, striking it with a Jamesian moral to include in the same letter to his father: "The 'picturesque'-ness that *we* now find there was the last thing present to the utilitarian minds of those who built them, and they make one realize how man's life is based historically on sheer force and will and fight, and how the inner ideal world only grows up inside and under the shelter of these brute tendencies."

This idea reappears in William's writings, notably "The Moral Equivalent of War" (1910), but to be noticed here is the implicit thesis, made fully explicit in his pragmatism, that we do not owe the past our contemplation or understanding; it rather owes us a challenge of some kind that, if met, means a specific triumph in the here-and-now. James heeded whatever in history could galvanize his moral and intellectual energies on behalf of future achievements, and the rest could be forgotten or, in lazy moments, perhaps indulged. This trait was observed by Henry: "He [William] professed amazement and even occasionally impatience at my reach of reminiscence—liking as he did to brush away old moral scraps in favour of new rather than to hoard and so complacently exhibit them."[4] It is not surprising, then, that after returning home in 1874 to Cambridge William should write to Henry, still in Florence: "Any gossip about Florence you can communicate will be greedily sucked in by me, who feel towards it as I do towards the old Albany of our childhood, with afternoon shadows of trees, etc. . . . All my moments here are inferior to those in Italy, but they are parts of a long plan which is good, so they content me more than the Italian ones which only existed for themselves."[5]

William manifested the same ambivalence, attraction, and revulsion during later travels to Italy. In a letter of 1882 from Venice he wrote to his father that "the spirit of the cheap young Italian swell has gradually stolen over my soul, who thinks the truest philosophy is to straddle about St. Mark's Place and watch the decay go on, with a pleasant smile on his face, a round topped hat stuck on the side of his head with a curl escaping beneath it on his forehead, a ready-made sack coat flung on his shoulders, and a six centime cigar between his teeth."[6] But side-by-side with these words are expressions of sadness at having to depart "the indescribable Italian charm," Italy that is "the most comfortable of all possible mediums to be plunged in," Italy with all its "glorious pictures." Italy represents for him beauty everywhere but decadence, too, the decay that only centuries-soaked soil can grow.

The opportunity of exploiting the tension between the old and the new had been handed to James, and he seized it. Positioned at the crossroads of two centuries, an American by birth and a cosmopolitan through travel, the stay-at-home brother of an expatriated novelist, and the grandson of an Irish immigrant, he savored fully where he was and what that meant. Out of his aesthetic and social sense of what distinguished a young country, slim on culture and tradition, from its elderly European relatives, he fashioned a philosophy that was instantly perceived by everyone to be American. Why not? Clearly, the temperament pulsating inside the philosophy, that gave it its special flavor, was self-consciously American.

Sending his impressions of San Francisco in 1898, he referred to its "sea-port nakedness, yet so new and American," also explaining his opting for Yosemite Valley rather than a trip down the coast because the latter would "involve too much humanity" and "on the whole I prefer the works of God to those of man." Except for the Alps, Europe also presented too much humanity and a superfluity of its artifacts. Three years later he wrote from Nauheim: "What I *crave* most is some wild American country. It is a curious organic-feeling need. One's social relations with European landscape are entirely different, everything being so fenced or planted that you can't lie down or sprawl." But even the most congested of American cities vied with the countryside for the pragmatist's admiration. The machine age had descended, but that was no cause for despair; its novelty was refreshing to the point of intoxication. He described the effects made on himself by New York City in 1907 to his brother Henry, calling the city a "cyclone," enjoying its pulse, and marveling at the powerful, beautiful subway.

It is an *entirely* new New York, in soul as well as in body, from the old one [his and Henry's birthplace], which looks like a village in retrospect. The courage, the heaven-scaling audacity of it all, and the *lightness* withal, as if there was nothing that was not easy, and the great pulses and bounds of progress, so many in directions all simultaneous that the coordination is indefinitely future, give a kind of *drumming background* of life that I never felt before.[7]

America, however, no more than any other place, could satisfy James's restlessness. In this country he longed for Europe but there he waxed nostalgic for New Hampshire or the Adirondacks. He traveled for escape, stimulation, and for convalescence. Always dogged by ill health, with symptoms, physical and mental, that have incited a wide range of diagnoses by his biographers, he as often sought Europe as he did the White Mountains as a place of healing. During the years 1899–1902 he was in bad shape, and, with the aim of repairing an impaired heart and a chronic neurasthenic condition, while composing *The Varieties of Religious Experience* (1902), he and his wife took to Europe.

Writing from Rome in 1900, the final decade of his life just under way, he displayed again the old ambivalence. Rome is unmatched for its collection of beauty, he declared, yet—and this, he thought, certainly disproves Bernard Berenson's dictum that beauty is rather suggested than literally seen—what Rome's artifacts suggest while delighting the eye is horrendous. "For the things the eyes most gloat on, the inconceivably corrupted, besmeared and ulcerated surfaces, and black and cavernous glimpses of interiors, have no suggestions save of moral horror." While considering how Giordano Bruno's statue reveals one of those "glorious" Italian inscriptions—A BRUNO, *il secolo da lui divinato qui dove il rogo arse* (here where the fire burned he made the century divine)—"here, where the faggots burned," James wrote, making "the tears come, for the poetic justice," but immediately adding "though I imagine B[runo] to have been a very pesky sort of crank, worthy of little sympathy had not the 'rogo' done its work for him."[8]

James's ambivalence was of course not confined to Italian encounters, although they were obviously among the more powerful experiences to bring it to eloquent expression. Nor was the ambivalence totally lost on James himself; on the contrary, it was an acknowledged aspect of how he saw things and a deliberately incorporated dimension of his philosophy. Temperamentally, he veered toward Manichaeism, perceiving duality everywhere—good and evil, beauty and ugliness, tradition and revolution—but he also leaned toward Hegelianism, locating the dualities not in Manichaean separateness but in a Hegelian simultaneous togetherness. Unlike Hegel's absolute, however, where the opposites blended monochromatically, James's metaphysics kept their separate colors equally vibrant while existentially fused in one mosaic.

Ambivalence and duality are helpful concepts for registering James's habit of discovering a defect in whatever was initially applauded or some merit in anything originally scorned. For a fuller, more accurate account, however, they are to be replaced by James's famous notion of pluralism that conveyed American associations such as the melting pot, individualism, checks and balances, inventiveness, dissent, and states-based democracy. Something less chauvinistic and more metaphysical was also meant. Pluralism is a larger idea that encompasses other features besides duality and ambivalance, and in explaining in his *Pragmatism* (1907) how pragmatism and pluralism connect, James referred to his friend and ally in Italy, Giovanni Papini.

Papini, a founder of Italian pragmatism that was based on the work of Charles Sanders Peirce, John Dewey, and William James, was then but twenty-six and disposed to address James as "Dear Master."[9] James admired the energy of Papini's writing, and, on the matter at hand, he especially liked Papini's statement that pragmatism tends to *unstiffen* theories and theorizing.[10] Neo-Hegelianism that dominated nineteenth-century philosophy was monistic, picturing the universe as an organic unity that can be conceptualized by a single system. The appearance of multiple and sometimes competing hypotheses is illusory, there being only one world or systematic reality and only one coherent theory for understanding it. This was monism, and, according to James and Papini, its product was dogmatism. A rigid, still style of philosophizing distinguished by high-flying abstract terminology and a priori arguments that rarely touched on everyday facts, monopolized the philosopher's sky.

James and Papini unstiffened such tightly knit theorizing by challenging the intellectual substitute for the Judeo-Christian tradition, known as the Hegelian Absolute, by denying the alleged oneness of the universe. Theirs more resembled David Hume's metaphysical world, a loosely related collection of atomic parts, wherein the character of the parts is not determined exclusively by alleged features of the collection itself. Pluralism asserted the independent reality of worldly parts, this in turn permitting a kind of random freedom, chance, and novelty that monism excluded. Careful not to be charged with dogmatism by simply decreeing monism's falsity, James presented pluralism as a rival hypothesis to be tested over the empirical long run, concluding:

Pragmatism, pending the final empirical ascertainment of just what the balance of union and disunion among things may be, must obviously range herself upon the pluralistic side. . . . [A] universe consolidated in every conceivable way, may turn out to be the most acceptable of all hypotheses. Meanwhile, the opposite hypothesis of a world imperfectly unified still, and perhaps always to remain so, must be sincerely entertained. This latter hypothesis is pluralism's doctrine.[11]

The pragmatic revolt against monism vented attitudes about the nature of reality, and about the nature of language as well. When James (unwittingly) set pragmatism on a popular course in 1898, crediting Peirce with originating it twenty years earlier, he never supposed that his trend-setting paper "Philosophical Conceptions and Practical Results" would launch a movement, never dreaming that it would reverberate back to him from traditional Italy. In that paper he had the role of words on his mind. Pragmatism was born as a theory about words, their meaning and function. "The words and thoughts of the philosophers are not exactly the words and thoughts of the poets—worse luck. But both alike have the same function. They are . . . blazes made by . . . the human intellect on . . . the otherwise trackless forest of human experience. They give you somewhere to go from. They give you a direction and a place to reach."[12]

It was a short step from this to the pragmatic theory of meaning. Criticizing traditional philosophy and absolute idealism in particular for promoting such propositions as "The universe is one" or "The absolute is all" but without showing what if any are their consequences, thus giving them the look of gibberish, James formulated the celebrated pragmatic maxim: "There can be no difference [in words] which doesn't *make* a difference—no difference in abstract truth which does not express itself in a difference of concrete fact, and of conduct consequent upon the fact, imposed on somebody, somewhere, and somewhen."[13] What, then, are meanings? Neither the vague intuitions, according to traditional theory, that supposedly accompany words, nor, as later thinkers like Ludwig Wittgenstein claimed, the conventional uses of words; instead, they are the experiential consequences of words. Two words mean the same if their experiential implications are identical; they mean something different if their implications differ.

Pragmatism as a theory of meaning sprouted immediately into a theory of truth. In *Pragmatism* and *The Meaning of Truth* (1909), James blended a "cash-value" view of meaning with a "cash-value" notion of truth; a "show-the-implications" doctrine of meaning became a "show-the consequences" theory of truth, and two traditional definitions of truth came under attack. The coherence theory, dear to the idealist's heart, held that propositions are true if they cohere or imply one another in helping to constitute a larger logical system; a proposition turns up false by not fitting with those already established. The problem for the theory is that, whereas coherence is one among several tests for truth, it is not by itself conclusive because a set of propositions all of which are mutually consistent or implicative may be totally false. Coherence, as a clever liar understands, guarantees consistency but not truth.

According to the correspondence theory, truth is the correspondence of a judgment or proposition with a fact. A problem here is the idea of correspondence itself. Is correspondence what roadmaps display relative to a highway system? Or is it the way numbers relate to things counted? Or the way that whole theories connect with experimentation? Or the kind of "correspondence" that twins in their appearances present?

Further problems embarrassed the correspondence theory. Some facts are negative: for example, that Papini is not here now. The statement "Papini is not here now" is true, but we seem unable to point to a corresponding fact as we can, however, for the statement "We are here now." Other facts are general, such as that all women are mortal or some fictional heroines are immortal, but these are not facts that even seem to hover in view as does the fact that is reported by "This is paper." What about future facts? If tomorrow it does rain and today I assert that it will, then I speak truly in asserting a fact, but is there today a fact to correspond to my true judgment made today? Or, since the corresponding fact must await tomorrow to be a fact, is today's uttered truth lacking the fact with which it needs to connect?

It surprised James that his 1898 paper led to a philosophical movement, that its arguments created such a flurry. Besides his American associates, there were sympathizers like F. C. S. Schiller in England, Wilhelm Jerusalem and Julius Goldstein in Germany, Ernst Mach in Austria along with the Vienna Circle members who were hatching logical positivism, and the Italian pragmatists. These included Mario Calderoni, Giovanni Amendola, Giovanni Vailati,

Giuseppe Prezzolini, and Giovanni Papini. Giulio C. Ferrari translated James's *The Principles of Psychology*, which pleased everyone
with its sales of 2,000 copies; he also contributed articles to *Leonardo*, the Italian pragmatists' journal from 1903 to 1907, that
strengthened James's influence in Italy. Dominique Parodi, mentioned by James as one of pragmatism's critics in his preface to *The
Meaning of Truth*, was another important participant in the movement.

Surprise upon surprise!—to hear a pragmatic revolution rum-
bling around Italy, that symbol of the "hoary eld." The Italian
thinkers, based in Florence, with *Leonardo* as their club's publicity
organ, seemed especially indebted to James and F. C. S. Schiller.
Attending the Fifth International Congress of Psychology in Rome
in 1905, James wrote that they were "apparently *really* inspired by
Schiller and myself (I never could believe it before, although Ferrari
had assured me)."[14] He praised their enthusiasm and its "literary
swing and activity" unknown in America, something "our damned
academic technics and Ph.D.-machinery and university organization prevents [sic] from ever coming to birth. These men, of whom
Ferrari is one, are none of them *Fach-Philosophers*, and few of them
teachers at all. It has given me a certain new idea of the way in
which truth ought to find its way to the world."[15]

Why did the Italian thinkers regard pragmatism, as Papini put it,
as "the doctrine which had from Peirce its name, from James its
fame"?[16] Without James, one supposes, Italian pragmatism would
have developed very differently, if at all. Independently of James,
of course, the scientific and experimental thrust of pragmatism,
alongside a growing alliance with formal logic, was invading world
philosophy. The pragmatist club in Florence knew very well that
there were varieties of pragmatism as represented by Peirce, Dewey,
Schiller, and James, and to a fair extent they reproduced that variety in their publications.

Giovanni Vailati, for instance, in 1906 wrote an essay "Pragmatism and Mathematical Logic," mostly outside the Jamesian mold
and influenced by Peirce and Giuseppe Peano.[17] Lauding *Leonardo*
for effecting interdisciplinary liaisons, Vailati's paper connected
pragmatism with contemporary work in mathematical logic. Logic
was now pragmatic in understanding logical and mathematical

postulates to be without "divine rights" like other propositions; which propositions are chosen for the role of postulates, thus determining which propositions are to be proven as theorems, is decided pragmatically. That is, the choice is made because the results are useful for specific purposes. As our objectives in mathematics and logic vary with the tasks at hand, so what is useful varies, and different propositions in different contexts get chosen as postulates or, as they were once called, self-evident propositions.

Pragmatism affects the logic of properties by insisting on the entirely relative character of the Aristotelian distinction between essential and accidental properties, and in this respect Vailati anticipated current rejections of that position known today as "essentialism." He noted the pragmatic bent of logicians who recognized the hypothetical nature of general propositions, and who, in treating "All mermaids are pretty" as meaning "If anything is a mermaid, then it is pretty," could assert that such a proposition is true without implying the existence of mermaids. It was a pretty thing to show this, because in mathematical logic, where things are notoriously less obvious, the consequences of showing it are considerably less trivial.

Vailati identified new issues concerning language and symbolism that had arisen from the contributions of pragmatic thinking to mathematical logic. Whereas Aristotle had sought definitions of isolated words, the new theory of definition required instead that words in use, as they function in phrases or sentences, are the proper definienda. In an especially interesting analysis of Peano's notion of "definition in abstraction," Vailati assists our grasp of what goes into the process of concept-formation; if a given relation displays certain properties of equality, Vailati observed, that fact can serve to create a new concept. For example, given that two straight lines parallel to a third are equal to each other, we can draw from that the fresh concept of *direction;* or, given that two quantities of goods exchanged for one and the same quantity of a third commodity are mutually exchangeable, we evolve the concept of *value*. Vailati concludes the essay with noting how, in line with the pragmatic maxim, mathematical logic now emphasizes that the same truths can be expressed in different notational systems. One system is chosen over another, not because it allegedly coincides with reality but simply because it is more useful for the task at hand.

In another paper "The Attack on Distinctions" in 1909, which also is not distinctly Jamesian, he defended pragmatism's insistence on drawing distinctions. Too much traditional philosophy, he argued, deliberately and tendentiously fudges distinctions that ought to be preserved. Consider the attempt, for example, to evaporate the line between affirmation and negation on the grounds that any affirmation, after all, can be rewritten as the negation of some other affirmation. The affirmation of "All S is P," it can be argued, is equivalent to denying the affirmation "Some S is not P"; if so, affirmation and negation are not ultimately distinct concepts. Vailati proposed that the distinction between affirming and negating something, like that between "east" and "west," is to some extent a relative one, but that, once the relativity conditions are specified and assumed to be in place, the distinction becomes both objectively valid and pragmatically useful. Vailati also opposed, in advancing an argument too dense for recapturing here, certain (unnamed) thinkers who would dissolve the border between determinism and indeterminism such that each position loses its hard edge with an intermediate position, representing a compromise between the two, finally emerging as the victor of the old debates. In view of his own famous arguments against determinism, against the claim that human acts and decisions are always determined by antecedent events in a manner that is outside the individual's control, James agreed of course with Vailati that the importance of preserving the distinction in this instance is sufficiently evident.[18]

What has been recounted thus far is actually more a prolegomenon to the story than the story itself of James's influence on the Italian pragmatists, because for that we must turn to the James-Papini relationship. Papini was a greedy reader, devouring ideas wherever dropped. Besides philosophers, he read Baudelaire, Dostoyevsky, Poe, and Whitman, names that suggest his range of interests. It is reported that he endured "a period of self-pity and neurasthenia, then of intense hero-worship directed toward all radicals, including William James whom he had once seen washing his neck."[19] However this spectacle may have reinforced his adoration, it was originally produced of course by James's writings, and we have yet to focus the ideas there that excited Papini most.

Jamesian pragmatism is considerably livelier than what our earlier sketch of it as a theory of meaning and truth might indicate. As I have emphasized elsewhere, his pragmatism is "subjective" in its justifying one's choices of belief and deed according to one's own subjective preferences when the objective evidence, as not rarely happens, is too weak to provide secure guidance.[20] James's pragmatism and his psychology are intimately related, but even more so are the pragmatism and his philosophy of religion. Filling in what was meant by equating truth with utility, workability, satisfactoriness, or cash value, he called truth *one species of good;* truth is whatever proves to be *good* in the way of belief. *"If theological ideas prove to have a value for concrete life, they will be true, for pragmatism, in the sense of being good for so much."*[21] It was this sentiment that propelled pragmatism into a movement and without which it would never have escaped graduate seminar rooms and their *Fach-Philosophers.*

Papini vibrated to James's themes for the same reasons that thousands attended his lectures. Pragmatism was intellectually exciting because it seemed to liberate the mind by making reality all but subservient to it. Reality, it declared, is not static but ever-changing, so truth is constantly in the making, made in great part by human ideas and actions; since the universe is in constant flux and the final word about it must remain mysterious, faith in an intensely personal religion and metaphysics is wholly rational. Jamesian pragmatism enthused its converts by assuring them that their personal beliefs and desires are part of a reality that is genuinely responsive to them, that its shape and the truths about it are largely fashioned by those beliefs and desires actively seeking their own verification. Pragmatism and James's will-to-believe philosophy, that subject to commonsense constraints one has the right to believe in the kind of reality that one prefers, clearly worked in tandem.

Agreeing with James that pragmatism is not a doctrine but a method, and in a formulation remarkably similar to Wittgenstein's years later, Papini asserted in a 1907 essay "What Pragmatism Is Like": "Pragmatism is really *less a philosophy than a method of doing without philosophy.*"[22] The pragmatist, so far as classical philosophy is concerned, is in revolt, determined to shun its pesky, perennial questions. "On the other hand, he will concern himself strenuously with *methods* and *instruments* of knowledge and action, because he will be sure that it is far more important to improve or to create methods of obtaining exact previsions, or of changing ourselves and others, than to sport with empty words around incomprehensible problems."[23] Here he echoes the Darwinian idea linking James, Dewey, and Peirce that to know is to act, not to contemplate, and theories in physics and chemistry are not pictures of reality but are rather instruments for happier adjustments by human organisms to their environments.

Papini sounded a more distinctly Jamesian note in claiming for the pragmatic method that it aims at whatever increases our power to act upon the world; here he was more in touch temperamentally than were other followers with what essentially distinguishes James's pragmatic method. It is in the end less a method for coming-to-know than it is for opting-to-act. The world presents us with risky choices, holding secret the evidence that reduces risk, so that a rational person, unlike the daredevil, delays while waiting for more evidence. But indefinite delay becomes paralysis, and James's pragmatism was a paralysis-breaking technique. When there is insufficient objective evidence to guide the choice of either A or B, then ask what are the likely consequences if A is selected, and expected different consequences if B is chosen; if the estimated consequences, say, of A are subjectively preferable, then go ahead, choose A! Such was James's pragmatic strategy for breaking the paralysis caused by insufficient evidence and opting—in a manner wholly rational— for theism rather than either agnosticism or atheism.

Employing this strategy, for temperaments like Papini's and James's, is like opening doors onto a hitherto closed-shut world. Or, quoting Papini's phrase that he so admired, James wrote in 1906 that pragmatism is a great corridor-theory, its method being "like a corridor in a hotel, from which a hundred doors open into a hundred chambers."[24] Papini was unrivaled among pragmatism's converts in his appreciation of its power to *inspire*, and, for James, he uniquely put that inspiration to work in opening a hundred imaginative doors. The vistas they opened onto had been closed to the obstructed, paralyzed will. The pragmatic method seemed to free the will by generating confidence in the personal, highly subjective bases for decision making—call it the opening of doors to life's choices.

The efficacy of the pragmatic method in terminating our Hamlet-like moods derives from its getting us to believe that our decisions, when the risks are large because the clues are small, should result from how we think about reality rather than from something inherent in reality itself. A vitality of thought bordering on passion is required for inducing what James and Papini called "the strenuous mood," for thereby freeing the will to believe in a world of desired possibilities that just might be realized were one to translate the belief into action. Nothing helps the paralyzed will so much as the swaggering thoughts of a passionate pragmatist.

So James found his man in Papini, admiring above all his passion. The academic pragmatist taught that doors could be opened, the passionate one proceeded to fling them open. Papini's enthusiasm for the new autonomy of personality and the authority of subjectivity led to his concept of Man-God *(Uomo-Dio)*. Conceding the bizarre nature of the idea, James nevertheless commented: "Why should not the divine attributes of omniscience and omnipotence be used by man as the pole-stars by which he may methodically lay his own course?" And, significantly, he added that Papini had made him more aware of the "full inwardness" of pragmatism, created "a tone of feeling well fitted to rally devotees and to make of pragmatism a new militant form of religious or quasi-religious philosophy."[25]

James was most impressed by Papini's *Il crepuscolo dei filosofi* that appeared in 1906, hailing the passion of its final chapter and certifying its author as pragmatism's most radical representative. That chapter, focusing on Nietzsche (the preceding ones covered Kant, Hegel, Schopenhauer, Comte, and Spencer), commands attention in light of the apparent similarities between the writings of Nietzsche and Papini. Stylistic and conceptual reverberations of Nietzsche, in addition to the obvious resemblance of his *Uomo-Dio* to Nietzsche's *Übermensch*, occur throughout Papini's work.

In *Un uomo finito* (1913) he explained his going beyond James's will to believe to the "will to do," fancying what it would be like if his will extended from his own body to everything beyond. "I pretended to start from a logical precept (pragmatism); but in my secret heart I was jealous of Divinity and eager to become a rival of Divinity."[26] Like Nietzsche, in seeking in philosophy something higher than art he was always returned to art, to poetic and dramatic bursts that, for James, expressed pragmatism's peculiar emotion but, for others, betrayed its sense. Since James was not a Nietzsche fan, having compared in his *The Varieties of Religious Experience* the writings of Schopenhauer and Nietzsche to the shriekings of two dying rats, why did he praise Papini's chapter on Nietzsche in the 1906 book?

James applauded, it would appear, Papini's severe criticisms of Nietzsche as well as the "passion" that bristled in those barbs. (Less passion than personal candor, I suggest, finding myself the former more on display in other of Papini's publications.) Papini's critique is personal and conversational in tone, the points of dissent rapidly listed and deprived of any sustained analysis. Nietzsche had a secret, Papini announced, hiding it with leonine roars, volcanic rumbles, and feverish laughs, but, sleuthing behind all the noise, Papini located it—a pathetic, chronic *weakness*.

Nietzsche's philosophy, according to Papini, grew out of his bad health, delicate constitution, and general weakness. Only weak men extol strength and power as Nietzsche did. The glorification of the human body and animal instinct, saying "Yea" to life no matter what, mounting what was in effect a monistic life philosophy, all these were born from the same deficient germ cell. Nietzsche's reaction to weakness was merely verbal, thus pointing to the underlying impotence of which the philosopher himself must have been painfully aware.

These were criticisms that James could favor, despite his and Papini's vulnerability to something of the same. He surely approved of Papini's jabs at Nietzsche's queer notion of eternal recurrence, the idea that each and every occurrence will recur infinitely and in identical detail, that every experience will return again and again without limit. (The idea has recently received popular attention in Milan Kundera's book, though not in the film, *The Unbearable Lightness of Being*.) The notion of eternal recurrence implies a deterministic view of history wherein we are helpless to control our individual destinies, and, since James's pragmatism had repeatedly fingered determinism as an arch enemy, Papini's blast was welcome support. Moreover, Nietzsche's attacks on Christianity and traditional morality were too easy and really self-serving, Papini claimed, giving the illusion of originality. James surely agreed that Nietzsche's perorations on religion were unbalanced, also that their corollary swipes at "the pessimistic attitude" were unrealistic. Papini echoed James in "What Pragmatism is Like" in maintaining that pessimism and optimism are both *pragmatic sentiments;* pessimism is needed, in addition to an ongoing hope, for clearly seeing the world's bleakness and the difficulties confronting the pragmatist's promise to ameliorate it. James may also have glimpsed between the lines of Papini's essay, despite its blatant iconoclasm, subtle hints of what years later would reconcile Papini and Christianity.

Herbert Spencer and his Darwinian philosophy had been a lifetime target of James's arrows, so he must have chuckled over Papini's likening Nietzsche's reverence for instinct to Spencer's regard for biological naturalism. "Both Spencer and Nietzsche are waiting for changes in the future, but both of them want man to bend his head in front of everything that exists out of necessity."[27] Nietzsche's thought was merely a "dithyrambic transfiguration" of Spencer; it was often beautiful poetry, as in *Also sprach Zarathustra,* but poor philosophy, due in part to his wanting to be known as a philosopher yet dismally failing himself to respect the discipline of philosophy. Papini, revealing some of the Jamesian ambivalence that was described earlier, quarreling with the thinker whom he most resembled, eventually passed a similar judgment on himself, confessing that he had allowed his youthful pragmatism to drift into lyrical phantasies; expressing sentiments also occurring in *Un uomo finito,* he attributed his subsequent maturity to having remained a man of theory. Formerly "blind when I set out to gain the lordship of the earth," he came to realize that "the true world I shall find only in my thoughts, in myself, and I can be master of it at my will, since I have but to seek it in myself, my innermost self."[28]

The passion that James found in Papini, that brought pragmatism's "full inwardness" into view, was a mode of philosophizing. It transformed theoretical thinking into a personal quest, and conversely; it turned arguments about meaning, truth, and reality into a personal drama. The quest was endless, the arguments inconclusive, and the drama a tense internal dialogue. Whatever was the source of their driven, sometimes tortured thinking, they shared a gadfly Socratic temperament. Perhaps they were the only two pragmatists actually to believe that Socrates was right: the goal of philosophy is the care of the soul, certainly one's own, but if he's not careful, the next fellow's, too.

Papini remarked that philosophers had considered changing only one of their tools, language. "They have not thought of the most important tool of all: the soul."[29] It is true, James said in the opening pages of *Pragmatism*, that philosophy bakes no bread, but "it can inspire our souls with courage . . . no one of us can get along without the far-flashing beams of light it sends over the world's perspectives. These give . . . to what it says an interest that is much more than professional."[30] Both thinkers shared the same remarkable premise, temperamentally rather than argumentatively based, that the care of one's soul demands change, novelty, revolution; and transformations that are external as well as inward. Sensing the reflections of himself in Papini's personality, James would not have been startled by his later association with Italian futurism.

Although he was not a colleague of Filippo Marinetti's when futurism was launched in 1909, and although he was not immediately sympathetic with the futurists' shouts of "Burn the museums" and "Let's kill the moonlight" and did not support Boccioni, Carrà, and Russolo when with yells and blows they delivered their "Manifesto" at Turin's theater in 1910 (the year of James's death), Papini had to be intrigued. "Futurism," he said, "has made people laugh, shout, and spit. Let's see if it can make them think."[31] After a period of resisting the movement, in 1913 Papini joined the critic and painter Ardengo Soffici in founding the influential futurist periodical, *Lacerba*. That Italian pragmatism contributed to an artistic and critical revolution known as futurism would have delighted James, in whose thought "the future" chimed on the hour. The futurist activity in the streets, not only in the museums, would have gratified his longing to witness the inner changes of heart and mind mirrored externally, not only in the classrooms.

James considered dedicating his *Pragmatism* to Papini, writing to Schiller: "What do you say to the following dedication of my vol. of lectures?—'To Schiller, Dewey, and Papini.' Don't you think Papini deserves it? With his *Uomo-Dio* he certainly has given a new kind of shove to the doctrine."[32] For whatever reasons, he decided differently, and the book honored John Stuart Mill. Perhaps at some level of his thinking it seemed fitting, for a book portraying philosophy as a quest without a grail, periodically exhibiting its own travail, to memorialize someone who, no longer part of it, was at rest. James was inclined to such thoughts. For the inscription on his sister Alice's urn, he chose a line from Dante—"ed essa da martiro e da essilio venne a questa pace" (from martyrdom and exile she came to this peace).[33] Pondering his own philosophical odyssey, Papini burst out: "To you, Dante—father Dante!—I owe a fierce longing for Paradise."[34] In musing about philosophy and himself, James, too, had Dante on his mind.

Notes

I want to thank two individuals for their invaluable assistance in preparing this paper: Dr. Monica Ricci for translating Italian items, especially the Giovanni Papini selections; and Dr. Roberta Sheehan for researching the James Collection at Houghton Library and for locating materials by or about Papini that are used here. For their contributions, substantial and generous, I am most grateful.

1. William James to F. C. S. Schiller, 28 December 1900, Rome, in *William James: Selected Unpublished Correspondence, 1885–1910*, ed. Frederick J. Down Scott (Columbus: Ohio State University Press, 1986), 243; William James to Josiah Royce, December 1892, Florence, in *The Letters of William James edited by his son Henry James* (Boston: The Atlantic Monthly Press, 1920), 2 vols., 1:332 (hereafter cited as *LWJ*).

2. William James to Alice James, 23 November 1873, Florence, *LWJ*, 1:176; Cambridge letter, 5 December 1869, in Ralph Barton Perry, *The Thought and Character of William James* (Boston: Little, Brown, 1935), 2 vols., 1:310 (hereafter cited as *RBP*). William James to Alice James, 17 December 1873, Rome, *LWJ*, 1:177–78.

3. William James to Henry James, Sr., 30 November 1873, Rome, *RBP*, 1:163.

4. Henry James, *A Small Boy and Others* (New York: Scribners, 1913), 68.

5. William James to Henry James, 18 April 1874, Cambridge, *RBP*, 1:355.

6. *RBP*, 1:385.

7. William James to Henry James, 1898, San Francisco, *LWJ*, 2:81; William James to Frances R. Morse, Nauheim 1901, *LWJ*, 2:158; William James to Henry James, 1907, New York City, *LWJ*, 2:264–65.

8. William James to Frances R. Morse, 1900, Rome, *LWJ*, 2:138–39.
9. *RBP*, 2:572.
10. *The Works of William James: Pragmatism* (Cambridge: Harvard University Press, 1975), 78.
11. Ibid., 79.
12. Appendix I, *Pragmatism*, 258.
13. Ibid., 260.
14. *RBP*, 2:387, 570.
15. *LWJ*, 2:227. The enthusiasm of the pragmatic movement beyond the campus appeared in later years to have influenced Benito Mussolini. For my recent discussion of this, see Gerald E. Myers, *William James: His Life and Thought* (New Haven: Yale University Press, 1986), 414–16, 592–93.
16. *RBP*, II:571.
17. Giovanni Vailati, "Pragmatism and Mathematical Logic," *The Monist* 16, no. 4 (October 1906): 481–91. (Originally published in *Leonardo*, February 1906.)
18. Vailati wrote an interesting paper "On Material Representation of Deductive Processes," *Journal of Philosophy, Psychology, and Scientific Methods* 5, no. 12 (4 June 1908): 309–16. The paper explores the sorts of metaphors that are often used for describing mental attitudes and processes, including making deductive inferences, concluding that such metaphors do not lead to the idea, apparently espoused by some (unnamed) thinkers, that deduction is neither a means of proof nor an ascertainment of truth.
19. Joseph Collins, *Idling in Italy: Studies of Literature and Life* (New York: Scribners, 1920), 95.
20. See Myers, *William James*, 291–306.
21. *Pragmatism*, 40.
22. Giovanni Papini, "What Pragmatism Is Like," *Popular Science Monthly* 71 (October 1907): 351–58.
23. Ibid., 352.
24. *The Works of William James: Essays in Philosophy* (Cambridge: Harvard University Press, 1978), 146. See also *Pragmatism*, 32. This calls to mind what James's sister Alice wrote in her diary (14 December 1889), reporting that James told her about his house in Chocorua in New Hampshire: "Oh, it's the most delightful house you ever saw; has 14 doors all opening outside." See *The Diary of Alice James*, ed. Leon Edel (New York: Penguin Press, 1982), 67–68.
25. *Pragmatism*, 147, 148.
26. G. Papini, *The Failure [Un uomo finito]* (New York: Harcourt, Brace, 1924), 131.
27. G. Papini, *Il crepuscolo dei filosofi*, revised ed. (Florence: Vallenchia, 1976), 142.

28. G. Papini, *Life and Myself* (New York: Brentano's, 1930), 9.
29. Papini, *The Failure*, 200.
30. *Pragmatism*, 10–11.
31. Quoted in Joshua C. Taylor, *Futurism* (New York: The Museum of Modern Art, 1961), 10.
32. Scott, *William James*, 425. See also *LWJ*, 2:267.
33. See *The Diary of Alice James*, 21.
34. Papini, *The Failure*, 139.

TEN

Listening to the Master:
William James and the "Making
of the New" in Italian Culture

CLAUDIO GORLIER

A N EBULLIENT, syncretic disposition ostensibly characterizes
and qualifies the cultural debate which took place in the
militant critical circles in Italy at the beginning of the twentieth
century. The burgeoning of a "new" literature, or at least of the
theory of a "new" literature, displayed an effort in conceptualiza-
tion which called for recourse to a real kaleidoscope of diverse and
often contradictory sources, repossessed and redefined to substanti-
ate the principle of a decisive breakthrough. In this context, a
number of little magazines and reviews played a pivotal role, vis-à-
vis the journals of the cultural establishment, no less than the
academic citadels of institutionalized literature, if we bear in mind
that two of the major Italian poets of the time, Carducci and
Pascoli, were also influential university professors and recognized
public figures. A mapping out of this territory must begin with
Leonardo, a review set up in Florence by Giovanni Papini and
Giuseppe Prezzolini and published from 1903 to 1907, whose "Programma sintetico" *(a synthetic program)* stands as a typical manifesto:

In LIFE they are *pagan* and *individualistic*—lovers of beauty and intelligence, worshipers of deep nature and of a full life, enemy of any form of
Nazarene submission and plebian servitude.
In THOUGHT they are *personalistic* and *idealistic*, that is, superior to any
system and to any limit, convinced that any philosophy is but a personal
way of life—denying any other existence beside thought.

In ART they love the ideal transfiguration of life and oppose the inferior forms of it; they aspire to beauty as the provocative representation and revelation of a deep and serene life.[1]

While we may grant the echoes from D'Annunzio's vitalism (although Prezzolini was indifferent to him) and from the gospel of literary aestheticism, the program clearly enunciated an iconoclastic rejection of a series of dominant shibboleths: evangelical Christianity, the literary categories of realism and naturalism, philosophical positivism, and to some degree idealism (namely, Croce's idealism). The program considered that "inferior forms of art" had mostly to do with *trivial literature* but also with the commercial exploitation of art and literature (D'Annunzio) and with the notion of "duplication" or "reproduction" denounced much later by Walter Benjamin. In point of fact, the "young people" ("un gruppo di *giovini*") who subscribed to the program purported an ideal of beauty which tended to replace the Ruskinian model—one of the most recurrent antecedents in the theoretical discussions of art in Italy at that time—with the notion of a free, creative role for the self, the "deepest and truest individual self" lyrically evoked by Prezzolini. Furthermore, from its very inception, *Leonardo* mustered a rather heterogeneous group of contributors. In Prezzolini's own words: "Here at *Leonardo* we are united more by what we hate than by the pursuit of common aims." Hence, the editorial policy developed in three successive stages: the first centered on a sort of conceptual deconstruction; the second was devoted to a cognitive reassessment; and the third was dominated by an increasing loyalty to the occult and was conducive to the principle of "magic realism" and the absolute primacy of the will. Delia Frigessi has aptly underscored the idea that the strongest and most consistent link between the "young people" of *Leonardo* emerges in the vindication of "thought" as a privileged function, which demands a stringent redicussion of general values.[2]

Since Papini and Prezzolini were self-educated intellectuals (Prezzolini insisted on his role as a *dilettante*) and cultural organizers more than original thinkers, they had to look for conceptual validation. Their favorite models included Nietzsche, Sorel, Bergson, and the exponents of American pragmatism. The intellectual venture of *Leonardo* was principally inspired by the discovery of pragmatism, and in 1905 William James met in Rome "the little band of pragmatists . . . who have taken my own writings, *entre autres, au grand sérieux*."[3] Not only did *Leonardo* channel pragmatism to Italy, but Papini, Giovanni Vailati, and other friends periodically met in Florence, forming what was called "The Pragmatic Club." In the preliminary statements on pragmatism, featured in *Leonardo* and later reprinted in book form under the title *Pragmatismo*, Papini stressed the disengaging function it performed: "Pragmatism is, rather than a philosophy, a method for doing *without philosophy*. . . . Pragmatism differs basically from all philosophies by the sheer fact that it is not . . . a philosophy, if, by philosophy, we mean metaphysics, a *Weltanschauung* and the like."[4]

These specific presuppositions significantly parallel a peremptory affirmation in the preface to *Il crepuscolo dei filosofi* (1906): "This book is mostly an attempt to do away with philosophy and with philosophers." They are expanded and culminate in the ingenious metaphor of the hotel corridor, almost literally translated by William James in his article on Papini and pragmatism. Pragmatism, according to Papini, is thus only a collection of attitudes and methods, and its chief characteristic is its armed neutrality in the midst of doctrines. It is like a corridor in a hotel, from which a hundred doors open into a hundred chambers. In one you may see a man on his knees praying to regain his faith; in another a desk at which sits someone eager to destroy all metaphysics; in a third a laboratory with an investigator looking for new footholds by which to advance upon the future. But the corridor belongs to all, and all must pass there. Pragmatism, in short, is a great *corridor theory*.[5]

In his attack on positivism and monism, Papini overemphasizes the plurality of solutions inherent in pragmatism. Antonio Santucci has perceptively observed that Papini was striving to build up a new cognitive synthesis derived from a complex project, to define the notion of an anthropoculture aimed at transforming the whole of society. "Science," Papini writes, "gives power. We must descend from thought to action." (Here Papini was possibly unaware of the ambivalence of his categorizing and of the later developments of its signifier, if not of its significance. The principle of action as the necessary fulfillment of thought would become a typical factor in the cultural statute of fascism.) The aggressive, intuitive, as well as

imaginative approach peculiar to Papini, appropriately reverber-
ated in his pseudonym *Gian Falco* (Johnny Hawk), is complemented by Prezzolini, alias *Giuliano il Sofista* (Julian the Sofist),
whose acceptance of pragmatism does not necessarily decry his
underlying, ironic skepticism, a safeguard against dogmatism.

It must be said that pragmatism is something more than a philosophy and
something better than a method; it is one of the activities of the soul. . . .
There is no need to speak of deception. James and Schiller are no less clever
than Peirce or Mach. In the country of *business* [in English in the original]
there is still a great deal of practical tact and a sense of the real; a *police-
man* [in English in the original] of psychology such as William James would
have already noticed the *piperie*, if there had been any. He has not, and
there isn't any.[6]

Nonetheless, in *Leonardo* we are confronted with two versions of
pragmatism, the "two sections" overtly described by Papini himself: "logical pragmatism and psychologic or magic pragmatism."
Giovanni Vailati and Mario Calderoni belong to the first "section,"
Papini and Prezzolini to the second. Vailati and Calderoni were
philosophers in the strict sense of the word, both isolated thinkers
who died very young and were rediscovered and reevaluated only
after World War II. A philosopher with a specific background in
science and mathematics and with a remarkable competence in
language analysis, Vailati would occasionally converge with Papini
and Prezzolini. In no way could he endorse their irrationalism and
share their interest in the occult, in magic, and in theosophy. Papini makes it clear in his preface to *L'altra metà* (1912):

The two things could not go together. I separated them. On the one hand
pragmatism, true pragmatism, the custodian of old induction, the prophet
of foresight . . . good English cloth with some American and Italian woof.
On the other hand the great thaumaturgical dream, never dead, never
renounced: man as Lord, soul as master of the world, will as mother of
miracles.[7]

The convergence of the "two sections" is certainly expedient to
the welding together of a cultural alliance, and it cannot conceal
the possible divergences, but some crucial interactions deserve special attention, for instance, when Vailati, whose main area of interest is mathematical logic, expounds a poignant comparison with
the creative process:

A theory becomes more perfect and closer to its ideal to the extent that he who builds it up is able to consider it as a mere creation of his own dictates. . . . This character of mathematical speculation . . . manifests the intimate and fundamental affinity between itself and the creative activity of the artist.[8]

It is no wonder that Papini and Prezzolini placed a premium on William James's *The Will to Believe*, whereas Vailati felt a closer affinity with Peirce. In stressing the pluralistic stance and the availability, so to speak, of pragmatism, Papini and Prezzolini seemed to enlarge on a central assumption in *The Will to Believe:*

To the very last, there are the various "points of view" which the philosopher must distinguish in discussing the world; and what is inwardly clear from one point remains a bare externality and datum to the other. The negative, the alogical, is never wholly banished.

While Vailati wanted to guarantee the objectivity of learning, Papini enhanced and ratified the centrality of belief. In this respect, he came very close to the proposition articulated by Gerald E. Myers, to the effect that "James's truth that subjectivity is obliquely cognitive, a blurry apprehension of objective realities, was the constant underpinning of his mysticism and his pragmatic equation of truth with what is satisfactory."[9] Yet Papini and Prezzolini took advantage of pragmatism as a springboard, and their protean intellectual unrest forced them beyond the boundaries of this experience. Whereas Prezzolini was gradually attracted to Croce's idealism, Papini transposed his principle of absolute will into the creation of a Man-God figure and the depiction of the splendid defeat of the individual who engages in the impossible quest for total and absolute knowledge at the price of his own destruction. In *Le memorie d'Iddio* (1911), God accepts the inevitability of His death at the hands of man, who created Him: "You are my fathers: it was only you gave me a soul and a will. . . . Now I only wish those who made me to unmake me, my inventors to be also my assassins." In the novel *Un uomo finito* (1913), the first-person narrator recounts his proud challenge and registers his failure:

"Being God! All men, Gods! This is the great dream, the impossible endeavour, the proud aim sought after. And I set it up as my program. . . . I am finished because I wanted to undertake too many things, and I am no longer anything because I wanted to be everything. . . . What did I want to

learn? What did I want to do? I did not know. Only knowing, knowing, knowing everything. . . . Either everything or nothing!"[10]

The most suitable land for such an adventure will be America, "where every credo finds a temple and every Moses a capital." Papini's abstract dream of an ideal America was mirrored in his enthusiasm for Walt Whitman, to whom he devoted an essay. *Un uomo finito* can be legitimately considered a turning point, in that it finalizes Papini's speculative project in a literary discourse. This occurs in spite of its unquestionable limits, due to the obsessive intrusion of the narrative self and of the assertive infrastructure. The "procession of centuries and of volumes" facing the protagonist, the symbol of an encyclopedia of learning, anticipate Borges's "Biblioteca de Babel"; and the avid reader trapped in his unabating and inordinate ambition foreshadows the plight of Roquentin in Sartre's *La Nausée*.

We are now in a position to verify the impact of the experimentation embodied by *Leonardo* on the literary avant-garde in Italy. Papini acted as an intermediary to futurism in his "reaction to an archaic tradition which benumbs a majority of the Italian intellectuals," as he observed in his pamphlet *Il mio futurismo* (1914). While he never actually joined the futurist movement, Papini ranks among its forefathers and among its fellow travelers. His editorship of *Lacerba*, another militant little review published in Florence between 1913 and 1915, displays a sort of critical sympathy with the movement. Many futurists, including F. T. Marinetti, contributed to *Lacerba* quite substantially. Yet Papini was careful not to identify with the movement, and the magazine was subject to abrupt changes of literary mood and conceptual content—a phenomenon far from unusual with Papini. "Similarly to Dante's damned," Papini denounced "the talented Italians [who] always keep their heads turned round—on the side of their ass." When he voiced his intention "to create also in Italy an atmosphere of avant-garde and of temerity, so as to allow and to bring in a new flowering of poetry," Papini expressed a view similar to that conveyed in the futurist manifestos. Luciano De Maria is right in pointing to a passage from *Stroncature* (1915), where Papini appropriated a futurist canon and utilized it for a fresh start, leading to a singular modernistic proposition: "Art is freedom and fun—pastime and recreation. . . . Art is a flourish, a dart, skill, music and flashing happiness." It has been correctly noted by Luigi Baldacci that the legacy of pragmatism clearly permeates Papini's view of futurism as a philosophy rather than a purely literary avant-garde, so that William James presides even over the definition of futurism in terms of an irrationalist variety of thought, a "superculture," at a stage when the reading of Nietzsche counteracted or at least complemented the influence of James. Theories matter—not in that they are true, but in that they suit our needs and help us to change the world: "great foolishness," Prezzolini preached, "is better than small wisdom." *L'altra metà*, inscribed to an avowed "Mephystophelic philosophy," betrayed a Nietzschean echo in its exploration of even the recognition of nothingness: all theories are useful in that they are false. Papini has subscribed to his own Faustian pact; in *L'uomo finito* and in *L'altra metà*, pragmatism is being tested, questioned, and enriched in the light of failure and desperation.[11]

At the moment when Papini formulated a ludic view of literature, Prezzolini championed the tragic sense of life which should pervade literature, and his friend promptly borrowed the suggestion. In a typical exchange of roles, Prezzolini elaborated a theory of lying as an indispensable dialectical counterstatement, and Vailati provided an extremely positive review of the book (*L'arte del persuadere*, 1907). There he praised Prezzolini's antidogmatic stand and his effort to describe the centrality of individual self-persuasion as opposed to indoctrination, the act of lying as a reaction against the propagation of undemonstrated ideas. Prezzolini's ostensible source was *The Will to Believe*, which Vailati was not inclined to take at face value. In any case, and the undeniable differences between the "two sections" notwithstanding, we should not fail to indicate the influence on both Papini and Prezzolini of Vailati's conception of the structural relationship between the two key principles of experience and of knowledge.

William James looked at the phenomenon of Italian pragmatism in terms of a cultural extrapolation. In keeping with his confession of being "poetry deaf," his knowledge of the Italian literary scene was almost nil; nor did he have any serious curiosity about the Italian classics, unlike at least two generations of Harvard scholars. He paid homage to the "inner spiritual Harvard . . . nursery of independent and lonely spirits" in a memorable address, but he never culturally associated with the Harvard charismatic figures, some of whom were the high priests of Italian culture in America. On the contrary, he proclaimed that "our undisciplinables are our proudest products." Ralph Barton Perry reminds us that "Lowell, Fields, Norton, Howells were friends. . . . To Henry [James] the New England men of letters were masters and colleagues. To William they were friends and sources of entertainment." Like Henry Adams, William James professed a much higher opinion of and esteem for the scientific group, from Asa Gray to Louis Agassiz. He probably ignored the existence at Harvard of the prestigious Dante Society. One notices a tinge of benevolent irony rather than of sincere admiration in his remarks on Charles Eliot Norton, one of the Harvard icons, in a letter to his sister Alice:

The way that man gets his name stuck to every greatness is fabulous. Dante, Goethe, Carlyle, Ruskin, Fitzgerald, Chauncy Wright [sic], and now Lowell! His name will dominate all the literary history of this epoch. 100 years hence, the *Revue des deux mondes* will publish an article entitled 'la vie de l'esprit aux etats-Unis vers la fin du XXme siècle; etude sur Charles Norton.[12]

As a tourist, William James was no passionate pilgrim. C. H. Grattan recalls that "William James's feeling for Europe almost exactly duplicated that of his father. It was a matter of attraction and of repulsion." Writing to his "beloved Sweetlington" (Alice James) in 1873 he announced: "To-day in Italy my spirits have risen," and he indulged in a touch of commonplace local color: "the beautifully good-natured easy-going expression of the faces of the railway officials." One year later he wrote to his brother Henry: "I suppose you are today percolating the cool arcades of Bologna and the faded beauties of Verona," and goes on to extol "the utter friendliness of Florence, of Rome," which "grow dear to me." But in 1883, in a letter to Thomas Davidson, he conceded that "Italy thoroughly disagrees with my loathsome nervous system." In 1905 he confessed: "The Greek lower orders seem far less avid and rapacious than the Southern Italians." The only positive element is confined to the appreciation of Italian painting. The discovery of Italy as a pragmatist province materialized into a pleasant and intriguing surprise. The article in the *Journal* on the Italian pragmatists, an "extraordinarily well-informed and gifted, and above all extraordinarily free and spirited and unpedantic group of writers," sounds high-pitched and, one would be tempted to add, suspiciously warm and complimentary, although James spelled out some prudent reservations, particularly on the Man-God theory:

> Sig. Papini lets his imagination work at stretching the limits. His attempt will be called Promethean or bullfroggian, according to the temper of the reader. It has decidedly an element of literary swagger and conscious impertinence, but I confess that I am unable to treat it otherwise than respectfully. . . . The program of a Man-God is surely one of the possible type-programs of philosophy. I myself have been slow in coming into the full inwardness of pragmatism. . . . In the writings of this youthful Italian, clear in spite of all their brevity and audacity, I find not only a way in which our English views might be developed farther with consistency . . . but also a tone of feeling well fitted to rally devotees and to make of pragmatism a new militant form of religious or quasi-religious philosophy.[13]

The correspondence between James and Papini sanctions an outspoken confirmation on the part of James. In reply to his first letter from Papini, James wrote: "you yourself are 'Gian Falco', I believe, and if so you have written a most decisive article on Nietzsche. Poor weak N.! but what an occasional command of language!" In a letter from Del Monte, California, dated 27 April 1906, James gave free rein to enthusiasm, and this attitude resulted in a phalanx of exclamation marks:

> My dear friend and master, Papini, I have just been reading your *Crepuscolo [sic] dei filosofi* and the February number of *Leonardo*, and great is the fortification of my soul. What a thing is genius! and you are a real genius! . . . You're such a brilliant, humorous and witty writer. It is splendid to see Italy renovating us all [curiously enough, James had originally written "herself," and then barred the word and corrected it to "us all"] in this way.

On 3 May 1906, Papini replied in French, and the humble recognition of his indebtedness to James betrays a genuine sincerity, in spite of its apparent servility (Papini was only twenty-five). I am quoting from Perry's translation:

> Dear Master, I have received your letter from Del Monte, and assure you that it has almost overwhelmed ["presque ému" in the original] me. To hear the master whom I have studied and whom I admire say to me things

that seem too flattering even for my pride (which, I might say, is not inconsiderable) [more bluntly, in the original, "très petit"] has been for me one of the most intense joys of my intellectual life.

James wrote again to Papini on 21 May 1906, from Cambridge:

To tell you the plain truth about your proposal to translate these recent essays of mine: it frightens me. I cannot believe that they could possibly have a market success, being, as they are, highly technical, polemical, abstract and unnatural for the most part. I expect to publish them some day in English, with one or two others still *in petto mio* [in Italian in the original], but only as a sort of appendix-volume containing the *indigestibilities* of my system. . . . Please *don't* translate this indigestible stuff now!

Papini resorted to inflated, almost prophetic language in a letter dated 3 July 1906, written in English: "Theories may die and you and I may very well, in two days or two years, have opposite opinions[,] but the inclination you show for my way of thinking and writing gives me a pleasure of a special kind that men of mere knowledge perhaps never feel." On 29 August 1906, Papini switched to Italian and duly apologized ("it is easier for me and possibly more helpful to you"). He reported on the mounting success of pragmatism in Italy with emphatic elation: "We are beginning to triumph!" In November of 1906, James refused to "contribute a preface" to the English translation of Papini's *Il tragico quotidiano:* "I admire that book greatly. . . . I fear very much that the English reader may fail to catch its significance, especially in translation." Then he resumed his favorite subject: "I think the attempt to convict us of *absurdity* by the rationalists is as discreditable as any thing I have seen in philosophy in my life time." Again in 1907, James was lavish in his praise in a postcard from Cambridge: "Your account of pragmatism is really stupendous, admirable." Three months later, on 13 June 1907, he made an incisive and acute observation on Bergson's Platonism: "*have* [doubly underlined] you read Bergson's new book? Perhaps the *divinest* thing in philosophy since Plato! and he has killed intellectualism stone-dead! —at last!" Further evidence of James's disinterested sympathy for Papini is to be found in the postscript of a letter to F. C. S. Schiller, where he took the *Uomo-Dio* theory into serious consideration: "What do you say to the following dedication of my Vol. of lectures?—'To Schiller, Dewey, and Papini.' Don't you think Papini deserves it? With his

Uomo-Dio he certainly has given a new kind of shove to the doctrine." Paradoxically, James, besides expressing his admiration, allowed himself a malicious comment at the totally groundless news of Papini's death in 1909: "Papini, I hear by rumor, recently died insane. Too bad! for he was indeed a genius. The *freest* I have known, even if he did delight a bit too much in *épater*-ing the *bourgeoisie*." [14]

Papini actually died in 1956, having had ample time to recant his juvenile transgressions, to have become a Roman Catholic convert, and to have given firm support to fascism. At William James's death in 1910 the pragmatist phase was virtually over, or it was undergoing a complex metamorphosis. In the aftermath of World War I, Papini could not conceive of any dynamic alternative to his own intellectual adventure, and passionately sought a reconciliation, what William James would have termed "a place of healing." He found it in religious and political orthodoxy. The issue of the political and ideological commitment of *Leonardo* and later of *La Voce* (the review, edited by Prezzolini, that replaced it with a wider range of contributors and areas of interests) leaves James untouched, and it would have been almost impossible for him to decode its complex implications from an American point of view. Yet the indictment of democracy as a degraded institution, which recurs in *Leonardo* and more conspicuously in *La Voce*, exhibits many similarities with Henry Adams's unsparing pronouncements on the subject. Beyond that, the upsurge of nationalism and expansionism sustained by Papini, Prezzolini, and their many friends might well have had a familiar ring to an American ear, especially after the Spanish-American War. Although Papini disagreed with Prezzolini on the point of the political and ideological emphasis implicit in the editorial policy of *La Voce*, the last and the most influential of the Florentine militant reviews, Prezzolini's design seems basically consistent with the notion of an "opposition politics" derived from that of an "opposition culture." As Alberto Asor Rosa has convincingly suggested, *La Voce* aimed at becoming the rallying point of different cultural and political currents antagonistic to the established system, an endeavor dramatically thwarted by the utopian project of a "party of the intellectuals," unable to resist the fatal temptations of elitism, nationalism, and an abstract palingenesis. The character of the ambiguous political attitudes held by the most representative exponents of the Italian "new" culture is still hotly debated. Marxist scholars are inclined to identify *Leonardo* and to a large degree *La Voce* and futurism as instances of derivative parochialism in literature and of reactionary thinking in politics. Antonio Gramsci's disparaging judgment of Prezzolini, "il chierichetto" (the altar boy), is a good case in point. But, regardless of the inadequacy of the creative achievements with respect to their theoretical premises, *Leonardo* and *La Voce* operated as cultural thoroughfares, as the hatcheries of the literature of the second and the third decades of the century in Italy.[15]

In considering whether the complex perspectives we encounter in *Leonardo* and *La Voce* can be reduced to derivative parochialism in literature and reactionary thought in politics, we must keep in mind three main points. First, the rhetoric of the occult in *Leonardo* and *La Voce*—although there was no room for any Madame Blavatsky in Roman Catholic Italy—has a wider European cultural frame of reference, and their plea for magic ushered in a tendency in the art and literature of many countries which we may describe as "magic realism." This magic realism, to which Italy made its original contribution, permeates the whole phenomenon of modern fantastic literature. Significantly enough, in his anthology of fantastic literature, Borges has included a short story by Papini, "L'ultima visita del gentiluomo malato" ("The Last Visit of the Sick Gentleman").

Second, the central notion of mysticism discussed by Papini (and partly borrowed from William James's *The Varieties of Religious Experience*) appears in many cognate forms. It acquires a specific later relevance in Wittgenstein's *Tractatus Logico-Philosophicus*, for example, as Gerald E. Myers remarks.[16] But it ought to be stressed that "mysticism" and "mystic" already possessed a strikingly similar valence in Coleridge's *Biographia Literaria* and *Aids to Reflection* and is manifest in nineteenth-century American transcendentalism. In this respect, Papini's attitudes form part of a continuing international dialogue throughout the nineteenth and twentieth centuries.

Third, one of *Leonardo*'s and *La Voce*'s political targets is undoubtedly socialism, along with the principle of egalitarianism or mass democracy. However, this critique also fits into a wider European perspective. We need only bear in mind the social views of Carpenter, Ortega, D. H. Lawrence, and Spengler—or Yeats and T. S. Eliot, for that matter.

The most that one can say is that the agenda of *Leonardo* and *La Voce* was marked by an ideological ambivalence and self-contradiction typical of most international cultural criticism in the early years of the twentieth century. The general equation of youth-revolution, for example, was evident in both Italy and the United States. *Leonardo*'s program was presented by a group of "young people" who were seen as the torchbearers of a new culture at large. Likewise, in 1921, Harold Stearns published *America and the Young Intellectual*. In order to convey the malaise of an unquiet young intelligentsia, disillusioned by the war and disdainful of politics as such, he formulated the emblematic question, "What *Can* a Young Man Do?" Even the Italian fascists equivocated with the question when they adopted an anthem entitled *Giovinezza (Youth)*, the first line of which runs as follows: "Giovinezza, giovinezza, primavera di bellezza" ("Youth, youth, springtime of beauty"). As late as 1931, when he published his autobiography, Lincoln Steffens could still confess that in his bewildered confrontation with the crisis of American democracy he was drawn to two alternative figures: Lenin and Mussolini. Finally, in December of 1922, less than two months after fascism had come to power in Italy, Prezzolini wrote in *La rivoluzione liberale* (Piro Gobetti's radical review): "With its violence, fascism has destroyed nothing but what we had destroyed with our thought in twenty years of criticizing: Italian democracy."[17] Left-wing and right-wing critics, as well as moderates, joined in the dismissal of pre-fascist democracy and of its conceptual and cultural foundations.

Mussolini's notorious interview given to the *Sunday Times* in 1926 should be carefully contextualized. At the time of *Leonardo* and *La Voce*, Mussolini was a revolutionary socialist who espoused nationalism, the optical self-justification, the political panacea bestowed on the Italian bourgeoisie by the ruling class, only on the eve of World War I. Whether he had a first-hand knowledge of pragmatism is quite irrelevant. "I learnt of William James the faith in action, that ardent will to live and fight," Mussolini was eager to avow. A plausible assumption. *Leonardo* and *La Voce* had been the testing ground for a considerable portion of the Italian intelligentsia, a swinging pendulum, as we have seen. In enacting his cultural or pseudocultural pantomime, Mussolini did his best to cash in on that momentum. He cunningly opened one of the doors in the corridor.

Notes

1. The "Programma sintetico" of *Leonardo* has been reprinted in Delia Frigessi, ed., *La cultura italiana del 1900 attraverso le riviste* (Turin: Einaudi, 1960), 1, 89. My translation.
2. Frigessi, *La cultura italiana*, 24–25.
3. Quoted in Ralph Barton Perry, *The Thought and Character of William James* (Boston: Little, Brown, 1935), 570.
4. Giovanni Papini, *Pragmatismo* (Milan: Libreria Editrice Milanese, 1913), 102ff. My translation.
5. Giovanni Papini, *Il crepuscolo dei filosofi* (Milano: Società Editrice Lombarda, 1960), vii. My translation. Cf. William James, "G. Papini and the Pragmatist Movement in Italy," *The Journal of Philosophy, Psychology, and Scientific Methods* 3, no. 13 (21 June 1906): 337–41.
6. Giuseppe Prezzolini, "Risposta a Calderoni," *Leonardo* 2 (November 1904): 7–9; reprinted in Frigessi, *La cultura italiana*, 172–76.
7. Giovanni Papini, *L'altra metà* (Ancona: Puccini, 1912), 1ff.
8. Giovanni Vailati, "La più recente definizione della matematica," *Leonardo* 2 (June 1904): 7–10; reprinted in Frigessi, *La cultura italiana*, 158–64. The title of the essay ("The Most Recent Definition of Mathematics") refers to Bertrand Russell's formulation. My translation. Cf. Antonio Santucci, "Papini e il pragmatismo," in *Giovanni Papini nel centenario della nascita*, ed. Sandro Gentili (Milan: Vita e Pensiero, 1983), 24–53.
9. William James, *The Will to Believe* (London: Longmans, Green, 1897), vii–xii. Cf. Gerald E. Myers, *William James: His Life and Thought* (New Haven: Yale University Press, 1986), passim.
10. Giovanni Papini, *Le memorie d'Iddio* (Florence: Casa Editrice Italiana, 1911), 85. My translation. Cf. *Un uomo finito* (Florence: Libreria della Voce, 1913), passim.
11. Giovanni Papini, *Il mio futurismo* (Florence: Edizioni de Lacerba, 1914), passim. My translation. Cf. Luciano De Maria, "Papini e le avanguardie," in Gentili, *Giovanni Papini*, 213–22. My translation. The quotation from *Stroncature* is in this essay. See also Luigi Baldacci, "Papini e *L'esperienza futurista*," in *Giovanni Papini nel centenario della nascita*, 266–78.

12. The letter to Alice James is quoted in Perry, *William James*, 418–19.
13. C. Hartley Grattan, *The Three Jameses* (New York: New York University Press, 1962), 133. The following letters are in *The Letters of William James, Edited by His Son Henry James* (Boston: The Atlantic Monthly Press, 1920), 1: 174–75; 1: 180–81; 2: 225. See also William James, "G. Papini and the Pragmatist Movement in Italy," passim.
14. The letter from Papini (3 May 1906) is given in English translation by Perry, *William James*, 572–73. I have checked a photocopy of the original in French, made available through the courtesy of the Primo Conti Foundation in Florence. Both the letter to F. C. S. Schiller and the note to James M. Cattell, commenting on the false news of Papini's death, are in *William James: Selected Unpublished Correspondence, 1885–1910*, ed. Frederick J. Down Scott (Columbus: Ohio State University Press, 1986), 425, 507. All the other letters quoted in this section are unpublished, and have been checked on photocopies made available through the courtesy of the Primo Conti Foundation in Florence.
15. Alberto Asor Rosa, *Dall'Unità a oggi*, volume 4:2 of Ruggiero Romano and Carrado Vivanti, comps. *Storia d'Italia* (Turin: Einaudi, 1975), 1257–59.
16. Gerald E. Myers, *William James: His Life and Thought* (New Haven: Yale University Press, 1986), 461.
17. Giuseppe Prezzolini, quoted in Renzo De Felice, "Prezzolini, la guerra, il Fascismo," *Giuseppe Prezzolini, 1882–1982*, ed. F. Pino Pongolini (Bellinzona: Dipartimento della Pubblica Educazione, 1983), 54. My translation.

ELEVEN *Henry James and the Literature of Italy*

LYALL H. POWERS

A RATHER surprising feature of Henry James's lifelong love affair with Italy is that it engendered only two published essays on Italian writers: "Matilde Serao" for the *North American Review* (March 1901), and "Gabriele D'Annunzio" for the *Quarterly Review* (April 1904). He did publish four reports on Italian actors, however, and they sound a note that anticipates the two essays in a significant way; so I want first to look at what James said of Ernesto Rossi in 1876 and of Tommaso Salvini in 1883. "Rossi is a superb stage figure, and every now and then he has a cry, a movement, a look, which goes straight to the mark" (*Scenic Art*, 46)—a look fraught with meaning, evidently. Of Salvini, James wrote

He is a magnificent creature . . . a great artistic nature. The admirable thing in this nature of Salvini's is that his intelligence is equal to his material powers; so that if the exhibition is, as it were, personal, it is not simply physical. He has a great imagination; there is a noble intention in all he does. (*Scenic Art*, 172)

James would praise, that is, Salvini's physical appearance as a palpable provable fact—the *look* of him—but even more so his ability to make that look meaningful. I will return to that "note" later.

James met Matilde Serao in Rome on the first Sunday in June 1894, at a luncheon given by Count Joseph Primoli. James was seated next to her and learned from her of Paul Bourget's "exaltation" to the Académie Française. The next day he wrote of this meeting to his old friend Grace Norton:

Did you ever hear of the Serao—the she-Zola of Italy?—or read any of her really "talented" fictions? She is a wonderful little burly Balzac in petticoats—full of Neapolitan life and sound and familiarity. *(Letters,* 3: 474)

He was evidently already acquainted with her work: his essay of 1901 informs us that he has "lately been giving a happy extension to an old acquaintance, dating from early in the eighties, with the striking romantic work of Matilde Serao" *(Lib. Amer.* 3: 957). And while the essay on D'Annunzio is ostensibly a review of five works in translation, James there exhibits a knowledge of D'Annunzio's publications that extends well beyond those five.

The question of why James restricted himself to two essays on Italian writers is challenging. More manageable is why he chose to write on those two, and in the space of only three years, just at that moment of his career. There is, first, the obvious Italian connection. The essays follow at a small distance his three-month visit to Italy in 1899; they are contemporary with *The Wings of the Dove* and *The Golden Bowl,* novels strongly Italianate in character and flavor, and with his essay of 1902 on Katherine de Kay Bronson's Venetian Casa Alvisi and his biography *William Wetmore Story and his Friends* in 1903. Then, James's important French connections would have kept him mindful of the "she-Zola of Italy," the "little burly Balzac in petticoats"; and Paul Bourget, among others, would have helped keep him abreast of the brilliant success in France of Gabriele D'Annunzio during the 1890s. Furthermore, in 1900 James reviewed Sidney Colvin's edition of the letters of Robert Louis Stevenson, whose friendship with James dated from publication of "The Art of Fiction"—about the moment when he began reading Serao. Clinging to the Stevenson connection would be the whole network of memories of the experimental decade that began with James's practice in the mode of Flaubert, Zola, and the other "grandsons of Balzac" and ended in January of 1895 with *Guy Domville.* The subsequent decade of experiment in narrative technique, that began with his discovery of "the divine principle of the Scenario" and the novels of the nineties, led to his fiction of the "major phase" and included his introductions for English translations of Flaubert's *Madame Bovary* and Balzac's *Les Deux Jeunes Mariées* (1902), his last essay on Zola (1903), and preparation in the fall of 1904 of his lecture "The Lesson of Balzac."

It was in great part the realistic-naturalistic aspect of Matilde Serao's fiction that would continue to attract James, even though his own experiments in narrative during the later nineties reflected a growing dissatisfaction with Zola's heavily documented, detailed descriptions and even with the Zolaesque aspect of Balzac's fiction. While Serao remained somewhat closer to Zola than James did, her published dissatisfaction with her French master was expressed in terms that James would choose to apply to Zola in his essay of 1903. Early in 1884 she spoke for the disenchanted followers of Zola: "Poveri apostoli! Il loro maestro a poco a poco descende alle funzioni di un meccanico senza talento" (*Domenica letteraria*, 13 January 1884, quoted in Gisolfi, 63). James would call Zola's *Vérité* "machine-minted" and attribute its weakness to Zola's succumbing to "the danger of the mechanical" (*Lib. Amer.* 3: 875).

His essay of 1901, however, still places Serao in the train of Zola but acknowledges an important difference, and in specifying that difference James sounds a recognizable echo from "The Art of Fiction"—to which we must give full attention in a moment; he praises her as "a vivid painter and a rich register of sensations and impressions" (*Lib. Amer.* 3: 957). There is particular significance in a further note of admiration for Serao's achievement, a note that hints at the possibility of her influence on James. He expresses his

admiration for the curious cluster of scenes that, in "Il Romanzo [della Fanciulla, 1885]," bears the title of "Nella Lava." . . . the real principle of "naturalism" . . . the famous "slice of life" . . . slices of shabby hungry maidenhood in small cockney circles . . . how little "story" is required to hold us when we get, before the object evoked and in the air created, the impression of the real thing. (*Lib. Amer.* 3: 963)

Here echo some of the familiar and crucial points of "The Art of Fiction": "A novel is in its broadest definition a personal, a direct impression of life; that, to begin with, constitutes its value, which is greater or less according to the intensity of the impression"—and again, "If experience consists of impressions, it may be said that impressions *are* experience"; to which James immediately added a word on the importance of "truth of detail" and of "the air of reality" (*Lib. Amer.* 2: 50, 53).

We ought to linger over James's attention to the "curious cluster of scenes" in "Nella Lava" ("In the Lava") and his recognition of "how little 'story' is required to hold us" under the right circumstances. That particular feature of Serao's fiction would understandably have interested the author of "A Bundle of Letters" (1879) and "The Point of View" (1882), and perhaps made some small contribution to James's later creation of the scantly plotted, "cubist" novel *The Awkward Age;* and *The Ambassadors* was sufficiently independent of plot to suffer the reversal of two of its chapters without appreciable loss of significance.

Furthermore, James's favorite among Serao's fictions, *Il Paese di Cuccagna* (1891), exhibits the very features he praised in "Nella Lava"—a cluster of scenes with little "story"; the same features characterize at least one other item of Serao's, a companion piece in *Il Romanzo della Fanciulla,* that is, "Telegrafi dello Stato." Here, indeed, the question of influence surfaces again from a slightly different angle: "Telegrafi dello Stato" might well have been in James's mind when he set down, in 1897, the beginnings of his own story of hungry maidenhood in a small cockney circle, specifically the circle of the post and telegraph office in a London greengrocer's —the story of the telegrapher in "In the Cage." There are certainly major differences between the two tales, but the few similarities are intriguing. In any case, at the end of the nineteenth century Matilde Serao would evidently have been a burly little lioness in the path of Henry James.

His appreciation of her work had, however, a severe limitation— a limitation that drew James's attention again in his appreciation of the work of Gabriele D'Annunzio. Serao's handling of the erotic, of what James felt obliged to refer to by its Italian term, *passione,* was what gave him serious pause. He begins by presenting her as an example of the benefit of the freedom accorded to European writers as opposed to the "rigour of convention" that binds the English and American writer. But use of that freedom to represent frankly relationships of a certain kind is artistically dangerous, James contends; and his objection has a moral basis, but that basis is signally different from the pernickety puritanical moralism that characterized his early criticism. In 1875, for example, he could ask rhetorically of the character of Sidonie Chèbe ("a young woman of depraved and licentious instincts") in Alphonse Daudet's *Fromont Jeune et Risler Aîné,* "If we are to write the natural history of the prostitute on this extended scale, on what scale shall we handle that of her betters?" (*Lib. Amer.* 2: 209). It is from quite another position that he can observe of *La Conquista di Roma* that

The effect . . . of the undertaking to give *passione* its whole place is that . . . no place speedily appears to be left for anything else . . . every relation in life but that over which Venus presides. (*Lib. Amer.* 3: 963)

And he concludes:

Love, at Naples and in Rome, as Madame Serao exhibits it, is simply unaccompanied with any interplay of our usual conditions. . . . It is not the passion of the hero and heroine that gives, that can ever give, the heroine and hero interest, but . . . it is they themselves, with the ground they stand on and the objects enclosing them, who give interest to their passion. (*Lib. Amer.* 3: 965)

In this reservation James's essay on Gabriele D'Annunzio most nearly resembles his essay on Matilde Serao. The 1904 essay opens with a familiar gambit—praise for the freedom D'Annunzio enjoyed and denigration of the comparable bondage imposed on writers in England and America. This makes him an interesting "case." James generously enough approves of D'Annunzio's talent as a novelist, and we readily detect in certain passages of the essay echoes of important comments in "The Art of Fiction" and of his praise, in the 1902 introduction to *Madame Bovary*, of Flaubert's artistry (the similarity would have pleased D'Annunzio):

So close is the marriage between his power of "rendering," in the light of the imagination, and whatever he sees and feels, that we should be much misled in speaking of his manner as a thing distinct from the matter submitted to it. The fusion is complete and admirable, . . . we see at no point where literature or where life begins or ends. (*Lib. Amer.* 3: 914)

An additional note of commendation further associates James's approval of D'Annunzio with his approval of Serao: the depiction of the multitudes at the shrine in the Abruzzi in *Il Trionfo della Morte*, he says, "has the mark of a pictorial energy for such matters not inferior to that of Zola."

But James had faulted Zola's system, in his essay of 1903: "breadth and energy supply the place of penetration. He rests to his utmost on his documents"—and so produces "the most extraordinary *imitation* of observation that we possess" (*Lib. Amer.* 3:878, 895). Now,

James would have known that D'Annunzio's work was eagerly embraced in France in the nineties as a refreshing alternative to naturalism; yet he will also fault D'Annunzio for weaknesses similar to Zola's. The defect of *Il Fuoco*, in James's eyes, is that it seems to be made of

material that the author had become possessed of, and not because, in its almost journalistic "actuality," it has any large meaning. We get the impression of a direct transfer, a "lift," bodily, of something seen and known, something not really produced by the chemical process of art, the crucible or retort from which things emerge for a new function. (*Lib. Amer.* 3: 930)

Here again James objects to the "*imitation* of observation," the absence of a meaningful and genial impression.

Such absence of penetrating observation and the consequent failure of significant representation is most serious when the erotic, *passione*, is in question; and it is in question, James contends, everywhere in D'Annunzio. His objection to that phenomenon in D'Annunzio's fiction is the same as his objection to it in Serao's. He indicts *Il Piacere*, *L'Innocente*, *Il Fuoco*, and even his favorite, *Il Trionfo della Morte*:

The plane of the situation [the sphere of exasperated sensibility] is thus visibly a singularly special plane; that, always, of the more or less insanely demoralized pair of lovers, for neither of whom is any other personal relation indicated either as actual or as conceivably possible. Here . . . is material rather alarmingly cut down as to range, as to interest and, not least, as to charm. (*Lib. Amer.* 3: 919)

The erotic, that is to say, is deprived of its potential significance in the characters' lives; consequently, the important relevance it bears to "the substance of the human spectacle" is seriously diminished if not actually erased. D'Annunzio "treats 'love' as a matter not to be mixed with life, in the larger sense of the word, at all," says James, but to be kept "Shut out from the rest of life, shut out from all fruition and assimilation" (*Lib. Amer.* 3: 941–42). His objection, as I say, is a fundamentally moral objection. That adjective needs an additional word of explanation; I will add it in a moment.

Just why this preoccupation with the treatment of the erotic in the fiction of Serao and D'Annunzio should have been entertaining

James's thoughts in the opening years of this century, the years of the major phase, is perhaps obvious enough. From 1895 onward, carnal confrontation in James's fiction, while never frequent or prolonged, nevertheless makes a significant contribution to his works, beginning with the kiss of Fleda Vetch and Owen Gereth. The essay on Serao coincides with James's beginning *The Ambassadors*. That novel is concerned with the illicit liaison of Chad Newsome and Marie de Vionnet and with the almost willfully obtuse Strether's fond hope that it is "a virtuous attachment." He defends the attachment even after he is obliged to recognize its true nature—as "virtuous" has perhaps changed its meaning for him. *The Ambassadors* thus seems a confirmed defense of adultery pragmatically justified; but a lingering question is whether Strether has turned his back on the great, grey Babylon rife with the smell of blood, refused Maria Gostrey's unambiguous offer, and sought the safety of the bloodless and uncarnal Woollet—out of reach of the temptations of man's simian relations.

The Wings of the Dove, sharing with *The Golden Bowl* its Italian flavor, gives sexual relations a prominence unusual in Jamesian fiction. Furthermore, it revives the polarity between spiritual and physical love that had characterized much of his earlier work; and of course in that polarity the spiritual is favored, as Kate Croy's grim recognition emphasizes—"Her memory's your love; you want no other." It would appear that James was finally working his way through the problem of the depiction of carnal relations and trying to sort things out and confront them honestly. The success of his effort is apparent in *The Golden Bowl*, where the old polarity, represented in the confrontation of Maggie Verver and Charlotte Stant, is resolved. Maggie enters the arena—as Milly never could with Kate Croy—and beats Charlotte at her own game, so to speak. The existence of the Principino, combined with Amerigo's last words to Maggie, evidently argue for the "moral" triumph of the princess. James's comments on the treatment of sexual passion in the fiction of Serao and of D'Annunzio apparently reflect the attitude of mind at work in the creator of *The Ambassadors*, *The Wings of the Dove*, and *The Golden Bowl*, and may be considered a kind of theoretic justification of the treatment of sexual passion in those three major novels. Final confirmation of James's position may be seen in the revised *Portrait of a Lady*—on which revision was begun only a couple of years after publication of the essay on D'Annunzio.

The moral basis, as I have called it, of James's attitude to the role of the erotic in fiction—explicitly enough present in the essays on Serao and D'Annunzio and strongly implicit in the fiction of the major decade of experiment from *The Spoils of Poynton* to the revised *Portrait of a Lady*—is firmly laid in James's essay of 1884, "The Art of Fiction." A brief reperusal of that essay will provide the additional word on the term "moral" that I promised a moment ago. I want to indicate that James's remarks on the conception and creation of works of fiction illuminate his view of the moral essence of fiction—and illustrate what he perhaps meant by the statement that "the deepest quality of a work of art will always be the quality of the mind of the producer" (*Lib. Amer.* 2: 64). Here is a familiar and most important passage from "The Art of Fiction":

the air of reality (solidity of specification) seems to me to be the supreme virtue of a novel . . . it is here that [the novelist] competes with his brother the painter in his attempt to render the look of things, *the look that conveys their meaning*, to catch the colour, the relief, the expression, the surface, *the substance of the human spectacle*. (*Lib. Amer.* 2: 53; my emphasis)

The *selection* of solidly specified details of a given aspect of setting or scene or character or action must work not as reproduction but as representation, not just to give "the look" of it but the meaning of it—"the substance of the human spectacle." There are two factors implicit in James's comment—significance and relevance: the representation must be careful to capture the significance of its object, and it must be careful to capture its essence—so as to convey its "substance" as part of the recognizably *human* spectacle, which is to say that it must be made *relevant* to the reader as to the human scene in general.

This representation, if it is to be usefully apprehended, must provoke intelligent participation in the reader; it must encourage him to *see* intelligently. Key statements in *The Ambassadors* suggest that such intelligent seeing is of fundamental importance to life: "Live all you can; it's a mistake not to," is Strether's advice to Little Bilham; yet when Bilham recalls that advice and asks him rhetorically, "Didn't you adjure me . . . to see all I can?" James does not have Strether "correct" Bilham but rather leaves intact the equation "To live is to see." *The Golden Bowl* adds to this equation the Jamesian stamp of fundamental morality. "I see," of course, means "I understand": it is a statement about intellectual perception or apprehension. Fanny Assingham is allowed the observation, "Stupidity carried to a certain point is immoral; and what is morality but high intelligence?"

Now, the problem with the erotic as James found it in the fiction of Serao and D'Annunzio is the failure that we recognize in pornography and prostitution: the immorality resides in the fact that the lovers and prostitutes are restricted to the deceptive "look of things" —a look, an appearance, that is without human significance and human relevance; it neglects the *meaning* of the persons involved as it reduces them to a single function, the sexual, and therefore in turn severely curtails the human relevance of that function and its real participation in "the substance of the human spectacle." This is not to claim, as the finical young James nearly did, that *all* portrayal of human sexual behavior is ipso facto immoral in the common meaning of that term, but that portrayal of sexual activity that lacks the necessary significance and relevance quite certainly is.

James the realist-naturalist of the mid-eighties begins that important passage in "The Art of Fiction" on the air of reality with the comment, you recall, "I am far from intending to minimize . . . the importance of exactness—or truth of detail." And elsewhere in the essay he adds a stern word of caution to his advice on being selective: "Art is essentially selection, but it is a selection whose main care is to be typical, to be inclusive" (*Lib. Amer.* 2: 58). That last word ("inclusive") is the problem: he would be understood to mean *representatively* inclusive—choosing the *detail* that carries the essential *truth*, seeing and expressing the world in a grain of sand and perhaps eternity in an hour. That is the quality he early praised in the acting of Ernesto Rossi and of Tommaso Salvini—the intelligent look that is essentially expressive, the imaginative dramatic presence that is personal but not "merely physical." This early admirer of Balzac and Zola has come to be wary of quantity of detail as opposed to quality: quantity, indeed, he came to fear as absolutely threatening—for himself as creative artist, for the reader confronted with artistic representation, and ultimately for the moral content of art and of life.

In his preface to *The Spoils of Poynton*, appropriately enough, he addresses the matter eloquently as he recalls being given the "germ" for the novel and his informant's unwillingness to hush: "I began to hear [all the details of the Scottish laird and his widowed mother] . . . I saw clumsy Life again at her stupid work . . . and I had once more the full demonstration of the fatal futility of Fact" (*Lib. Amer.* 3: 1140). That is a near companion to his comment, sometimes misunderstood, criticizing novels of Thackeray, Dumas père, and Tolstoi in the preface to *The Tragic Muse:*

A picture without composition slights its most precious chance for beauty. . . . [W]hat do such large loose baggy monsters, with their queer elements of the accidental and the arbitrary, artistically *mean*? . . . There is life and life, and as waste is only life sacrificed and thereby prevented from "counting," I delight in a deep-breathing economy and an organic form. (*Lib. Amer.* 3: 1107–8)

Behind both of these attitudes—concerning the provenance of a story and the manner of its artistic depiction—lies the common assumption that one is writing for a similarly attuned audience, readers on whom "nothing is lost." For the acutely attentive reader, the deepest quality of James's art is finally its moral message. The moral content, thus, is everywhere at one with—and at its best indistinguishable from—the artistic form in which it is embodied. That morality consists in the recognition and espousal of the fundamental importance for mature human life of clear vision, alert consciousness, accurate and unprejudiced perception of the given elements of our world as in themselves they truly are—or as far as it is possible to do so; in the discovery of and respect for the significance and relevance of those elements, the people and things around us.

Certainly James constantly urges the moral necessity of distinguishing between people and things and of recognizing the evil of treating people as though they were things—for example, Mrs. Light's treatment of Christina, the manipulation of Isabel by Serena Merle and Gilbert Osmond, the plight of Verena Tarrant and of little Maisie and of Miles and Flora, Kate Croy's attempted use of Milly and Charlotte's of Maggie. Yet the morality extends as well to things, in an interesting way. In his excellent study *The Phenomenology of Henry James*, Paul Armstrong observes: "Even an appropriate aesthetic appreciation of a work of art must evoke and cherish the subjectivity lodged in it" (144).

The Spoils of Poynton brilliantly illustrates this embracing moral attitude—which includes, by the way, an interesting emphasis on the *reflexive* nature of moral vision and behavior (similar to Faulkner's constant equation of murder and suicide). The evil of Mrs. Gereth, the connoisseur and collector, is not the crude love of possession: it is that her attitude to the collectibles robs them of their "life" and so leaves them inert—as a house left vacant may lose its "spirit." She is an idolater: the items in her life are rendered opaque by her vision, for she sees only "the look of things." Obviously, Mrs. Gereth treats Fleda Vetch and her own son, Owen, as things, to a considerable extent: they are in her eyes of less importance than the items in her collection. But that immorality is extended—and its reflexiveness emphasized—by James's depiction of her attitude to the "old things." The declension of Fleda's view of Mrs. Gereth goes through an instructive series of steps. In chapter 4:

The truth was simply that all Mrs. Gereth's scruples were on one side and that her ruling passion had in a manner *despoiled her of her humanity*. (My emphasis)

The great wrong Owen had done her . . . was his failure from the first to understand what it was to have a mother at all, to appreciate the beauty and sanctity of the character. . . . One's mother, . . . the only kind Mrs. Gereth cared for, was a subject for poetry, for *idolatry*. (Chapter 5, my emphasis)

And in chapter 7: "Wherever she was, she was *herself the great piece in the gallery*" (my emphasis). Fleda also serves to underline the contrast between the "wretched things" at Ricks and the costly spoils at Poynton.

The poor furnishings of the maiden aunt who had lived at Ricks continue to assert their significance: their look conveys a meaning; and that meaning is redolent of human relevance, as the long paragraph concluding chapter 5 makes clear. "Fleda was moved. . . . The more she looked about the surer she felt of the character of the maiden-aunt . . . : the maiden-aunt had been a dear; she would have adored the maiden-aunt." The point is eloquently reiterated on Fleda's return to Ricks, in the penultimate chapter. She explains to Mrs. Gereth:

"Ah, the little melancholy, tender, tell-tale things: how can they not speak to you and find a way to your heart? It's not the great chorus of Poynton. . . . This is a voice so gentle, so human, so feminine—a faint, far-away voice with the little quaver of a heart-break. . . . It's a kind of fourth dimension. It's a presence, a perfume, a touch. It's a soul, a story, a life."

Fleda's perception basically resembles the discovery Maggie Verver makes of the golden bowl, especially as she gathers its constituent pieces into her own hands—"for love." I am speaking here of the reflexive nature of morality as Henry James and others (Faulkner, as I have said) understand it: it is contained, I think, in a familiar admonition that James knew well but perhaps understood less as the prescriptive "thou shalt love" and more as the descriptive "thou wilt love thy neighbor as thyself."

Now the perception, depiction, and moral statement involved in the treatment of what James called "the great relation of men and woman, the constant world renewal" are part and parcel of the unified attitude I have been discussing. The treatment of the erotic in the fiction of Matilde Serao and of Gabriele D'Annunzio, James found, was like Mrs. Gereth's treatment of Owen and Fleda and the old things. The characters in their fiction, he believed, were robbed of their human significance and relevance, rendered inert, deprived of real life, when passione was at issue. James's two essays on the literature of Italy were an important part of his establishing to his own satisfaction his whole artistic and human position, a fusion of the aesthetic and the ethical, at the turn of the century: that is, that failure of moral vision is destructive of life—including one's own.

Bibliography

Key to Works by Henry James

Letters—Henry James Letters, ed. Leon Edel, vol. 3, 1883–1895. Cambridge: Harvard University Press, 1980.
Lib. Amer. 2—Literary Criticism: Essays on Literature, American Writers,

English Writers, ed. Leon Edel. New York: Literary Classics of the United States, 1984.

Lib. Amer. 3—*Literary Criticism: French Writers, Other European Writers, The Prefaces to the New York Edition*, ed. Leon Edel. New York: Literary Classics of the United States, 1984.

Scenic Art—*The Scenic Art: Notes on Acting and Drama 1872–1901*, ed. Allan Wade. New Brunswick, N.J.: Rutgers University Press, 1948.

Other Works Cited

Armstrong, Paul B. *The Phenomenology of Henry James*. Chapel Hill: University of North Carolina Press, 1983.

Gisolfi, Anthony M. *The Essential Matilde Serao*. New York: Las Americas Publishing Company, 1968.

TWELVE *William Wetmore Story and His Friends: The Enclosing Fact of Rome*

DENIS DONOGHUE

O N 23 DECEMBER 1903, Henry James wrote to the duchess of Sutherland, thanking her for liking *William Wetmore Story and His Friends* well enough to write to him about it. The book was, he confessed, "the operation of making bricks without straw and chronicling (sometimes) rather small beer with the effect of opening champagne":

Story was the dearest of men, but he wasn't massive, his artistic and literary baggage were of the slightest and the materials for a biography *nil*. Hence (once I had succumbed to the amiable pressure of his children), I had really to *invent* a book, patching the thing together and eking it out with barefaced irrelevancies—starting above all any hare, however small, that might lurk by the way. It is very pleasant to get from a discriminating reader the token that I have carried the trick through. But the magic is but scantly mine—it is really that of the beloved old Italy, who always *will* consent to fling a glamour for you, whenever you speak her fair.[1]

Not only did James think that Story failed to be massive; he regarded him as "thinner than thin." There was no subject, he complained to William Dean Howells, before he had written the book, commenting there was "nothing in the man himself to write about": "There is nothing for me but to do a *tour de force*, or try to—leave poor dear W.W.S. *out*, practically, and make a little volume on the old Roman, Americo-Roman, Hawthornesque and other bygone days."[2]

Indeed, James regarded Story as a dabbler, something of a clown, and he never forgot the dismal experience of having to listen to him reading, to an audience of four, his five-act tragedy on the history of Nero. As James reported the evening to Charles Eliot Norton, on 13 March 1873, Story "got through three acts in three hours, and the last two were resumed on another evening when I was unavoidably absent." The performance, he continued, "was the result much less of an inward necessity, I surmise, than of a most restless ambition, not untinged with—what an impertinent little word stands for, beginning with v and ending with y."[3] In *William Wetmore Story and His Friends* James does not use the word *vanity*, but he refers to "talkative emphasis" when he quotes one of Story's early letters to James Russell Lowell.

The *tour de force* to which James referred showed itself as a possibility when he realized that under the excuse of writing a biography of Story he could paint a group portrait of the American and English friends whom Story and his wife entertained at their apartment in the Palazzo Barberini—the Brownings, Margaret Fuller, William Page, Landor, Hawthorne, and many more. James could also draw upon his own experience of Rome when he first visited it in 1869. The book, as Leon Edel has noted, is judiciously titled: *William Wetmore Story and His Friends From Letters, Diaries, and Recollections;* it was written as a chore and to keep a promise exacted from James by Story's son Waldo.

In the event, the book was a commercial success, especially in America, and some readers took it more seriously than James intended. I think James was embarrassed, as much as pleased, when Henry Adams wrote to say that the book was the life not only of Story but of every such American of his generation, including Charles Sumner, Emerson, Lowell, Longfellow, Adams, and indeed James himself, each of whom was an ignorant bourgeois Bostonian trying to make himself something else. James's reply evaded the large issue and pleaded that the biographical form itself made its subjects seem thin, "throws a chill upon the scene, the time, the subject, the small mapped-out facts."[4]

It must appear that the book started under the worst possible auspices: a thin subject and an unwilling biographer who had better and more urgent things to be doing, including a novel to be called *The Golden Bowl.* It is true that some of James's pages are barefaced

fillers of space, and that other pages, more agreeably written, are
merely workmanlike. I have in view, as an example of professionally respectable but otherwise unexciting work, James's account of
the episode in *The Marble Faun* where Hawthorne sends Miriam to
visit the sculptor in his studio and to see the statue of Cleopatra; as
Hawthorne acknowledged in his preface to the book, the statue was
Story's work, and one of his most successful. James's account of this
episode in *The Marble Faun* is charming so far as it goes, but he
demands far less of the book than he did in his early biography of
Hawthorne, published in 1879, where he takes the book seriously
enough to find it a faulty production. He still likes "its laxities of
insistence, its timidities of indication, its felicities of suggestion, its
sincerities of simplicity and, most of all, its total vague intensity,
so curiously composed of all these,"[5] but he no longer cares enough
about it to pursue the questions which troubled him in the biography, even though these included questions about an American
imagination trying to cope with a Roman scene.

These pages in *William Wetmore Story and His Friends* are, then,
professionally adequate, but unexacting. Indeed, the book came
alive only under one form of pressure, that of remembrance, especially the act of remembrance incited by James's thoughts of Rome.
In that respect, the book is of a piece with the affectionate record
of Italy, of Florence, which James spoke of again in his preface to
the New York Edition of *Roderick Hudson*. The principle of remembrance is often intimated and at least once in the book on Story it
is described: "the value of the pleasure derived from the act itself,
the act of remembrance lively almost to indiscretion."[6]

But the pleasure was nothing unless it consisted in renewed relations, personal and social in the immediately recalled instance, and
at a further remove the sense of one's general relatedness to lives
otherwise gone. It was this general sense which prompted James, in
The Portrait of a Lady, to let Isabel drive out to the Campagna and
there to drop her sadness into the silence of lonely places—an
attempted release James had already come upon, as Q. D. Leavis
has shown, in *Little Dorrit* and *Middlemarch*.

The principle of remembrance was simple enough. As James gives
it in the book on Story, "to live over people's lives is nothing unless

we live over their perceptions, live over the growth, the change, the varying intensity of the same—since it was by these things they themselves lived."[7] But it would not answer if one merely lived over these perceptions in any sequence that came to one's mind, a procedure no better than random: the "living over" had somehow to bespeak the mutual relation of parts, a sense of the whole, for which the best analogy was spatial, as in the felt unity of a great house. In recalling the Palazzo Barberini, James pondered again, as he reported, "the old mystery of the strong effect that resides in simplicity and that yet is so far from merely consisting of it."[8] Simplicity is the form in which mutually acknowledged relations are recognized, and it is the work of remembrance to produce them under that sense of responsibility.

What is remembered need not be a great thing in itself. Some of the liveliest recollections in the book on Story are incited by recalling Mrs. Procter, "mother of Adelaide Procter the poetess, the ornament of anthologies when anthologies are not, as we may say, pedantic."[9] The liveliness is of the kind which enabled James, having reported that Mrs. Procter had had a falling-out with Kinglake to the extent of not speaking to him thereafter for a quarter of a century," immediately to add: "She was magnificent."

But it is unnecessary to draw a sharp line between James's remembrance of minor people and of the Rome in which they figured. He makes this clear again when he comes to refer to *Roba di Roma*, Story's guidebook to Rome and its environs which he assembled in 1863. In 1909 James assembled his own early essays on Venice, Rome, Florence, Siena, Ravenna, and other Italian places, and published them as *Italian Hours*. In that context, *Roba di Roma* is hardly a book to make James feel jealous—it is a rambling, garrulous work—except that it disclosed on Story's part a degree of intimacy with Italy which James could not claim. His reference to *Roba di Roma* is characteristically generous:

The golden air, as I look over its pages, makes a mist; I read them again in the light of old personal perceptions and emotions; I read, as we say, too much into them, too many associations, pictures, *other* ineffaceable passages. . . . [The book] summed up, with an extraordinary wealth of statement, with perpetual illustration and image, the incomparable entertainment of Rome, where almost everything alike, manners, customs, practices, processes, states of feeling, no less than objects, treasures, relics, ruins, partook of the special museum-quality.[10]

In James's memory of Rome, revived now by *Roba di Roma*, virtually everything was at least interesting. "To read these passages over", he says, "is to taste and feel again the very air of early rambles, when one was always agaze; to hear the sounds, to smell the dust, to give one's self up once more as to the thing that was ancient and noble even when homely or sordid, the thing that might be mean but that yet couldn't be vulgar."[11]

The act of remembrance had a further and this time a more painful responsibility, to evoke places and manners which in 1903 were chiefly to be recognized as having been destroyed. When James recalls the artist's life, whether the particular artist was Story, or Page, or Browning, or lesser men like Eugene Benson and Rollin Tilton, he has to report that the blissful conditions in which they first saw Rome were now largely defaced. The artist life, he said, "in the romantic conditions and with the romantic good faith, is a thing of the past; the Campagna, near the walls of Rome, has been for the most part cruelly curtailed and cockneyfied; the hotels, huge and overflowing, the paradise now of the polyglot element, much more copious than of old and more strident, outface the palaces and entertain, gloriously, themselves and each other."[12] James found still more acute reason for his sense of loss when he made his final visit to Italy in 1907; just as he discovered in 1904 that America was no longer the place he had known. All the more reason, in both cases, for the renewed act of remembrance, because only by its ministry could he find, as he said in the book on Story, that "the softer tone lives still, on the spot, in a fond memory here and there, and echoes of the old evenings in especial, of the Roman balls, say, before the days of mourning, even yet fall upon the ear."[13]

In fact, the work of James's last years is best understood not as an intermittently indulged "backward glance" but as an elaborate reconsideration and recovery of old experience; he is endlessly engaged in circling back upon former places and intimations, the poignancy in most cases issuing from a sense of difference and change, the mitigating advantage being the consideration that at least he, the mindful artist, is still here to bear witness and tribute to what other people have forgotten or never known. In the only note we have for *William Wetmore Story and His Friends*, long before James had written a line of it, he jotted this down:

For W. W. Story. Beginning. "The writer of these pages— (the scribe of this pleasant history?) is well aware of coming late in the day. . . . BUT the very gain by what we see, *now*, in the contrasted conditions, of happiness of old Rome of the old days."XXXXX[14]

The book, in the event, became a balancing of that loss and this gain. The conditions of the old Rome have changed in nearly every respect for the worse: the former state of things must be recovered by documents, such as Story's letters to his friends, but more strenuously by one's own remembrance. The modern artist who has known Rome in both sets of conditions sees it the more clearly, and makes a finer picture.

It follows that James's technique is one of survey and distantiation. He is writing, in 1902, of the Roman atmosphere from about 1849, when Story and his wife started going to Italy, and concentrating on the years from 1856 when they settled permanently in Rome. The conditions, as James construes them, remained much as they were till 1869, when he himself started going to Italy, and he considers that the changes became decisive in 1870 with the Franco-Prussian War. At the beginning of the book, and on several occasions thereafter, he speaks of Story and his generation as precursors, "the *éclaireurs*, who have gone before." They were the ones, "the tentative generation," American artists for the most part or at least men and women who aspired to the practice of art, who first tried the experiment of living a certain form of life in Rome. They made it easier for their successors, men and women of James's generation, to maintain, as Americans, a relation to Italy, and to know what such a relation would entail. An American relation to Rome, which would involve residence there or at least periodic visits of some duration, was a paradigm, a possible way of living, and there was every need to understand it. It might be taken as the type of any and every American relation to Europe, though of course James recognized that residence in England or France or Germany would entail, at least, different nuances. In *William Wetmore Story and His Friends*, as elsewhere, James thought of it as a bristling situation, that of a consciousness, American by birth and fate and in varying degrees by choice, encountering a more complicated world in Europe, with whatever consequence. His interest in the situation coincided with his wonder at the sight of a mind somehow becoming more perceptive, but he thought it made for a still richer mixture if the mind continued to be, in some sense, what it always was. When he refers to Story and his friends as precursors, he means to distinguish this mixture of conditions and motives, and to imply that his own mixture is bound to be different. The precursive situation is well enough outlined by this passage near the beginning of the book:

The dawn of the American consciousness of the complicated world it was so persistently to annex is the more touching the more primitive we make that consciousness; but we must recognise that the latter can scarcely be interesting to us in proportion as we make it purely primitive. The interest is in its becoming perceptive and responsive, and the charming, the amusing, the pathetic, the romantic drama is exactly that process. The process, in our view, must have begun, in order to determine the psychological moment, but there is a fine bewilderment it must have kept in order not to anticipate the age of satiety.[15]

James does not bother to say, what is obvious enough, that the psychological moment corresponded to a certain historical, social, and economic moment; it coincided with particular conditions— the relative inexpensiveness of Italy in relation to the American dollar, the extensive development of European railways, the weather of Rome, and the ease of escaping from it to any of the charming hill towns surrounding it or further afield—conditions which made the psychological moment feasible.

The mixture of trial and error, perceptiveness and bewilderment, in the American mind of Story's generation made it a matter of peculiar interest to James. These men and women colonized Rome, and made it easier for James's generation to enjoy the satisfactions of being "settled partakers of the greater extension." The advantage of the earlier generation was that everything for them was a surprise; the fate of the later was that many things were found to be matters chiefly of regret.

The precursive relation is what concerns James in the first several chapters of the book, and his metaphors of annexation and colonization imply that the enterprise is continuous. Story and his friends ran ahead, set up field stations, made the rudimentary domestic arrangements; the main body of the army then followed and enjoyed the comforts of a settled perceptiveness. But as the book goes on, the precursors seem to lose their standing; they become echoes, ghosts, and shades. The act of remembrance is still performed, but what is recovered is a sequence of traces. It is as if the forerunners had died off, which they mainly had, leaving behind them at most a certain defunctive music. A letter from Mrs. Gaskell about Hawthorne starts up an echo. Trying to recapture what James does not scruple to call the "Arcadian" time, he speaks of his "impulse to recover any echo of an echo (as I might have held a sea-shell to my ear)."[16] Changing the metaphor but not the impulse, he speaks of Story and his friends as "the hovering ghosts." One of Story's references to General McClellan is described as having "a spectral actuality," renewing the feeling of that moment in the middle of the Civil War, "that feeling of the time which so often makes itself intense as from the sense of its only chance, of foreknowing that it will scarce be the feeling of any other time."[17]

In yet another version of the impulse, what James recovers is called a shade, and I cannot be sure that he distinguishes at all between shades and ghosts. Referring to Siena, where Story and his wife spent the summer of 1857 and several later summers, James says that the town "is peopled for us to-day with wandering shades —impalpable phantoms of lightly-dressed precursors that melt, for every sense, into the splendid summer light . . ."[18] Presumably he calls them shades rather than ghosts because for the moment he is content to see them casting a shadow or otherwise darkening the light of summer before yielding to it. Later in the book, referring to himself as "the chronicler with a sense of shades," he describes the congenial years in England, before the dreaded year 1870, when it was still possible to remain "unconscious of the emphasised rule of the mob." In that case the shades are distinguishable from ghosts by knowing that they have been defeated by rough force, rather than by merely having died. But James sometimes uses the word shade in a more genial sense, as if he meant merely some figure that arrests one's memory without striking fear in it. "We wander here still among shades," he says at one point, as if the wandering were an easy stroll. And there is at least one reference in which James, requiring us to make a distinction between shades and ghosts, apparently thinks of ghosts as the more terrible of the species. Alluding to Colonel Hamley, who introduced Story to the Blackwoods, he remarks that "his name meets me, as it comes up, with that imputed recognition to which we have responded for every figure in our dim procession, he too being, in his degree, one of the friendly, the less ghostly, shades."[19]

I try to distinguish between echoes, ghosts, and shades, if only because James's first word, *precursor*, seems to be neutral; it leaves open the question of the precise relation between precursors and successors, even though in a military or imperial vocabulary those who are sent ahead are deemed to be expendable in an emergency. The important people are those who come later. But James is not so bound by this figure as to confine himself to such a discrimination.

It is true that in one version of the precursive relation, the precursors are patronized. James tended to give pioneers the kind of honor which is compatible with their being naïfs. He writes of his predecessors in the art of the novel as if they deserved the greater respect, considering that they did not know what they were about, and had no standards by which they might be guided. He condescended to Fielding and Jane Austen and Hawthorne in much the same way as to Emerson and Thoreau and Margaret Fuller: they did well, given that there was little they thought of doing. When Story first comes to Europe, he exhibits what James calls "the good faith of the young American for whom Europe meant, even more than now, culture, and for whom culture meant, very much more than now, romantic sentiment."[20] As a sculptor, Story was naive and quite untrained; he did not know what good sculpture was or where he might go to discover it; he was "the victim, all innocent at first, and unconscious, of an order of things from which standards were absent."[21] As a poet, Story loved the lyric and dramatic forms, and never discovered why such love was not enough to produce great poems. As an expatriate, Story never understood the price he paid for the felicity of that condition, though James is evidently willing to believe that Story at least knew that some price was in question. He concedes, without producing much evidence for the concession, that Story was alert to the matter:

He therefore never failed of any plenitude in feeling—in the fullness of time and on due occasion—that a man always pays, in one way or another, for expatriation, for detachment from his plain primary heritage, and that this tax is levied in an amusing diversity of ways. . . . He could suspect, on plenty of evidence, the definite, the homely proof of the pudding—the show, as to *value*, of the general heterogeneous production to which the general charmed life could point. He could suspect it—which was all that was necessary for the prime lucidity—at the same time that he could do it justice and feel how things happen and how the case stood and how, if Boston had never been Rome, so Rome could never be Boston; and also how, in a word, they had all danced to good music and in the noblest ballroom in the world.[22]

James does not measure, in that passage, the extent to which Boston failed to be Rome, or the extent to which Rome declined to be Boston. He seems to think the question sufficiently answered by its having been mentioned, and he assumes that Story at least gave it occasional thought in the intervals of the Roman dance. But it is hard to be sure, in this part of the book, whether he is reporting what Story thought or thinking on Story's behalf on an issue—the question of expatriation—crucial to both of them.

The question is of interest, of course, because it is a variant of the other question, which pervades the book: how may an American, specifically an American artist, "take" Europe; in the particular case, "take" Rome? On the whole, James felt that Story's way of taking Rome was charming, and would have been splendid if only there had been more to the taker. Other ways of taking it were variously exemplified by Longfellow, Lowell, and Hawthorne, men who resorted to Rome betimes but not for long enough to think of weighing it in a balance against Boston. In the book on Story, James found Longfellow "interesting for nothing so much as for the secret of his harmony (harmony of situation and sense I of course mean) and for the way in which his 'European' culture and his native kept house together." They kept house together, James speculates, perhaps because Longfellow had "worked up his American consciousness to that mystic point . . . at which it could feel nothing but continuity and congruity with his European."[23] Hawthorne was in a more difficult state: as James presents him, he was too simple, too provincial to make anything of Rome, too untutored even to divine that others might make a lot of it. Notoriously, James patronized

Hawthorne, and thought him in the end a lightweight, but he admitted that Hawthorne had made himself an artist by just being American enough: there were possibilities in such resilience. As for Lowell, "his theory," as James said, "was that of the American for whom his Americanism filled up the measure of the needful; his practice was that of freely finding room for any useful contribution to the quantity from without." Put like that, it seems a nearly perfect formula, and it allows for smiling occasions of disproportion, on which the theory is put into question by some extraordinarily catching practice.

But it is not precisely James's theory. James, in the book on Story as elsewhere, held to a riskier program; he did not assume that his Americanism would fill up the measure of the needful, but that it evidently would not. The measure would have to be filled, in his case, by whatever in addition we find issuing from England, France, and Italy. It was T. S. Eliot, not James, who made the extraordinary statement that "it is the final perfection, the consummation of an American to become, not an Englishman, but a European—something which no born European, no person of any European nationality, can become."[24] But Eliot said this in a memorial essay on James. I assume that he was not recommending any such "becoming" as a general program for Americans, but merely pointing to a certain possibility, a paradigm which a particular American might pursue. I do not think James pursued it, even in Rye, but he opened his being an American to every risk entailed by the quantity and the quality of experience from without. When he considered the price exacted from Story for the blessing of expatriation, he must have reckoned that his own theory and his far more telling practice raised the same question.

James recognized differences of theory, as of one's general stance, toward the question of America and Europe, or Boston and Rome. But I think he saw, at least for himself, two possibilities, either of which would keep him safe. The first was a matter of concentration, and in the context of Story and his friends he saw the lack of it in Elizabeth Barrett Browning and in Story, just as he saw the force of it in Robert Browning. Browning testified to the possibility of a double identity: one could be a man of the world and at the same time one could be fully at home to the demands of an exacting art. While Story was distracted and diverted from his main task by everything he saw and heard in Rome, Florence, and Siena, so that he never fully became any of the several things he sought to become —sculptor, poet, dramatist—Browning never allowed anything, even the experience of living in Florence, to become too much for him:

That weight of the whole mind which we have also speculatively invoked was a pressure that he easily enough, at any point, that he in fact almost extravagantly, brought to bear. And then he was neither divided nor dispersed.[25]

By comparison, and James tries to avoid saying it bluntly, Mrs. Browning could never sufficiently mind her own business; she could never keep any of her mind intact above its engrossments. The cause of Italy, its daily ramification, so preoccupied her that she quite let down "her inspiration and her poetic pitch." "We are less edified than we ought to be," as James concluded.[26] Similarly with Story. He "was not with the last intensity a sculptor":

Had he been this he would not, in all probability, have been also with such intensity (so far as impulse and eagerness were concerned) so many other things; a man of ideas—of other ideas, of other curiosities. . . . He was as addicted to poetry as if he had never dreamed of a statue, and as addicted to statues as if he were unable to turn a verse.[27]

James does not commit the indelicacy of saying that Story and Mrs. Browning were alike, but he leaves it to the reader to observe that they were alike in having not enough indifferences; they did not have enough objects of interest toward which, on particular occasions, their tenderness was a matter of choice. With Mrs. Browning, it was always Italy, with Story it might be anything. Clearly, James had the contrast with Robert Browning especially in view when he said of Story:

How could he be, our friend, we sometimes find ourselves wondering, so restlessly, so sincerely aesthetic, and yet, constitutionally, so little insistent? We mean by insistence, in an artist, the act of throwing the whole weight of the mind, and of gathering it at the particular point (when the particular point is worth it) in order to do so.[28]

Story irritated James and was most of all a scandal in his eyes because he allowed himself to become in Italy "the prey to mere beguilement." He was, in the end, merely an amateur, a tourist, even though he spent many years among compelling reasons for being something much more.

James's clear implication, throughout *William Wetmore Story and His Friends*, is that so long as an artist throws the full weight of his mind upon the work in hand, and does not allow himself to be promiscuously beguiled, he is secure anywhere. Browning was the supreme type of that capacity, and his being English did not alter his suggestive case: he showed the best way of being a foreigner in Italy. What James, in his essay on *The Ring and the Book*, called "Browning's own particular matchless Italy" was something Story could never have possessed, because he was not with sufficient intensity an artist. But there were still further possibilities, which James divined as if they lay beyond Browning. It is for us to say that they were Jamesian, and I find the most complete indication of them, as a matter of theory, in a passage of *William Wetmore Story and His Friends* and again in the preface to *The Aspern Papers*.

In the preface, recalling that he got wind of his story in Florence, he says:

It was in Florence years ago; which is precisely, of the whole matter, what I like most to remember. The air of the old-time Italy invests it, a mixture that on the faintest invitation I rejoice again to inhale—and this in spite of the mere cold renewal, ever, of the infirm side of that felicity, the sense, in the whole element, of things too numerous, too deep, too obscure, too strange, or even simply too beautiful, for any ease of intellectual relation. One must pay one's self largely with words, I think, one must induce almost any 'Italian subject' to *make believe* it gives up its secret, in order to keep at all on working—or call them perhaps rather playing—terms with the general impression.[29]

James does not further explain what the relation should be between the Italian subject and the mind that responds to it, apart from saying, a few sentences later:

So, right and left, in Italy—before the great historic complexity at least—penetration fails; we scratch at the extensive surface, we meet the perfunctory smile, we hang about in the golden air. But we exaggerate our gathered values only if we are eminently witless. It is fortunately the exhibition in all the world before which, as admirers, we can most remain superficial without feeling silly.[30]

James does not say how one might, as an American artist in Italy, avoid being superficial, as Story, for instance, was bound to be superficial and was regularly silly. But the notion of paying one's self largely with words, in default of complete possession of the Italian subject, is elaborated in the book on Story. What James intuits is that a decent response to Rome might take one of two forms. In one, the passionate pilgrim would see himself condemned to be superficial, indeed, but not dismayed by that discovery. He would feel somewhat as Roderick Hudson felt, in the chapter called "Rome" and while he is still in possession of himself. He is for the moment one of those spirits, as James describes them, "with a deep relish for the artificial element in life and the infinite superpositions of history."[31] Roderick does not pretend to understand these matters, but he is still good enough to bring his curiosity to attend upon them. In *William Wetmore Story and His Friends* James cannot help giving his own sense of Rome, under the guise of attributing some of it to Story, but he is usually vigilant in indicating where his own responsibility for such perceptions begins and ends. "The Roman air, for us," he said, "insistently pervades and tinges; so that—to make my own confession at least complete—I see no circumstance too trite, no image too slight, to be bathed by it in interest and in beauty."[32] To what extent Story felt what James felt, we have to guess for ourselves, but in any event the city is there, and the responsibility it imposes must at least be acknowledged. If one pays one's respect in words, the words are bound to fall ridiculously short.

That is the first form, in which if we compare the object with our expression of it, the relation is humiliating. But there is a second possibility, in which the comparative question can be evaded. It is as if James were saying, to testify to this possibility in the experience of Rome: "only recognise the spirit of the place, surrender yourself to that, and it won't matter that your sense of anything in particular is puny." If the pilgrim obeys this instruction, he finds every inequality removed. In this connection, James recalls meeting Matthew Arnold at the Palazzo Barberini:

He had been, in prose and verse, the idol of my previous years, and nothing could have seemed in advance less doubtful than that to encounter him face to face, and under an influence so noble, would have made one fairly stagger with a sense of privilege. What actually happened, however, was that the sense of privilege found itself positively postponed; when I met him again, later on, in London, *then* it had free play. It was, on the Roman evening, as if, for all the world, we were *equally* great and happy, or still more, perhaps, equally nothing and nobody; we were related only to the enclosing fact of Rome, before which every one, it was easy to feel, bore himself with the same good manners.[33]

James goes on to explain that this sense of equality, of equal submission to the spirit of Rome, would not have been possible in London, Paris, or New York, cities, he says, in which the spirit of the place has long since lost any advantage it may ever have practiced over the spirit of the person:

So, at any rate, fanciful as my plea may appear, I recover the old sense— brave even the imputation of making a mere Rome of words, talking of a Rome of my own which was no Rome of reality. That comes up as exactly the point—that no Rome of reality was concerned in our experience, that the whole thing was a rare state of the imagination.[34]

I derive from this passage, and from other passages of similar bearing, that there are indeed two ways of proceeding, faced with the Rome of reality. The first is to try to be responsive at every point and to every particular, even while discovering that one's response is trivial in comparison with its object. It is to try, given a subject, as James told Mrs. Humphry Ward in another connection, to "work one's self into the presence of it." And of course to fail: the city will not give up its secret. The second way is by not competing, by assenting so wholeheartedly to the spirit of the place that the mere details, momentous and historic as they are, may be taken for granted. This relation, then, may be expressed, without humiliating oneself in the process, by paying oneself largely with words; by creating in one's mind and demeanor a Rome of words, and by not worrying at all about their adequacy or their applicable force. The value of the words as making reference to a city or as somehow describing it is alternative to this second response, by which the chosen words pay tribute to the object by not even offering to emulate it.

It is clear, too, that this second form of responsiveness can indeed be regarded as barefaced irrelevancy, but James was not prepared to give up the privilege of what he called "subjective amplification." Coming to the end of the book on Story, he leads himself into a theme of the great prefaces, the question of a subject. He has referred to "our conviction of the puerility of any pretended estimate of property in *subject*." Then he drives the conviction further:

A subject is never anything but his who can make something of it, and it is the thing made that becomes the property. But as between the thing made and the making the distinction is not to be seized, it is to the treatment alone that the fact of possession attaches—from which it is superfluous to warn us off.[35]

But, to go back to James's starting point: what if the subject, Story's life in this case, is not worth the treatment, the spirit expended upon it? The glib answer is that in that case we have a new subject, the result of James's determination to take responsibility for every occasion, however slight, and to work it for more than, on any ordinary valuation, it was worth. But James took an artist's pride, even when a subject was apparently thin, in seeing what he could make of it, how ample it might appear to become under his treatment.

When James went back to Rome in 1907, he found—as I have mentioned—much changed. Of course all was not lost, and James's act of remembrance had the effect of making the recalled and re-covered thing nearly as satisfying as if it were, in addition, still actual, still present. "The city of his first unpremeditated rapture shines to memory, on the other hand," he reported of the mature visitor in *Italian Hours*, "in the manner of a lost paradise the rustle of whose gardens is still just audible enough in the air to make him wonder if some sudden turn, some recovered vista, mayn't lead him back to the thing itself."[36] In a remarkable chapter called "A Few Other Roman Neighbourhoods" in *Italian Hours* James, strolling through the Villa d'Este, fancies that the ruined fountains are themselves waiting to be remembered in their first play and movement:

The ruined fountains seemed strangely to wait, in the stillness and under cover of the approaching dusk, not to begin ever again to play, also, but just only to be tenderly imagined to do so; quite as everything held its breath, at the mystic moment, for the drop of the cruel and garish exposure, for the Spirit of the place to steal forth and go his round.[37]

James is writing in "the spirit of the postscript," making last-minute additions to documents of an otherwise lost time. He recalls not only Rome but the first agitated consciousness which, as a young man, he brought to it. He sees himself as precursor to the mature visitor he is now; as a shade among shades:

No one who has ever loved Rome as Rome could be loved in youth and before her poised basketful of the finer appeals to fond fancy was actually upset, wants to stop loving her; so that our bleeding and wounded, though perhaps not wholly moribund, loyalty attends us as a hovering admonitory, anticipatory ghost, one of those magnanimous life-companions who before complete extinction designate to the other member of the union their approved successor.[38]

James is writing in 1909, looking back nearly forty years to his first sight of Rome. He is thinking of earliness and lateness, of himself as *éclaireur* and now as successor to himself. The idiom is that of *William Wetmore Story and His Friends*, but with a difference: James is not inclined to patronize the young man he was. Indeed, the figure of the magnanimous life-companion has the opposite effect. The thing itself is Rome, loved as the young James loved her: the nuptial relation signified as much. The designated successor cannot be supposed entirely to fill the place left by the young man: he cannot be more than a worthy substitute. His worth, indeed, consists in the degree and force of his remembrance: without that, he would be a usurper or, at best, merely posthumous to the only consciousness that matters.

Notes

1. *Henry James Letters*, vol. 4, *1895–1916*, ed. Leon Edel (Cambridge: Harvard University Press, 1984), 302.
2. Henry James to William Dean Howells, 25 January 1902, ibid., 224–25.
3. *Henry James Letters*, vol. 1, *1843–1875*, ed. Leon Edel (Cambridge: Harvard University Press, 1974), 353.
4. Henry James to Henry Adams, 19 November 1903, *Letters*, 4: 289.
5. Henry James, *William Wetmore Story and His Friends: From Letters, Diaries, and Recollections* (London: Thames and Hudson, n.d.) 2: 87.
6. Ibid., 1: 15.
7. Ibid., 1: 125.
8. Ibid., 1: 341.
9. Ibid., 1: 224.
10. Ibid., 2: 131.
11. Ibid., 2: 132–33.
12. Ibid., 1: 348.

13. Ibid., 1: 348.
14. *The Complete Notebooks of Henry James*, ed. Leon Edel and Lyall H. Powers (New York: Oxford University Press, 1987), 183.
15. James, *William Wetmore Story and His Friends*, 1: 6–7.
16. Ibid., 1: 275.
17. Ibid., 2: 126.
18. Ibid., 2: 3.
19. Ibid., 1: 188.
20. Ibid., 1: 294.
21. Ibid., 1: 333.
22. Ibid., 1: 312.
23. Ibid., 2: 287.
24. T. S. Eliot, "In Memory," *The Little Review* 5, no. 4 (August 1918): 44.
25. James *William Wetmore Story and His Friends*, 2: 227.
26. Ibid., 2: 55.
27. Ibid., 2: 84.
28. Ibid., 2: 216.
29. Henry James, *Literary Criticism* (New York: Library of America, 1984), 1173.
30. Ibid., 1174.
31. Henry James, *Novels 1871–1880* (New York: Library of America, 1983), 227.
32. James, *William Wetmore Story and His Friends*, 1: 328.
33. Ibid., 2: 208.
34. Ibid., 2: 209.
35. Ibid., 2: 234–35.
36. Henry James, *Italian Hours* (London: Century, 1986; reprint), 217–19.
37. Ibid., 219.
38. Ibid., 217.

THIRTEEN *Italy and the Artist in Henry James*

AGOSTINO LOMBARDO

T HERE is the story of one's hero, and then, thanks to the intimate connection of things, the story of one's story itself. I blush to confess it, but if one's a dramatist one's a dramatist, and the latter imbroglio is liable on occasion to strike me as really the most objective of the two." These well-known words from the preface to *The Ambassadors* rightly point out the constant presence, in any work of art, of *another* story (sometimes a "figure" deeply hidden in "the carpet," sometimes a more evident sign) which is the story of the artist. All artistic language is in fact, I believe, a metalanguage—the artist always speaks of himself, and not in a merely autobiographical sense but *qua* artist; he speaks of his own social and psychological condition, of his relationship (and his struggle) with his instrument—and one is reminded of Shakespeare's continual references, in the Sonnets, to the ink, the pen, the paper he is using, or the lines he is drawing; or, in the plays, of the innumerable allusions to the theater, the stage, the actors, the costumes. If this, however, is true of all art, it is true to an exceptional degree of American literature, in which the problem of the artist, from Charles Brockden Brown to Poe and Hawthorne, from Melville to Whitman and Crane, from Pound, Eliot, and Wallace Stevens to Salinger and Saul Bellow, is not only important but indeed central and decisive, so that its most distinctive feature seems to me the vigorous presence, and often the predominance, of the *other* story, the *other* imbroglio. And it is true of Henry James.

Both owing to his American heritage and to his connections with aestheticism, James brings indeed this general trend to its extreme consequences—thus anticipating the whole movement of modern, and postmodern, literature, in which the real object of the writing is precisely the relationship and struggle I have mentioned, the conflict of the writer with that "written word" which, as James notes in *Italian Hours* ("Italy Revisited"), "stands for something that eternally tricks us." There are of course novels (such as *Roderick Hudson* and *The Tragic Muse*) and stories which directly analyze the situation of the "heroes and martyrs of the artistic ideal" and in which the *other* story therefore is explicit; and it is obviously explicit in the prefaces, which can be read, as I have tried to suggest elsewhere (see the introduction to the Italian edition of the Prefaces, Rome 1986—first published 1956), as a *novel* on the artist and on the artistic process. But it is present, implicitly, in the whole *corpus* of James's works, and not only in the general sense of a metalanguage always interacting with the language, but in the more particular sense of fictional situations which are, at the same time, metaphors of both the human and the artistic experience; of fictional characters behind which (think of Isabel Archer) one sees the lineaments of the artist; of fictional images and symbols which, while suggesting the secret texture of the "garden of life" (as in the case of the golden bowl) also point to the mysteries of the garden of art, or, if you like, of the "house of fiction." Indeed, the famous passage in the preface to *The Portrait of a Lady* seems to me emblematic of this intermingling of human and artistic experience (which is probably the greatest and most original contribution of Henry James to modern culture). The "artistic" problem is clearly, here, also a "human" problem, the house of fiction is clearly also the house of life, the multiplicity of the aesthetic points of view is also the multiplicity (and ambiguity) of our vision of life:

The house of fiction has in short not one window, but a million—a number of possible windows not to be reckoned, rather. . . . But they have this mark of their own that at each of them stands a figure with a pair of eyes, or at least with a field-glass, which forms, again and again, for observation, a unique instrument, insuring to the person making use of it an impression distinct from every other. He and his neighbours are watching the same show, but one seeing more where the other sees less, one seeing black where the other sees white, one seeing big where the other sees small, one seeing coarse where the other sees fine.

Of such a unique fictional universe, based upon reality and at the same time constantly and tenaciously meant to include and represent the artistic experience, Italy had inevitably to become not only an essential but the most important component. And I say inevitably in spite (and perhaps because) of the limits of James's knowledge of our country. America, England, and France he knew, from what we can call a "realistic" point of view, much better, much more precisely. He knew their manners, their social and political problems, their attitudes, their language, their literature, and their theater. Italy, in spite of his many travels and sojourns, of his immutable love and veritable passion, he knew, I must say, very little, as all the critics who have touched this subject, from Leon Edel and Mario Praz, the masters of us all, to F. O. Matthiessen and Sergio Perosa, from Robert Gale to Cristina Giorcelli (the author of a fine book on James and Italy—Rome 1968) have convincingly demonstrated. Italy is not an Arcadia, for James, as I shall try to show, and his "dream" is different from that traced by Van Wyck Brooks in his admirable book. But all the same, it is not a real country—if by real we mean a country composed not only of landscapes and works of art and relics of the past, but of social classes, political problems, and daily life (such as that which Howells tried to represent in *Venetian Life*). And one thinks of the extremely scarce contact he had with Italians ("I have been nearly a year in Italy," he wrote to Grace Norton in 1874, "and have hardly spoken to an Italian creature save washerwomen and waiters")—which is one of the reasons for his extremely slow penetration into our culture, as is amply proved by the valuable bibliographical material prepared by Donatella Izzo. One thinks, too, of the almost complete lack, in his fiction, of Italian characters that are not conventional, "literary," or indeed operatic. Or of the frequent misspelling—almost Shakespearian, one would say—of Italian words and idioms ("Basta! Basta!" seems the only exact one). Or of his rather vague knowledge (with the exception of D'Annunzio and, of all writers, Matilde Serao) of Italian literature. There are of course, here and there, especially in *Italian Hours*, very acute observations (even, if few, political ones): but there is no doubt that the Italy of the Unity, the Italy still living and creating its *Risorgimento*, does not really exist for James. It certainly exists for James much less than

France, or the England in which he decided to live (while he could *not* live in modern Italy), or the United States, which he had left so early. What exists is the Italy of the past—and not so much of the historical past (history being for James, as for Stephen Dedalus, a "nightmare," "the terrible human past" mentioned in *The Portrait of a Lady* and dramatized in *The Sense of the Past*) as of the artistic one.

On the other hand, Italy (and here we can start seeing the difference between Henry James and the other "travellers to Italy") is not only, for him, an immense museum (a living Louvre) which enables him to see and penetrate works of art that would otherwise be inaccessible—such as the *Cena* of "the beautiful, tragical Leonardo," "the saddest work of art in the world" and still, "battered, defaced, ruined as it is . . . one of the greatest" (*Italian Hours*; but see also "Travelling Companions"). Italy is not only a place which gives him the possibility—much more than was the case for Hawthorne—to deepen and enlarge his appreciation of painting and sculpture and architecture, guided also by his reading of Ruskin. And Italy is not only a series of those picturesque landscapes, towns, streets, churches, *piazze* and *piazzette* which he describes with inimitable elegance and subtlety in his essays and in his fiction. All these elements, the artistic and the natural ones, as well as the literary filters (Hawthorne, Stendhal) through which James received his impressions, blend in a greater unity, a larger image such as that symbolically suggested by a "sublime afternoon" in Naples, at Posilippo (i.e., Posillipo):

Here, as happened, were charming wise, original people even down to delightful amphibious American children, enamelled by the sun of the Bay as for figures of miniature Tritons and Nereids on a Renaissance plaque; and above all, on the part of the general prospect, a demonstration of the grand style of composition and effect that one was never to wish to see bettered. The way in which the Italian scene on such occasions as this seems to purify itself to the transcendent and perfect *idea* alone—idea of beauty, of dignity, of comprehensive grace, with all accidents merged, all defects disowned, all experience outlived, and to gather itself up into the mere mute eloquence of what has just incalculably *been*, remain forever the secret and the lesson of the subtlest daughter of History. (*Italian Hours*)

Italy is first and foremost, for James, a metaphor of art which all elements—natural, artistic, historical, human—contribute to form, and all his writings on Italy seem to me the repeated attempts on one side to represent it on the page, giving it form, body, reality (*this* reality) and on the other, deeper side, to unveil its meaning. It is a process we often find in American literature: in Melville, when he gives a body to, and at the same time tries to interpret, to "read," the White Whale; in Hawthorne, when he represents and accurately describes the Scarlet Letter and at the same time tries to discover its symbolic meaning. But one thinks first and above all of Shakespeare's *Antony and Cleopatra*—a play often evoked by James in his "Italian" writings (Christina Light, in *Roderick Hudson*, is compared to Cleopatra)—where the desperate attempt, on the part of the poet, but also on the part of the characters, to give reality to Cleopatra's features, to fix them on the page, to trace them with words, is essentially the endeavor to identify the lineaments and the meaning of the art of which Cleopatra, like Italy for James, is the metaphor.

This is why Italy *had* to become the most important component of James's universe. Already in his first "Italian" pages, such as the letters of Nora Lambert in *Watch and Ward* or the reportage of "Travelling Companions" and of "At Isella," Italy is perceived in this metaphorical light and the attempt is only superficially that of describing beautiful landscapes or buildings or works of art, or that of merely expressing the enthusiasm of the "passionate pilgrim" in front of the materialization of his Italian dream. Under this surface a deeper intent lives and operates, which becomes more evident and indeed central while new colours and lines are added to the mysterious and protean painting: the Siena of *Confidence*; the Rome of *Roderick Hudson*, "The Last of the Valerii," "Adina," "Daisy Miller," "Longstaff's Marriage," "Georgina's Reasons," *The Portrait of a Lady*, "The Solution" (as well as the invisible one of *The Golden Bowl*); The Florence of "The Madonna of the Future," "The Diary of a Man of Fifty," "The Pupil," *The Portrait* itself; the Venice of *The Aspern Papers*, "The Pupil," again, *The Princess Casamassima* (through Hyacinth Robinson's letter) and, of course, *The Wings of the Dove*—all these cities, palaces, churches, works of art, and ruins have specific narrative functions, symbolic as they are of moral situations. This quality, with regard to Venice, has recently been discussed in Venice in a symposium published as *Henry James e Venezia*, ed. Sergio Perosa, 1987.

But they are also stages of James's journey through the artistic experience, parts of the great Portrait of Italy he was trying throughout his life to paint. A portrait to which innumerable touches are added in other novels and stories where Italy is present in a less direct way (for instance, through Gloriani in *The Ambassadors*), in the essays of *Italian Hours*, in articles on Italian authors, or actors, in the autobiographical writings, the letters, the notebooks; in *William Wetmore Story and His Friends*; in *The American Scene*, where Italy is not only frequently evoked but is indeed offered as a model of form to a formless America; and in the prefaces. The prefaces, in fact, because of their explicit dealing with the artistic experience, bristle with such touches, with allusions to those cities and places, with evocations meant to recapture "the loved Italy . . . so much more loved than one has ever been able, even after fifty efforts, to say!" But they also stress the difficulty of the great attempt:

It was in Florence years ago; which is precisely, of the whole matter, what I like most to remember. The air of the old-time Italy invests it, a mixture that on the faintest invitation I rejoice again to inhale—and this in spite of the mere cold renewal, ever, of the infirm side of that felicity, the sense, in the whole element, of things too numerous, too deep, too obscure, too strange, or even simply too beautiful, for any ease of intellectual relation. One must pay one's self largely with words, I think, one must induce almost any "Italian subject" to *make believe* it gives up its secret, in order to keep at all on working—or call them perhaps rather playing—terms with the general impression. . . . So, right and left, in Italy—before the great historic complexity at least—penetration fails; we scratch at the extensive surface, we meet the perfunctory smile, we hang about in the golden air.

One is reminded, in reading this passage, of Edgar Allan Poe's "The Poetic Principle," when he writes of "a certain petulant, impatient sorrow at our inability to grasp now, wholly, here on earth, at once and forever, those divine and rapturous joys, of which *through* the poems, or *through* the music, we attain to but brief and indeterminate glimpses." And indeed for James, as for Poe, the artist, although given supreme lucidity and control and insight (to the point that the novelist is the supreme model of the fictional character), has no superhuman or mystical faculties: the "portrait of Italy," therefore, is always incomplete, always "in progress"—

like any artistic text, like Cleopatra's portrait, Cleopatra's "infinite variety" being in fact that of the artistic text, ungraspable, ever-changing, protean like the sea in front of Stephen Dedalus—and these are the qualities Italy has for James. France, England, even London, "the great grey Babylon", the United States, can for James all be defined, judged, calculated, because they belong to a measurable, and therefore representable, reality. But Italy belongs, one would say with Antony, to a "new heaven," a "new earth," and therefore its "figure in the carpet" is traceable only up to a certain point. Hence we find the patient addition, page by page, of new elements; hence the continual, hard tension of the representation of things Italian; the use of symbols (more frequent in the "Italian" stories and novels than in the others); the Poe-esque sense of frustration, of inadequacy, of impotence in front of words which, as in Eliot's "Burnt Norton," "strain, / Crack and sometimes break, under the burden, / Under the tension, slip, slide, perish, / Decay with imprecision, will not stay in place, / Will not stay still."

Italy, then, is no Arcadia, for Henry James. Identified as it is with the artistic experience, and even with the artistic text, the relationship with it produces all the anxiety, the strenuous effort, the struggle which the artist's job itself produces. Neither is it Arcadia for those characters—"the candid children of the West," "the disinherited of Art"—which in a sense repeat, explicitly or disguisedly, within the fictional world the experience of their author. If the European "connection" is always hard for the American "innocents," it may still offer, in England or in France, moments of quiet, peace, and even happiness. But this cannot happen in Italy. The "most beautiful country in the world," the garden of Europe, assumes for these characters the qualities of Rappaccini's garden (Hawthorne's great story is mentioned, significantly, in "Travelling Companions"), with its "flowers gorgeously magnificent" which, like Beatrice herself, are deadly poisonous—and it is perhaps not casual that in describing his Italian experience, in the preface to *The Reverberator*, James uses the metaphor of poison:

A part of the adventure had been the never-to-be-forgotten thrill of a first sight of Italy, from late in the summer of 1869 on; so that a return to America at the beginning of the following year was to drag with it, as a lengthening chain, the torment of losses and regrets. The repatriated victim of that unrest was, beyond doubt, acutely conscious of his case: the fifteen months just spent in Europe had absolutely determined his situation. The nostalgic poison had been distilled for him.

And further on:

I had from as far back as I could remember carried in my side, buried and unextracted, the head of one of those well-directed shafts from the European quiver to which, of old, tender American flesh was more helplessly and bleedingly exposed, I think, than to-day: the nostalgic cup had been applied to my lips even before I was conscious of it.

Neither is it coincidental, perhaps, that if (in that very *Tempest* on which James wrote a fascinating essay) Gonzalo sees the beautiful island of his utopia transformed into the "fearful country" which he wants to abandon, Roderick Hudson asks Rowland Mallet to be taken out of "this terrible Italy where everything mocks and reproaches and torments and eludes me! Take me out of this land of impossible beauty."

With very few exceptions ("The Chaperon" is the most significant) Italy is thus, for James's characters, an experience of sorrow. They are surrounded by beautiful landscapes and magnificent palaces and works of art, but this vision never results in happiness. On the contrary, such extraordinary beauty does but underline the "negative" result of the Italian pilgrimage. Italy is a perfect, serene object only in the imagination—in reality it hides—like the golden bowl—cracks, perplexities, and deceit. The story of Isabel Archer is even emblematic, from this point of view, and we can read her "meditative vigil," in the glorious chapter 42, not only as the revelation to her of Osmond's nature but as a revelation of what the Italian experience has done to her:

It was not her fault—she had practised no deception; she had only admired and believed. She had taken all the first steps in the purest confidence, and then she had suddenly found the infinite vista of a multiplied life to be a dark, narrow alley with a dead wall at the end. Instead of leading to the high places of happiness, from which the world would seem to lie below one, so that one could look down with a sense of exaltation and advantage, and judge and choose and pity, it led rather downward and earthward, into realms of restriction and depression where the sound of other lives, easier and freer, was heard as from above, and where it served to deepen the feeling of failure.

Italy is sorrow; Italy is solitude and renunciation; Italy is illusion, a stage where men and objects wear masks, creating a show in the presence of which the American "dreamers" find themselves like Eliot's Gerontion face to face with history: "Think now / History has many cunning passages, contrived corridors / And issues, deceives with whispering ambitions, / Guides us by vanities." And Italy is, above all, death. That death already appears, however obliquely, in "Travelling Companions" and is the inevitable conclusion of the artistic experience (and illusion) in "The Madonna of the Future" and in *Roderick Hudson*, the novel of 1875 which is the reference point, and the foil, of many of my observations, the identification of Italy and the artistic experience being explicit and central in it (as it was in Hawthorne's *The Marble Faun*, the book that must have been its model); it is the death which interrupts so abruptly the Roman adventure of Daisy Miller, which appears in "Georgina's Reasons," and is secretly announced in Hyacinth's letter from Venice in *The Princess Casamassima*. Indeed Hyacinth's suicide is due to the betrayal of his political and social ideas after the "discovery" of "this impossible, abominable old Venice" and of

the monuments and treasures of art, the great palaces and properties, the conquests of learning and taste, the general fabric of civilisation as we know it, based if you will upon all the despotisms, the cruelties, the exclusions, the monopolies and the rapacities of the past, but thanks to which, all the same, the world is less of a "bloody sell" and life more of a lark. . . .

It is the death enacted in *The Aspern Papers*, "The Pupil," and, of course, the admirable *The Wings of the Dove*, again in that Venice of which, in the essay of 1892 on "The Grand Canal" *(Italian Hours)* James writes that "the essential character of the most melancholy of cities resides simply in its being the most beautiful of tombs. Nowhere else has the past been laid to rest with such tenderness, such a sadness of resignation and remembrance."

Such a vision of Italy (and of Venice) has, of course, many sources and antecedents. One thinks of the Elizabethan dramatists and especially of Shakespeare—the Shakespeare of *The Merchant of Venice*, for instance, and above all of *Othello*, one of the plays most present (with *The Tempest*) in James's imagination (to the point that Othello's condition seems to me the archetype of that of Christopher Newman and of many aspects of the "international theme"). One thinks of the Gothic novel, both in its English and its American versions, and of the whole American tradition, culminating in Hawthorne (present in *Roderick Hudson* but also in "The Last of the Valerii" and "Daisy Miller"). One thinks of the English romantics, from Byron (so subtly evoked in *The Aspern Papers*) to Keats and Shelley; of Goethe, Stendhal, Browning, and Ruskin; of the Anglo-American "colony" remembered in *William Wetmore Story and His Friends*. But all these sources, suggestions, and intimations are absorbed and transcended by that identification of Italy with the artistic experience which I have tried to trace and, at the same time, by the intuition, on the part of James, that art (as Poe had suggested) is inevitably connected with death. This connection (already present in Hawthorne's evocation of Beatrice Cenci) is rendered more evident and plastic in the splendid description of the Bronzino painting observed by Milly Theale in *The Wings of the Dove:*

She found herself, for the first moment, looking at the mysterious portrait through tears. Perhaps it was her tears that made it just then so strange and fair—as wonderful as he [Lord Mark] had said: the face of a young woman, all magnificently drawn, down to the hands, and magnificently dressed; a face almost livid in hue, yet handsome in sadness and crowned with a mass of hair rolled back and high, that must, before fading with time, have had a family resemblance to her own. The lady in question, at all events, with her slightly Michaelangelesque squareness, her eyes of other days, her full lips, her long neck, her recorded jewels, her brocaded and wasted reds, was a very great personage—only unaccompanied by joy. And she was dead, dead, dead.

The characters suffer, in Italy, and die, because the artist, in order to create, must "die into life" (as Keats wrote in *Hyperion*) and because the artistic object inevitably leads to that absolute, sacred moment which is death. The work of art seems indeed to me to be built upon a double process: the form creates a positive world of beauty, harmony, and even joy and, at the same time, impairs and destroys it, revealing its ephemeral, illusory, untrue nature (a great example of this is Keats's *Ode on a Grecian Urn*). What remains true is the human condition with its destiny of sorrow, mystery, and death. This is true of all art; and it is certainly true of the Jamesian text. James, following Flaubert, leads the novel to its highest consciousness by creating perfect narrative architectures, organic fictional worlds which seem entirely autonomous and completely self-referential. But James is just as conscious that these worlds are artifacts: he knows, like Coleridge, or Poe, or Baudelaire, that their harmony and order are illusory, that paradises can only be artificial, that truth is a hell that art cannot exorcise. In all his works, then, and especially in the "Italian" ones, we can distinguish the double process by which through the representation of life, and beauty, and joy we are led to the vision of death. A significant example is that of the sweet, and serene, and beautiful Gardencourt, in *The Portrait of a Lady*, which, like time in Proust, contains the seeds of decadence and death. But the greatest is that, again, of *The Wings of the Dove:* for "the potential heiress of all the ages," menaced by death, James builds a world of beauty which we can certainly define as the world of art—and the more so since its form and substance is that of Venice. But, like Prince Prospero's palace in Poe's "The Mask of the Red Death," this world is not sufficient to keep death away—death is in Milly but death is also in Venice ("Phoenix City and Sepulchre," to use a pregnant image of Leon Edel) and the supreme symbol of beauty becomes, as in Thomas Mann, or in Pound, a tomb—a mausoleum evocative of that in which Cleopatra hides herself and dies (for ever hiding her lineaments, her portrait).

Thus, it does not really matter if James's Italy is not real in the sense mentioned at the beginning of this paper and if we Italians do not find it a faithful picture of our country, and manners, and history. Its reality lies in another sphere, which is that of the artistic experience, of the drama of the artist. And Italy is inevitably, I must again say, at the basis of James's most important works and indeed masterpieces not only because of his never-to-be-extinguished love and nostalgia ("many things come and go, but Italy remains") but above all because it is especially through Italy, the Italian stories, the Italian experience, that James realizes that for him the *other* story is in fact *the* story and that the theme of the artist is his *main* theme. But there is a fundamental difference,

however, from the artists—like Wilde and D'Annunzio—of aestheticism, as well as from our contemporary postmodern writers.
Italy is *the* great metaphor of art, but the relationship with art so
pregnantly represented through the relationship of the characters
with Italy is, in its turn, for James, symbolic of the human condition. By adding, through Italy and the Italian stories, the artistic
element to his fictional universe (and to the "international theme")
James also shows the necessity of art, its centrality in the human
experience not as "decoration" or "ornament" but as a metaphor of
life, the revelation of truth, the knowledge of our destiny.

Contributors

DENIS DONOGHUE is the Henry James Professor of English and American Letters at New York University. He is the author of *Ferocious Alphabets, Connoisseurs of Chaos, Reading America, Thieves of Fire, The Sovereign Ghost, The Arts Without Mystery*, and many other studies of British and American literature and culture.

LEON EDEL, the Henry James Professor of English and American Letters (Emeritus) at New York University, is the author of the Pulitzer Prize winning biography *Henry James* (five volumes), the editor of the four-volume *Henry James: Letters*, and the compiler, with Dan H. Laurence and James Rambeau, of *A Bibliography of Henry James*. His other works include *Henry James: Les Années Dramatiques, James Joyce: The Last Journey, The Psychological Novel, Literary Biography*, and (with Gordon Ray) *Henry James and H. G. Wells*.

DANIEL MARK FOGEL, Professor of English at Louisiana State University, is the founder and editor of the *Henry James Review* (1979–). His works include *Henry James and the Structure of the Romantic Imagination* and various essays on modern literature in quarterlies like the *Wallace Stevens Journal* and the *Journal of Modern Literature*. He is also the editor of *New Essays on The Portrait of a Lady*.

CLAUDIO GORLIER is Professor of English at the University of Turin.

JOSEPHINE GATTUSO HENDIN is Professor of English at New York University. Her critical studies include *The World of Flannery O'Connor, Vulnerable People: A View of American Fiction Since 1945*, and various essays and studies, including "Experimental Fiction" in the *Harvard Guide to Contemporary American Writing*.

241

AGOSTINO LOMBARDO, Professor and Chairman of the Department of English at the University of Rome "La Sapienza," is the author of *La poesia inglese dall'estetismo al simbolismo*, *Il dramma pre-shakesperiano*, *La ricerca del vero*, and *Un rapporto col mondo*, *saggio sui racconti di Nathaniel Hawthorne*. He has translated and edited works by Shakespeare, Dr. Johnson, Boswell, Trollope, Hawthorne, and Henry James. He is the editor of both *Studi Americani* and *Studi Inglesi*.

BONNEY MACDONALD is Assistant Professor of English at Union College. The author of *Henry James's Italian Hours: Revelatory and Resistant Impressions*, she has also assisted R. W. B. Lewis in the preparation of the new edition of *The Art of the Novel* by Henry James.

GERALD E. MYERS is the author of *William James: His Life and Thought*, *The Spirit of American Philosophy*, and *Self: An Introduction to Philosophical Psychology*. He is the coeditor of *Self, Religion, and Metaphysics*, *Pathology and Consciousness*, *Philosophical Essays on Dance*, and *Emotion: Philosophical Studies*. He is Professor of Philosophy at Queens College of the City University of New York.

SERGIO PEROSA is Professor and Chairman of the Department of English at the University of Venice. He is the author of *Henry James and the Experimental Novel*, *American Theories of the Novel, 1793–1903*, and *The Art of F. Scott Fitzgerald* and is the editor of *L'Euro-America di Henry James* and *Henry James e Venezia*. President of the European Association for American Studies, Professor Perosa has has translated and edited the works of many American writers, including Emily Dickinson, Washington Irving, John Berryman, and Henry James.

LYALL H. POWERS is the author of *A Guide to Henry James*, *Henry James: An Introduction and Interpretation*, and *Henry James and the Naturalist Movement*, as well as *Faulkner's Yoknapatawpha Comedy* and *A Bibliography of American Periodicals, 1850–1910*.

He is the editor of *The Portable Henry James, Studies in The Portrait of a Lady, Henry James's Major Novels: Essays in Criticism* and, with Leon Edel, of *The Complete Notebooks of Henry James*. He is Professor of English at the University of Michigan.

MARIA ANTONIETTA SARACINO, who teaches at the University of Rome "La Sapienza," is the translator and editor of *Alice James: Il diario, 1889–1892*, published by La Tartaruga (Milan) in 1985.

ADELINE R. TINTNER, President of the Henry James Society, is an independent scholar trained in European literature and art history. In addition to scores of articles on American literature and art, her publications include *The Museum World of Henry James, The Book World of Henry James: Appropriating the Classics, The Pop World of Henry James: From Fairy Tales to Science Fiction*, and, with Leon Edel, *The Library of Henry James*.

JAMES W. TUTTLETON, Professor of English and Associate Dean of the Graduate School of Arts and Science at New York University, is the author of *Thomas Wentsworth Higginson* and *The Novel of Manners in America*. He has edited *Henry James's The American* (Norton Library), *Washington Irving: History, Tales and Sketches* (Library of America), and *Voyages and Discoveries of the Companions of Columbus* for the thirty-volume *The Complete Writings of Washington Irving*.

Index